Enterprise Networking, Security, and Automation Labs and Study Guide (CCNAV7)

Allan Johnson

‧ı|ı·ı|ı· Networking
CISCO Academy

Cisco Press

221 River St.

Hoboken, NJ 07030 USA

Enterprise Networking, Security, and Automation Labs and Study Guide (CCNAv7)

Published by
Cisco Press
221 River St.
Hoboken, NJ 07030 USA

1 2020

Library of Congress Control Number: 2020906042

Student ISBNs:

ISBN-13: 978-0-13-663469-0
ISBN-10: 0-13-663469-9

Instructor ISBNs:

ISBN-13: 978-0-13-663471-3
ISBN-10: 0-13-663471-0

Editor-in-Chief
Mark Taub

Director, ITP Product Management
Brett Bartow

Alliances Manager, Cisco Press
Arezou Gol

Senior Editor
James Manly

Managing Editor
Sandra Schroeder

Development Editor
Ellie Bru

Project Editor
Mandie Frank

Copy Editor
Kitty Wilson

Technical Editor
Dave Holzinger

Editorial Assistant
Cindy Teeters

Designer
Chuti Prasertsith

Composition
codeMantra

Proofreader
Charlotte Kughen

CISCO

Warning and Disclaimer

This book is designed to provide information about the Cisco Networking Academy Switching, Routing, and Wireless Essentials (CCNAv7) course. Every effort has been made to make this book as complete and as accurate as possible, but no warranty or fitness is implied.

The information is provided on an "as is" basis. The authors, Cisco Press, and Cisco Systems, Inc. shall have neither liability nor responsibility to any person or entity with respect to any loss or damages arising from the information contained in this book or from the use of the discs or programs that may accompany it.

The opinions expressed in this book belong to the author and are not necessarily those of Cisco Systems, Inc.

Trademark Acknowledgments

All terms mentioned in this book that are known to be trademarks or service marks have been appropriately capitalized. Cisco Press or Cisco Systems, Inc., cannot attest to the accuracy of this information. Use of a term in this book should not be regarded as affecting the validity of any trademark or service mark.

Special Sales

For information about buying this title in bulk quantities, or for special sales opportunities (which may include electronic versions; custom cover designs; and content particular to your business, training goals, marketing focus, or branding interests), please contact our corporate sales department at corpsales@pearsoned.com or (800) 382-3419.

For government sales inquiries, please contact governmentsales@pearsoned.com.

For questions about sales outside the U.S., please contact intlcs@pearson.com.

Feedback Information

At Cisco Press, our goal is to create in-depth technical books of the highest quality and value. Each book is crafted with care and precision, undergoing rigorous development that involves the unique expertise of members from the professional technical community.

Readers' feedback is a natural continuation of this process. If you have any comments regarding how we could improve the quality of this book, or otherwise alter it to better suit your needs, you can contact us through email at feedback@ciscopress.com. Please make sure to include the book title and ISBN in your message.

We greatly appreciate your assistance.

CISCO.

Americas Headquarters
Cisco Systems, Inc.
San Jose, CA

Asia Pacific Headquarters
Cisco Systems (USA) Pte. Ltd.
Singapore

Europe Headquarters
Cisco Systems International BV Amsterdam,
The Netherlands

Cisco has more than 200 offices worldwide. Addresses, phone numbers, and fax numbers are listed on the Cisco Website at **www.cisco.com/go/offices**.

Cisco and the Cisco logo are trademarks or registered trademarks of Cisco and/or its affiliates in the U.S. and other countries. To view a list of Cisco trademarks, go to this URL: www.cisco.com/go/trademarks. Third party trademarks mentioned are the property of their respective owners. The use of the word partner does not imply a partnership relationship between Cisco and any other company. (1110R)

About the Contributing Author

Allan Johnson entered the academic world in 1999, after 10 years as a business owner/operator, to dedicate his efforts to his passion for teaching. He holds both an M.B.A. and an M.Ed. in training and development. He taught CCNA courses at the high school level for 7 years and has taught both CCNA and CCNP courses at Del Mar College in Corpus Christi, Texas. In 2003, Allan began to commit much of his time and energy to the CCNA Instructional Support Team, providing services to Networking Academy instructors worldwide and creating training materials. He now works full time for Cisco Networking Academy as Curriculum Lead.

About the Technical Reviewer

Dave Holzinger has been a curriculum developer, project manager, author, and technical editor for Cisco Networking Academy in Phoenix since 2001. Dave works on the team that develops Cisco Networking Academy's online curricula, including CCNA, CCNP, and IT Essentials. He has been working with computer hardware and software since 1981. Dave has certifications from Cisco, BICSI, and CompTIA.

Contents at a Glance

Contents

Command Syntax Conventions

The conventions used to present command syntax in this book are the same conventions used in the IOS Command Reference. The Command Reference describes these conventions as follows:

- **Boldface** indicates commands and keywords that are entered literally as shown. In actual configuration examples and output (not general command syntax), boldface indicates commands that are manually input by the user (such as a **show** command).

- *Italic* indicates arguments for which you supply actual values.

- Vertical bars (|) separate alternative, mutually exclusive elements.

- Square brackets ([ ]) indicate an optional element.

- Braces ({ }) indicate a required choice.

- Braces within brackets ([{ }]) indicate a required choice within an optional element.

Introduction

This book supports instructors and students in Cisco Networking Academy, an IT skills and career-building program for learning institutions and individuals worldwide. Cisco Networking Academy provides a variety of curriculum choices, including the very popular CCNA curriculum. It includes three courses oriented around the topics of Cisco Certified Network Associate (CCNA) certifications.

Enterprise Networking, Security, and Automation Labs and Study Guide is a supplement to your classroom and laboratory experience with Cisco Networking Academy. To be successful on the exam and achieve your CCNA certification, you should do everything in your power to arm yourself with a variety of tools and training materials to support your learning efforts. This *Labs and Study Guide* provides just such a collection of tools. Used to its fullest extent, it will help you gain knowledge as well as practice skills associated with the content area of the Enterprise Networking, Security, and Automation v7 course. Specifically, this book will help you work on these main areas:

- Explain how single-area OSPF operates in both point-to-point and broadcast multiaccess networks.

- Implement single-area OSPFv2 in both point-to-point and broadcast multiaccess networks.

- Explain how vulnerabilities, threats, and exploits can be mitigated to enhance network security.

- Explain how ACLs are used as part of a network security policy.

- Implement IPv4 ACLs to filter traffic and secure administrative access.

- Configure NAT services on the edge router to provide IPv4 address scalability.

- Explain how WAN access technologies can be used to satisfy business requirements.

- Explain how VPNs and IPsec secure site-to-site and remote access connectivity.

- Explain how networking devices implement QoS.

- Implement protocols to manage the network.

- Explain the characteristics of scalable network architectures.

- Troubleshoot enterprise networks.

- Explain the purpose and characteristics of network virtualization.

- Explain how network automation is enabled through RESTful APIs and configuration management tools.

Labs and Study Guide similar to this one are also available for the other two courses: *Introduction to Networks Labs and Study Guide* and *Switching, Routing, and Wireless Essentials Labs and Study Guide*.

Who Should Read This Book

This book's main audience is anyone taking the Enterprise Networking, Security, and Automation course of the Cisco Networking Academy curriculum. Many Academies use this *Labs and Study Guide* as a required tool in the course; other Academies recommend the *Labs and Study Guide* as an additional resource to prepare for class exams and the CCNA certification.

The secondary audiences for this book include people taking CCNA-related classes from professional training organizations, those in college- and university-level networking courses, and anyone wanting to gain a detailed understanding of routing. However, the reader should know that the content of this book tightly aligns with the Cisco Networking Academy course. It may not be possible to complete some of the "Study Guide" sections and Labs without access to the online course. Fortunately, you can purchase the *Enterprise Networking, Security, and Automation v7.0 Companion Guide* (ISBN: 9780136634324).

Goals and Methods

The most important goal of this book is to help you pass the 200-301 Cisco Certified Network Associate exam, which is associated with the Cisco Certified Network Associate (CCNA) certification. Passing the CCNA exam means that you have the knowledge and skills required to manage a small, enterprise network. You can view the detailed exam topics at http://learningnetwork.cisco.com. They are divided into six broad categories:

- Network Fundamentals
- Network Access
- IP Connectivity
- IP Services
- Security Fundamentals
- Automation and Programmability

The Enterprise Networking, Security, and Automation v7 course covers introductory material in the last four bullets. The previous two courses, Introduction to Networks v7 and Switching, Routing, and Wireless Essentials v7, cover the material in the first two bullets.

Each chapter of this book is divided into a "Study Guide" section followed by a "Labs and Activities" section. The "Study Guide" section offers exercises that help you learn the concepts, configurations, and troubleshooting skills crucial to your success as a CCNA exam candidate. Each chapter is slightly different and includes some or all of the following types of exercises:

- Vocabulary matching exercises
- Concept questions exercises
- Skill-building activities and scenarios
- Configuration scenarios
- Packet Tracer exercises
- Troubleshooting scenarios

The "Labs and Activities" sections include all the online course labs and Packet Tracer activity instructions. If applicable, this section begins with a Command Reference that you will complete to highlight all the commands introduced in the chapter.

Packet Tracer and Companion Website

This book includes the instructions for all the Packet Tracer activities in the online course. You need to be enrolled in the Enterprise Networking, Security, and Automation Companion Guide v7 course to access these Packet Tracer files.

Four Packet Tracer activities have been created exclusively for this book. You can access these unique Packet Tracer files at this book's companion website.

To get your copy of Packet Tracer software and the four unique files for this book, please go to the companion website for instructions. To access this companion website, follow these steps:

Step 1.   Go to www.ciscopress.com/register and log in or create a new account.

Step 2.   Enter the ISBN: 9780136634690.

Step 3.   Answer the challenge question as proof of purchase.

Step 4.   Click on the Access Bonus Content link in the Registered Products section of your account page to be taken to the page where your downloadable content is available.

How This Book Is Organized

This book corresponds closely to the Cisco Networking Academy Switching, Routing, and Wireless Essentials v7 course and is divided into 14 chapters:

- **Chapter 1, "Single-Area OSPFv2 Concepts":** This chapter reviews single-area OSPF. It describes basic OSPF features and characteristics, packet types, and single-area operation.

- **Chapter 2, "Single-Area OSPFv2 Configuration":** This chapter reviews how to implement single-area OSPFv2 networks. It includes router ID configuration, point-to-point configuration, DR/BDR election, single-area modification, default route propagation, and verification of single-area OSPFv2 configuration.

- **Chapter 3, "Network Security Concepts":** This chapter reviews how vulnerabilities, threats, and exploits can be mitigated to enhance network security. It includes descriptions of the current state of cybersecurity, tools used by threat actors, malware types, common network attacks, IP vulnerabilities, TCP and UDP vulnerabilities, network best practices, and cryptography.

- **Chapter 4, "ACL Concepts":** This chapter reviews how ACLs are used to filter traffic, how wildcard masks are used, the creation of ACLs, and the difference between standard and extended IPv4 ACLs.

- **Chapter 5, "ACLs for IPv4 Configuration":** This chapter reviews how to implement ACLs. It includes standard IPv4 ACL configuration, ACL modifications using sequence numbers, applying an ACL to vty lines, and extended IPv4 ACL configuration.

- **Chapter 6, "NAT for IPv4":** This chapter reviews how to enable NAT services on a router to provide IPv4 address scalability. It includes descriptions of the purpose and function of NAT, the different types of NAT, and the advantages and disadvantages of NAT. Configuration topics include static NAT, dynamic NAT, and PAT. NAT64 is also briefly discussed.

- **Chapter 7, "WAN Concepts":** This chapter reviews how WAN access technologies can be used to satisfy business requirements. It includes descriptions of the purpose of a WAN, how WANs operate, traditional WAN connectivity options, modern WAN connectivity options, and internet-based connectivity options.

- **Chapter 8, "VPN and IPsec Concepts":** This chapter reviews how VPNs and IPsec are used to secure communications. It includes descriptions of different types of VPNs and an explanation of how the IPsec framework is used to secure network traffic.

- **Chapter 9, "QoS Concepts":** This chapter reviews how network devices use QoS to prioritize network traffic. It includes descriptions of network transmission characteristics, queuing algorithms, different queueing models, and QoS implementation techniques.

- **Chapter 10, "Network Management":** This chapter reviews how to use a variety of protocols and techniques to manage the network, including CDP, LLDP, NTP, SNMP, and syslog. In addition, this chapter discusses the management of configuration files and IOS images.

- **Chapter 11, "Network Design":** This chapter reviews the characteristics of scalable networks. It includes descriptions of network convergence, considerations for designing scalable networks, and switch and router hardware.

- **Chapter 12, "Network Troubleshooting":** This chapter reviews how to troubleshoot networks. It includes explanations of network documentation, troubleshooting methods, and troubleshooting tools. This chapter also demonstrates how to troubleshoot symptoms and causes of network problems using a layered approach.

- **Chapter 13, "Network Virtualization":** This chapter reviews the purpose and characteristics of network virtualization. It includes descriptions of cloud computing, the importance of virtualization, network device virtualization, software-defined network, and controllers used in network programming.

- **Chapter 14, "Network Automation":** This chapter reviews network automation. It includes descriptions of automation, data formats, APIs, REST, configuration management tools, and Cisco DNA Center.

Single-Area OSPFv2 Concepts

The "Study Guide" portion of this chapter uses a variety of exercises to test your knowledge of how single-area Open Shortest Path First (OSPF) operates in both point-to-point and broadcast multiaccess networks. There are no labs or Packet Tracer activities for this chapter.

As you work through this chapter, use Chapter 1 in *Enterprise Networking, Security, and Automation v7 Companion Guide* or use the corresponding Module 1 in the Enterprise Networking, Security, and Automation online curriculum for assistance.

Study Guide

OSPF Features and Characteristics

In this section, you review basic OSPF features and characteristics.

Components of OSPF

OSPF is a link-state routing protocol that was developed as an alternative for the distance vector protocol Routing Information Protocol (RIP). OSPF uses the concept of areas. A network administrator can divide the routing domain into distinct areas that help control routing update traffic. A link is an interface on a router. Information about the state of a link is known as link-state information; this information includes the network prefix, prefix length, and cost.

The components of OSPF include

- **Router protocol messages:** OSPF routers exchange routing information using five types of packets. List them.

    - _____

    - _____

    - _____

    - _____

    - _____

- **Data structures:** OSPF messages are used to create and maintain three OSPF databases. List and briefly describe each of them in a few words.

    - _____

    - _____

    - _____

- **Algorithm:** OSPF route calculations are based on Dijkstra's _____ algorithm, which accumulates the cost to reach a destination. This algorithm then builds a tree that is used to calculate the best routes to install in the routing table.

Link-State Operation

OSPF routers use the link-state routing process to reach a state of convergence where the LSDBs of all routers in the area have the same topology table. List and briefly describe the five steps in the link-state routing process.

_____

_____

_____

_____

_____

Single-Area and Multiarea OSPF

OSPF can be implemented in one of two ways:

- **Single-area OSPF:** All routers are in one area. Best practice is to use area 0.

- **Multiarea OSPF:** OSPF is implemented using multiple areas, in a hierarchical fashion. All areas must connect to the backbone area (area 0), as shown in Figure 1-1. Routers interconnecting the areas are referred to as area border routers (ABRs).

Figure 1-1   A Multiarea OSPF Topology

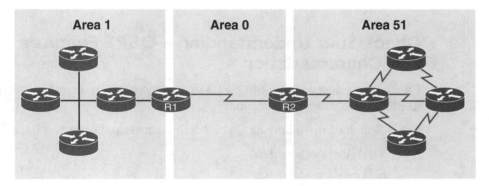

List and briefly describe three advantages of using multiarea OSPF.

- _____

- _____

- _____

OSPFv3

OSPFv3 is the version of OSPF used for exchanging IPv6 prefixes. OSPFv3 has the same functionality as OSPFv2 but uses IPv6 as the network layer transport, communicating with OSPFv3 peers and advertising IPv6 routes. OSPFv3 also uses the SPF algorithm as the computation engine to determine the best paths throughout the routing domain. OSPFv2 and OSPFv3 each have separate adjacency tables, OSPF topology tables, and IP routing tables, as shown in Figure 1-2.

Figure 1-2   OSPFv2 and OSPFv3 Data Structures

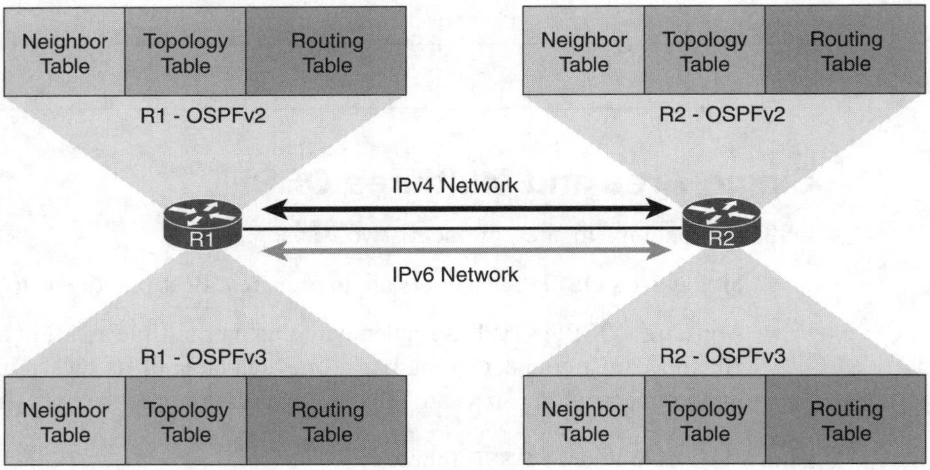

Check Your Understanding—OSPF Features and Characteristics

Check your understanding of OSPF features and characteristics by choosing the BEST answer to each of the following questions.

1. Which of the following OSPF components is associated with the neighbor table?

   a. Dijkstra's algorithm

   b. Link-state database

   c. Routing protocol messages

   d. Adjacency database

   e. Forwarding database

2. Which of the following OSPF components is responsible for computing the cost of each route?

   a. Dijkstra's algorithm

   b. Link-state database

   c. Routing protocol messages

   d. Adjacency database

   e. Forwarding database

3. Which of the following OSPF components is associated with the topology table?

   a. Dijkstra's algorithm

   b. Link-state database

   c. Routing protocol messages

   d. Adjacency database

   e. Forwarding database

4. Which of the following OSPF components is associated with the routing table?

    a. Dijkstra's algorithm

    b. Link-state database

    c. Routing protocol messages

    d. Adjacency database

    e. Forwarding database

OSPF Packets

In this section, you review how OSPF packet types are used in single-area OSPF.

Types of OSPF Packets

The following list describes the five different types of OSPF packets. Each packet serves a specific purpose in the OSPF routing process. Fill in the name for each packet type.

- _____: Used to establish and maintain adjacency with other OSPF routers

- _____: Contains an abbreviated list of the sending router's link-state database and is used by receiving routers to check against the local link-state database

- _____: A request for more information about any entry in the DBD

- _____: Used to reply to LSRs as well as to announce new information

- _____: Confirms receipt of an LSU

Link-State Updates

Receiving an OSPF Hello packet on an interface confirms for a router that there is another OSPF router on the link. OSPF then begins the process of establishing adjacency with the neighbor.

Routers initially exchange Type _____ packets. This type of packet is an abbreviated list of the sending router's LSDB and is used by receiving routers to check against the local LSDB.

The receiving routers use a Type _____ packet to request more information about an entry in the DBD.

The Type _____ packet is used to reply to an LSR packet.

Then, a Type _____ packet is sent to acknowledge receipt of the LSU.

In Table 1-1, indicate which OSPF packet type matches each LSA purpose.

Table 1-1   Identify OSPF Packet Types

LSA Purpose	OSPF Packet Type				
	Hello	DBD	LSR	LSU	LSAck
Discovers neighbors and builds adjacencies between them.					
Data field is empty.					
Asks for specific link-state records from router to router.					
Sends specifically requested link-state records.					
Contains a list of the sending router's LSDB.					
Can contain seven different types of LSAs.					
Checks for database synchronization between routers.					
Confirms receipt of a link-state update packet.					
Maintains adjacency with other OSPF routers.					

Hello Packet

Every OSPF message includes the header, as shown in Figure 1-3. Also shown in the figure are the fields of the OSPF Hello packet. Fill in the missing field names.

Figure 1-3   OSPF Message Format

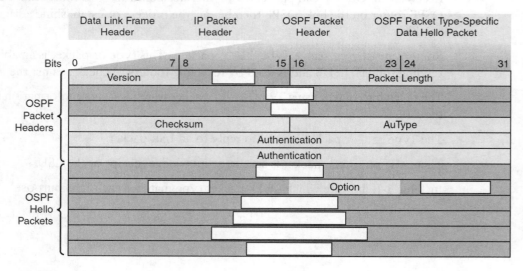

Check Your Understanding—OSPF Packets

Check your understanding of OSPF packets by choosing the BEST answer to each of the following questions.

1. Which of the following OSPF packets contains an abbreviated list of the LSDB of the sending router?

   a. Type 1: Hello packet

   b. Type 2: DBD packet

   c. Type 3: LSR packet

   d. Type 4: LSU packet

   e. Type 5: LSAck packet

2. Which of the following OSPF packets do routers use to announce new information?

   a. Type 1: Hello packet

   b. Type 2: DBD packet

   c. Type 3: LSR packet

   d. Type 4: LSU packet

   e. Type 5: LSAck packet

3. Which of the following OSPF packets do routers use to request more information?

   a. Type 1: Hello packet

   b. Type 2: DBD packet

   c. Type 3: LSR packet

   d. Type 4: LSU packet

   e. Type 5: LSAck packet

4. Which of the following OSPF packets is responsible for establishing and maintaining adjacency with other OSPF routers?

   a. Type 1: Hello packet

   b. Type 2: DBD packet

   c. Type 3: LSR packet

   d. Type 4: LSU packet

   e. Type 5: LSAck packet

5. Which of the following OSPF packets is used to confirm receipt of an LSA?

   a. Type 1: Hello packet

   b. Type 2: DBD packet

   c. Type 3: LSR packet

   d. Type 4: LSU packet

   e. Type 5: LSAck packet

6. Which of the following is used with a Hello packet to uniquely identify the originating router?

   a. Hello Interval

   b. Router ID

   c. Designated Router ID

   d. Network Mask

   e. Dead Interval

OSPF Operation

In this section, you review how single-area OSPF operates.

OSPF Operational States

When an OSPF router is initially connected to a network, it attempts to

- Create adjacencies with neighbors

- Exchange routing information

- Calculate the best routes

- Reach convergence

In Figure 1-4, record the five states that occur between the *Down state* and the *Full state*.

Figure 1-4   Transitioning Through the OSPF States

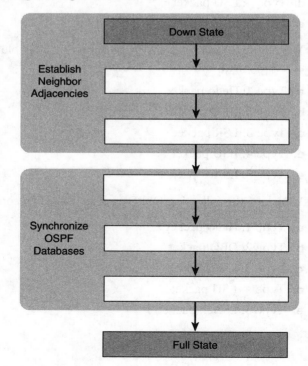

In Table 1-2, indicate which OSPF state matches each state description.

Table 1-2   Identify the OSPF States

State Description	OSPF States						
	Down	Init	Two-Way	Ex-Start	Exchange	Loading	Full
Routes are processed using the SPF algorithm.							
A neighbor responds to a Hello.							
Hello packets are received from neighbors and contain the sending router ID.							
On Ethernet links, elect a designated router (DR) and a backup designated router (BDR).							
No Hello packets received.							
Router requests more information about a specific DBD entry.							
Routers exchange DBD packets.							
Routers have converged.							
The LSDB and routing tables are complete.							
A new OSPF router on the link sends the first Hello.							
Exchange of DBD packets initiated.							
Negotiation of the master/slave relationship and DBD packet sequence number.							

The Need for a DR

Describe the two challenges regarding OSPF LSA flooding in multiaccess networks.

- _____

- _____

For each multiaccess topology in Figure 1-5, indicate how many adjacencies would be formed if the DB/BDR process were not part of OSPF operations.

Figure 1-5   Multiaccess Topologies

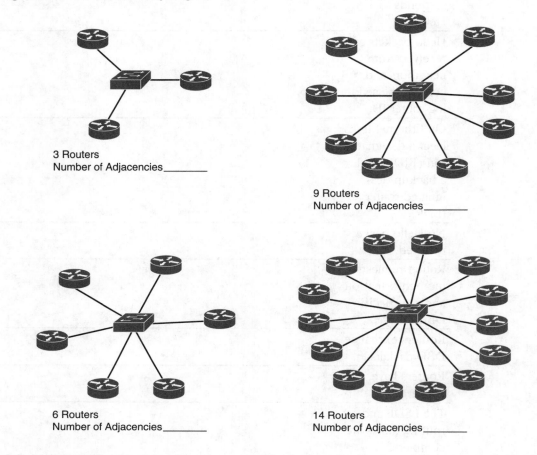

3 Routers
Number of Adjacencies_____

9 Routers
Number of Adjacencies_____

6 Routers
Number of Adjacencies_____

14 Routers
Number of Adjacencies_____

LSA Flooding with a DR

Briefly describe how the designated router (DR) reduces the impact of LSA flooding.

_____

_____

Check Your Understanding—OSPF Operation

Check your understanding of OSPF operation by choosing the BEST answer to each of the following questions.

1. During this OSPF state on multiaccess networks, the routers elect a designated router (DR) and a backup designated router (BDR).

   a. Down state

   b. Init state

   c. Two-Way state

   d. ExStart state

   e. Exchange state

   f. Loading state

   g. Full state

2. During this OSPF state, routers send each other DBD packets.

   a. Down state

   b. Init state

   c. Two-Way state

   d. ExStart state

   e. Exchange state

   f. Loading state

   g. Full state

3. An OSPF router enters this state when it has received from a neighbor a Hello packet that contains the sending router's router ID.

   a. Down state

   b. Init state

   c. Two-Way state

   d. ExStart state

   e. Exchange state

   f. Loading state

   g. Full state

4. During this OSPF state on point-to-point networks, the routers decide which router initiates the exchange of DBD packets.

   a. Down state

   b. Init state

   c. Two-Way state

   d. ExStart state

   e. Exchange state

   f. Loading state

   g. Full state

5. During this OSPF state, routers have converged link-state databases.

 a. Down state

 b. Init state

 c. Two-Way state

 d. ExStart state

 e. Exchange state

 f. Loading state

 g. Full state

6. During this OSPF state, no Hello packets are received.

 a. Down state

 b. Init state

 c. Two-Way state

 d. ExStart state

 e. Exchange state

 f. Loading state

 g. Full state

7. During this OSPF state, the link-state databases are fully synchronized.

 a. Down state

 b. Init state

 c. Two-Way state

 d. ExStart state

 e. Exchange state

 f. Loading state

 g. Full state

Labs and Activities

There are no labs or Packet Tracer activities in this chapter.

Single-Area OSPFv2 Configuration

The "Study Guide" portion of this chapter uses a variety of exercises to test your knowledge and skills related to implementing single-area OSPFv2 in both point-to-point and broadcast multiaccess networks. The "Labs and Activities" portion of this chapter includes all the online curriculum labs and Packet Tracer activity instructions.

As you work through this chapter, use Chapter 2 in *Enterprise Networking, Security, and Automation v7 Companion Guide* or use the corresponding Module 2 in the Enterprise Networking, Security, and Automation online curriculum for assistance.

Study Guide

OSPF Router ID

In this section, you review how to configure an OSPFv2 router ID.

OSPF Reference Topology

Figure 2-1 shows the reference topology, and Table 2-1 shows the addressing scheme used for the OSPF point-to-point configurations in this chapter.

Figure 2-1   OSPF Point-to-Point Reference Topology

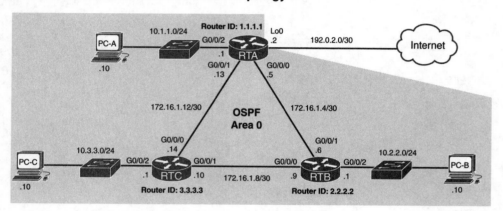

Table 2-1   Addressing Table

Device	Interface	IPv4 Address	Subnet Mask	Default Gateway
RTA	G0/0/0	172.16.1.5	255.255.255.252	N/A
	G0/0/1	172.16.1.13	255.255.255.252	N/A
	G0/0/2	10.1.1.1	255.255.255.0	N/A
	Lo0	192.0.2.2	255.255.255.252	N/A
RTB	G0/0/0	172.16.1.9	255.255.255.252	N/A
	G0/0/1	172.16.1.6	255.255.255.252	N/A
	G0/0/2	10.2.2.1	255.255.255.0	N/A
RTC	G0/0/0	172.16.1.14	255.255.255.252	N/A
	G0/0/1	172.16.1.10	255.255.255.252	N/A
	G0/0/2	10.3.3.1	255.255.255.0	N/A
PC-A	NIC	10.1.1.10	255.255.255.0	10.1.1.1
PC-B	NIC	10.2.2.10	255.255.255.0	10.2.2.1
PC-C	NIC	10.3.3.10	255.255.255.0	10.3.3.1

Router IDs

Every router requires a router ID to participate in an OSPF domain. The router ID can be defined by an administrator or automatically assigned by the router. The router ID is used by other OSPF routers to uniquely identify neighbors. Briefly explain the two ways an OSPF-enabled router uses the router ID.

- _____

- _____

Router ID Order of Precedence

Complete the flowchart in Figure 2-2 to indicate the order of precedence a router uses to choose the router ID. The two diamond shapes are questions. The rectangle at the bottom is a decision.

Figure 2-2   Router ID Order of Precedence

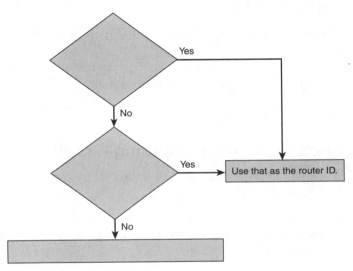

Configure a Loopback Interface as the Router ID

Instead of relying on a physical interface, the router ID can be assigned to a loopback interface. Typically, the IPv4 address for this type of loopback interface should be configured using a 32-bit subnet mask (255.255.255.255). This effectively creates a host route. A 32-bit host route would not get advertised as a route to other OSPF routers.

Refer to Figure 2-1 and Table 2-1. Enter the commands and router prompt to configure RTA with a Loopback 0 interface using IP address 1.1.1.1/32.

_____

_____

Explicitly Configure a Router ID

Refer to Figure 2-1 and Table 2-1. Instead of configuring a loopback interface on RTA, you can explicitly configure the router ID. Record the commands and router prompt to configure RTA with a router ID of 1.1.1.1 for OSPF process 1.

_____

_____

Modify the Router ID

Say that you changed the router ID on RTA to 1.1.1.2. You check to see if RTA is using the new router ID and notice that it is still using the old router ID, 1.1.1.1. What command did you enter to show the following output?

RTA# _____

```
Routing Protocol is "ospf 1"
  Outgoing update filter list for all interfaces is not set
  Incoming update filter list for all interfaces is not set
  Router ID 1.1.1.1
```

In what two ways can you have RTA change the router ID it is using?

_____

Which way is preferred, and how do you do it?

_____

Check Your Understanding—OSPF Router ID

Check your understanding of OSPF router ID by choosing the BEST answer to each of the following questions.

1. True or false: In the **router ospf** *process-id* command, the *process-ID* value, which can any number between 1 and 65,535, is globally significant. It must be the same on all routers in the OSPF area.

   a. True

   b. False

2. Which of the following applies to the router ID? (Choose two.)

   a. The router ID cannot be defined by an administrator.

   b. The router ID is not used to determine the backup designated router (BDR).

   c. The router ID is used to determine the designated router (DR).

   d. The router ID uniquely identifies the router.

   e. The router ID is not required.

3. Which of the following is the order of precedence for choosing the router ID?

   a. 1. Router ID that is explicitly configured

      2. Lowest IPv4 loopback address

      3. Lowest active IPv4 address that is configured

   b. 1. Router ID that is explicitly configured

      2. Lowest active IPv4 address that is configured

      3. Lowest IPv4 loopback address

   c. 1. Router ID that is explicitly configured

      2. Highest IPv4 loopback address

      3. Highest active IPv4 address that is configured

d. 1. Highest IPv4 loopback address

2. Router ID that is explicitly configured

3. Highest active IPv4 address that is configured

e. 1. Highest IPv4 loopback address

2. Highest active IPv4 address that is configured

3. Router ID that is explicitly configured

Point-to-Point OSPF Networks

In this section, you review how to configure single-area OSPFv2 in a point-to-point network.

The network Command Syntax

The basic syntax for the **network** command is as follows:

```
Router(config-router)# network network-address wildcard-mask area area-id
```

- With the *network-address wildcard-mask* syntax, any interfaces on a router that match the network address in the **network** command are enabled to send and receive OSPF packets.
- The **area** *area-id* syntax specifies the OSPF area for this network. When configuring single-area OSPFv2, the convention is to use area 0.

The Wildcard Mask

The wildcard mask is typically the inverse of the subnet mask for the network configured on the interface. In Table 2-2, fill in the dotted-decimal subnet mask and wildcard mask for each address.

Table 2-2   Calculate the Wildcard Mask

Network/Prefix	Dotted-Decimal Subnet Mask	Wildcard Mask
172.30.0.0/16		
192.168.200.128/20		
10.100.200.53/30		
192.168.226.96/27		
172.17.2.128/25		
10.0.0.0/8		
172.24.4.0/23		

Configure OSPF Using the network Command

Refer to Figure 2-1 and Table 2-1. Record the commands, including the router prompt, to configure OSPF process 1 on RTA. Include the router ID and **network** commands, using a wildcard mask based on the subnet mask.

```
RTA(config)# _____
```

_____

_____

_____

Record the commands, including the router prompt, to configure OSPF process 1 on RTB. Include the router ID and **network** commands, using a quad-zero wildcard mask.

```
RTB(config)# _____
```

_____

_____

_____

Configure OSPF Using the ip ospf Command

Refer to Figure 2-1 and Table 2-1. Record the commands, including the router prompt, to configure OSPF process 1 on RTC. Include the router ID and then show the commands to configure OSPF on the interface.

```
RTC(config)# _____
```

_____

_____

_____

_____

_____

_____

Passive Interface

List and briefly described the three ways that sending out unneeded messages on LANs affects the network.

- _____

- _____

- _____

Configure Passive Interfaces

Refer to Figure 2-1 and Table 2-1. Record the commands to configure RTA, RTB, and RTC with the appropriate passive interfaces.

```
RTA(config)# _____
```

_____

```
RTB(config)# _____
```

_____

```
RTC(config)# _____
```

_____

Packet Tracer Exercise 2-1: Point-to-Point Single-Area OSPFv2 Configuration

Now you are ready to use Packet Tracer to apply your knowledge about configuring single-area OSPFv2 in a point-to-point network. Download the file LSG03-0201.pka from the companion website for this book and open it. Refer to the Introduction of this book for specifics on accessing files.

Note: The following instructions are also contained within the Packet Tracer Exercise.

In this Packet Tracer activity, you will configure point-to-point single-area OSPFv2.

Requirements

Use the following requirements and your documented commands from the "Point-to-Point OSPF Networks" section to configure RTA, RTB, and RTC with single-area OSPFv2:

- Explicitly configure router IDs.
- Configure the network command on RTA, using a wildcard mask based on the subnet mask.
- Configure the network command on RTB, using a quad-zero wildcard mask.
- Configure the **ip ospf** interface command on RTC.
- Configure passive interfaces.

All PCs should be able to ping each other. PC-B and PC-C will not be able to ping the loopback interface on RTA. Your completion percentage should be 100%. If it is not, click Check Results to see which required components are not yet completed.

Multiaccess OSPF Networks

In this section, you review how to configure the OSPF interface priority to influence the DR/BDR election in a multiaccess network.

OSPF Designated Router

Recall that, in multiaccess networks, OSPF elects a DR and a BDR as a solution to manage the number of adjacencies and the flooding of link-state advertisements (LSAs). The DR is responsible for collecting and distributing LSAs sent and received.

What multicast IPv4 address does a DR use to send OSPF messages to all OSPF routers?

Briefly describe the role of the BDR.

All other OSPF routers are called DROTHERs (for "DR other"). What multicast IPv4 address do DROTHERs use to send OSPF messages to the DR?

OSPF Multiaccess Reference Topology

Figure 2-3 shows the reference topology, and Table 2-3 shows the addressing scheme used for the OSPF multiaccess configurations in this chapter.

Figure 2-3   OSPF Multiaccess Reference Topology

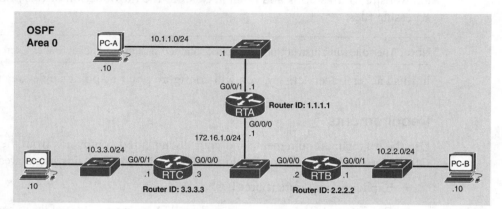

Table 2-3   Addressing Table

Device	Interface	IPv4 Address	Subnet Mask	Default Gateway
RTA	G0/0/0	172.16.1.1	255.255.255.0	N/A
	G0/0/1	10.1.1.1	255.255.255.0	N/A
RTB	G0/0/0	172.16.1.2	255.255.255.0	N/A
	G0/0/1	10.2.2.1	255.255.255.0	N/A
RTC	G0/0/0	172.16.1.3	255.255.255.0	N/A
	G0/0/1	10.3.3.1	255.255.255.0	N/A
PC-A	NIC	10.1.1.10	255.255.255.0	10.1.1.1
PC-B	NIC	10.2.2.10	255.255.255.0	10.2.2.1
PC-C	NIC	10.3.3.10	255.255.255.0	10.3.3.1

Assume that all routers in Figure 2-3 boot at the same time. Which routers would be elected DR and BDR?

DR: _____

BDR: _____

Verify OSPF Multiaccess Router Roles

In Example 2-1, fill in the command you would use to display the highlighted information about the multiaccess OSPF configuration on the G0/0/0 interface for RTA.

Note: Output in this chapter is from Packet Tracer 7.3 and may differ slightly from the output in your version of Packet Tracer or on real routers. However, the important OSPF details are the same.

Example 2-1   Getting Detailed Information for an OSPF Interface

```
RTA# _____
GigabitEthernet0/0/0 is up, line protocol is up
  Internet address is 172.16.1.1/24, Area 0
  Process ID 1, Router ID 1.1.1.1, Network Type BROADCAST, Cost: 1
  Transmit Delay is 1 sec, State DROTHER, Priority 1
  Designated Router (ID) 3.3.3.3, Interface address 172.16.1.3
  Backup Designated Router (ID) 2.2.2.2, Interface address 172.16.1.2
  Timer intervals configured, Hello 10, Dead 40, Wait 40, Retransmit 5
    Hello due in 00:00:01
  Index 2/2, flood queue length 0
  Next 0x0(0)/0x0(0)
  Last flood scan length is 1, maximum is 1
  Last flood scan time is 0 msec, maximum is 0 msec
  Neighbor Count is 2, Adjacent neighbor count is 2
    Adjacent with neighbor 3.3.3.3   (Designated Router)
    Adjacent with neighbor 2.2.2.2   (Backup Designated Router)
  Suppress hello for 0 neighbor(s)
RTA#
```

What command do you use for RTA to quickly discover the status of adjacencies with other OSPF routers, as shown in Example 2-2?

Example 2-2   Getting Adjacency Information for OSPF Routers

```
RTA# _____
Neighbor ID     Pri   State       Dead Time   Address      Interface
3.3.3.3          1    FULL/DR     00:00:39    172.16.1.3   GigabitEthernet0/0/0
2.2.2.2          1    FULL/BDR    00:00:39    172.16.1.2   GigabitEthernet0/0/0
RTA#
```

DR Failure and Recovery

For the following questions, refer to Figure 2-3.

The router ID on RTA is changed to 4.4.4.4. Which router is the DR?

_____

The RTC fails. Which router becomes the DR? _____

Which router becomes the BDR? _____

RTC rejoins the network. Which router is the DR?

_____

Assume that all the above actions have occurred. Also assume that the network administrator can simultaneously reset the OSPF process on all three routers, forcing a DR/BDR election. Which routers are now DR and BDR?

_____

Configure OSPF Priority

A better method for ensuring which routers are DR and BDR is to configure the OSPF priority by using the **ip ospf priority** interface configuration command.

Assume the following requirements for the router in Figure 2-3:

- RTA should be the BDR. However, its priority should not be the default value.
- RTB should be the DR. Its priority should be set to the highest possible value.
- RTC should never be the DR or BDR.

Record the commands, including the command prompts, to configure the priority for each router.

RTA(config)# _____

_____

RTB(config)# _____

_____

_____

What command, including router prompt, forces a new DR/BDR election?

_____

What command, other than **show run**, can you use to verify the OSPF priority on the local router?

_____

What command can you use to verify the OSPF priority of the adjacent OSPF routers?

_____

Modify Single-Area OSPFv2

In this section, you review how to implement modifications to change the operation of single-area OSPFv2.

Cisco OSPF Cost Metric

The Cisco cost of an interface is inversely proportional to the bandwidth of the interface. Therefore, a higher bandwidth indicates a lower cost.

What is the formula used to calculate OSPF cost in Cisco IOS?

_____

What is the default value for the reference bandwidth?

_____

In Table 2-4, record the Cisco IOS cost for each of the interface types.

Table 2-4   Cisco ISO Default OSPF Cost Values

Interface Type	Reference Bandwidth/Default Interface Bandwidth	Cost
10 Gigabit Ethernet	100,000,000/10,000,000,000	
Gigabit Ethernet	100,000,000/1,000,000,000	
Fast Ethernet	100,000,000/100,000,000	
Ethernet	100,000,000/10,000,000	

If you did the calculations correctly, you can see that, by default, 10 Gigabit Ethernet, Gigabit Ethernet, and Fast Ethernet all have the same cost value. IOS rounds to the nearest integer, so the cost value cannot be less than 1.

Adjust the Reference Bandwidth

What are the router prompt and command syntax to change the reference bandwidth to a higher value so that 10 Gigabit Ethernet, Gigabit Ethernet, and Fast Ethernet all have different values?

The value is entered in Mbps, so what is a good value to enter to change the resulting cost values so that each is a different value?

Record the command to set the reference bandwidth on RTA. All three routers would then be configured with the same value.

% OSPF: Reference bandwidth is changed. Please ensure reference bandwidth is consistent across all routers.

OSPF Accumulates Cost

Figure 2-4 shows the point-to-point topology from earlier, now with OSPF cost labels. The **auto-cost reference-bandwidth** command has been configured on all three routers.

Figure 2-4   OSPF Point-to-Point Reference Topology with Cost Values

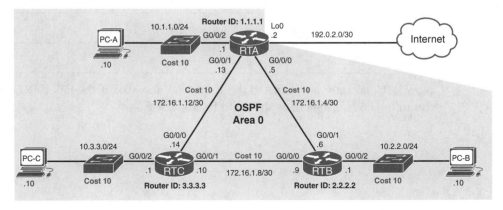

In Example 2-3, record the commands used to display the route information for 10.3.3.0/24. Fill in the missing cost values.

Example 2-3   Finding the OSPF Cost for RTA to Reach 10.3.3.0/24

```
RTA# _____

O       10.3.3.0/24 [110/___] via 172.16.1.14, 00:10:10, GigabitEthernet0/0/1

RTA# _____
Routing entry for 10.3.3.0/24
Known via "ospf 1", distance 110, metric ___, type intra area
   Last update from 172.16.1.14 on GigabitEthernet0/0/1, 00:10:22 ago
   Routing Descriptor Blocks:
   * 172.16.1.14, from 3.3.3.3, 00:10:22 ago, via GigabitEthernet0/0/1
       Route metric is ___, traffic share count is 1


RTA#
```

Manually Set OSPF Cost Value

In Figure 2-4, notice that, from RTC's perspective, the link between RTA and RTB has equal-cost paths, as shown in Example 2-4. RTC would load balance traffic to this network.

Example 2-4   OSPF Equal-Cost Paths

```
RTC# show ip route ospf | begin 172.16.1.4
O       172.16.1.4 [110/20] via 172.16.1.13, 00:21:28, GigabitEthernet0/0/0
                   [110/20] via 172.16.1.9, 00:21:28, GigabitEthernet0/0/1

RTC#
```

However, the administrator might want RTC to prefer the route to RTA over the route to RTB. Also, RTB should use the route to RTA to get to the 172.16.1.12 network. Record the commands, including the router prompt, to configure the link between RTB and RTC with a cost of 40.

_____

_____

_____

Now RTC has only one route to the 172.16.1.4 network. If the link to RTA fails, the route through RTB is installed, as shown in Example 2-5.

Example 2-5   Verifying One Route and Testing Failover to the Backup Route

```
RTC# show ip route ospf | begin 172.16.1.4

O       172.16.1.4 [110/20] via _____


RTC# conf t

RTC(config)# int g0/0/0

RTC(config-if)# shutdown

%LINK-5-CHANGED: Interface GigabitEthernet0/0/0, changed state to administratively
down

%LINEPROTO-5-UPDOWN: Line protocol on Interface GigabitEthernet0/0/0, changed
state to down

00:35:21: %OSPF-5-ADJCHG: Process 1, Nbr 1.1.1.1 on GigabitEthernet0/0/0 from FULL
to DOWN, Neighbor Down: Interface down or detached

RTC(config-if)# end

RTC# show ip route ospf | begin 172.16.1.4

O       172.16.1.4 [110/50] via _____


RTC#
```

Modify OSPFv2 Intervals

OSPF routers must use matching Hello intervals and Dead intervals on the same link. The default interval values result in efficient OSPF operation and seldom need to be modified. However, you can change them.

Again refer to Figure 2-4. Assuming that the current intervals are 10 and 40, document the commands necessary to change these OSPFv2 intervals on the link between RTB and RTC to a value four times greater than the current value.

_____

_____

_____

_____

_____

Note that it is not necessary to configure the Dead interval as long as the desired interval is four times the Hello interval. IOS automatically increases the Dead interval to four times the configured Hello interval.

What command displays the output shown in Example 2-6?

Example 2-6   Verifying the Hello and Dead Intervals on RTC

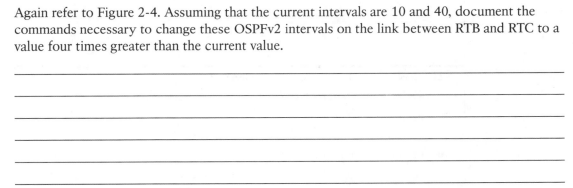

```
RTC# _____

   Timer intervals configured, Hello 40, Dead 160, Wait 160, Retransmit 5

RTC#
```

Note: This filtered command does not work in Packet Tracer.

Default Route Propagation

In this section, you review how to configure OSPF to propagate a default route.

Propagate and Verify a Default Route

In Figure 2-4, there is a simulated link to the internet. Record the commands to configure RTA with a default route, using Loopback 0 as the exit interface. Then record the commands to configure RTA to propagate the default route to RTB and RTC.

_____

_____

_____

On RTB and RTC, the routing table should now have a default route and should be able to ping the Loopback 0 interface on RTA, as shown in Example 2-7.

Example 2-7   Verifying That RTB and RTC Have a Default Route

```
RTB# show ip route | include Gateway
Gateway of last resort is 172.16.1.5 to network 0.0.0.0
RTB# ping 192.0.2.2

Type escape sequence to abort.
Sending 5, 100-byte ICMP Echos to 192.0.2.2, timeout is 2 seconds:
!!!!!
Success rate is 100 percent (5/5), round-trip min/avg/max = 0/0/0 ms

RTB#
```

```
RTC# show ip route | include Gateway
Gateway of last resort is 172.16.1.13 to network 0.0.0.0
RTC# ping 192.0.2.2

Type escape sequence to abort.
Sending 5, 100-byte ICMP Echos to 192.0.2.2, timeout is 2 seconds:
!!!!!
Success rate is 100 percent (5/5), round-trip min/avg/max = 0/0/1 ms

RTC#
```

Packet Tracer Exercise 2-2—Modify a Point-to-Point Single-Area OSPFv2 Configuration

Now you are ready to use Packet Tracer to apply your knowledge about modifying single-area OSPFv2 in a point-to-point network. Download the file LSG03-0202.pka from the companion website for this book and open it. Refer to the Introduction of this book for specifics on accessing files.

Note: The following instructions are also contained within the Packet Tracer Exercise.

In this Packet Tracer activity, you will modify a point-to-point single-area OSPFv2 configuration.

Requirements

Use the following requirements and your documented commands from the "Modify Single-Area OSPFv2" and "Default Route Propagation" sections to modify the single-area OSPFv2 configuration on RTA, RTB, and RTC:

- Adjust the reference bandwidth so that Gigabit Ethernet links have an OSPF cost of 10.
- Modify the OSPF cost between RTB and RTC to be 40.
- Modify the Hello and Dead intervals between RTB and RTC to be four times the current default value.
- Configure RTA with a default route that uses Loopback 0 as the exit interface.
- Propagate the default route to RTB and RTC.

All PCs should be able to ping each other and the Loopback 0 interface on RTA. Your completion percentage should be 100%. If it is not, click Check Results to see which required components are not yet completed.

Verify Single-Area OSPFv2

In this section, you review how to verify a single-area OSPFv2 implementation. Commands that are particularly useful for determining that OSPF is operating as expected include the following:

- **show ip ospf neighbor**
- **show ip protocols**
- **show ip ospf**
- **show ip ospf interface**

Note: The output shown in this section is from Packet Tracer. In some cases, the output may not match output on real equipment. However, the important information is shown. In addition, Cisco regularly changes the output for **show** commands. Therefore, you should get comfortable with focusing on the important information displayed as opposed to whether the command output exactly matches what is shown between different IOS implementations.

Verify OSPF Neighbors

Example 2-8 shows the output for the **show ip ospf neighbor** command, which provides a quick overview of the status of neighbor adjacencies.

Example 2-8   The *show ip ospf neighbor* Command

```
RTA# show ip ospf neighbor
Neighbor ID      Pri   State      Dead Time    Address        Interface
2.2.2.2            1   FULL/DR    00:00:36     172.16.1.6     GigabitEthernet0/0/0
3.3.3.3            1   FULL/DR    00:00:36     172.16.1.14    GigabitEthernet0/0/1
RTA#
```

List four reasons two routers may not form an adjacency.

- _____

- _____

- _____

- _____

Verify OSPF Protocol Settings

Example 2-9 shows the output for the **show ip protocols** command. Using this command is a quick way to verify vital OSPF configuration information.

Example 2-9   The *show ip protocols* Command

```
RTA# show ip protocols
*** IP Routing is NSF aware ***
Routing Protocol is "ospf 1"
  Outgoing update filter list for all interfaces is not set
  Incoming update filter list for all interfaces is not set
  Router ID 1.1.1.1
  It is an autonomous system boundary router
  Redistributing External Routes from,
  Number of areas in this router is 1. 1 normal 0 stub 0 nssa
  Maximum path: 4
  Routing for Networks:
    10.1.1.0 0.0.0.255 area 0
    172.16.1.4 0.0.0.3 area 0
    172.16.1.12 0.0.0.3 area 0
  Passive Interface(s):
    GigabitEthernet0/0/2
  Routing Information Sources:
    Gateway         Distance      Last Update
    1.1.1.1              110      00:10:15
    2.2.2.2              110      00:08:20
    3.3.3.3              110      00:08:20
  Distance: (default is 110)
RTA#
```

Verify OSPF Process Information

Example 2-10 shows the output for the **show ip ospf** command. This command is particularly useful for showing OSPF area information in a multiarea OSPF configuration.

Example 2-10   The *show ip ospf* Command

```
RTA# show ip ospf
 Routing Process "ospf 1" with ID 1.1.1.1
 Supports only single TOS(TOS0) routes
 Supports opaque LSA
 SPF schedule delay 5 secs, Hold time between two SPFs 10 secs
 Minimum LSA interval 5 secs. Minimum LSA arrival 1 secs
 Number of external LSA 1. Checksum Sum 0x00fecf
 Number of opaque AS LSA 0. Checksum Sum 0x000000
Number of DCbitless external and opaque AS LSA 0
 Number of DoNotAge external and opaque AS LSA 0
 Number of areas in this router is 1. 1 normal 0 stub 0 nssa
 External flood list length 0
    Area BACKBONE(0)
        Number of interfaces in this area is 3
        Area has no authentication
        SPF algorithm executed 3 times
        Area ranges are
        Number of LSA 6. Checksum Sum 0x03f8a3
        Number of opaque link LSA 0. Checksum Sum 0x000000
        Number of DCbitless LSA 0
        Number of indication LSA 0
        Number of DoNotAge LSA 0
        Flood list length 0
 RTA#
```

Verify OSPF Interface Settings

Example 2-11 shows output for the **show ip ospf interface** command. This command is useful for displaying the router ID, the type of network, OSPF cost, OSPF intervals, and DR/BDR information in a multiaccess network.

Example 2-11   The *show ip ospf interface* Command

```
RTA# show ip ospf interface GigabitEthernet 0/0/0
GigabitEthernet0/0/0 is up, line protocol is up
  Internet address is 172.16.1.5/30, Area 0
  Process ID 1, Router ID 1.1.1.1, Network Type BROADCAST, Cost: 1
  Transmit Delay is 1 sec, State BDR, Priority 1
  Designated Router (ID) 2.2.2.2, Interface address 172.16.1.6
  Backup Designated Router (ID) 1.1.1.1, Interface address 172.16.1.5
  Timer intervals configured, Hello 10, Dead 40, Wait 40, Retransmit 5
    Hello due in 00:00:00
  Index 3/3, flood queue length 0
  Next 0x0(0)/0x0(0)
  Last flood scan length is 1, maximum is 1
  Last flood scan time is 0 msec, maximum is 0 msec
  Neighbor Count is 1, Adjacent neighbor count is 1
    Adjacent with neighbor 2.2.2.2   (Designated Router)
  Suppress hello for 0 neighbor(s)
```

Example 2-12 shows output for the **show ip ospf interface brief** command, which is useful for quickly verifying the following information:

- What interfaces are participating in OSPF
- What networks are being advertised (with the IP address/mask)
- The cost of each link
- The network state
- The number of neighbors on each link

Example 2-12   The *show ip ospf interface brief* Command

```
RTA# show ip ospf interface brief
Interface    PID   Area         IP Address/Mask     Cost   State  Nbrs F/C
Gi0/0/0      1     0            172.16.1.5/30       10     P2P    0/0
Gi0/0/1      1     0            172.16.1.13/30      30     P2P    1/1
Gi0/0/2      1     0            10.1.1.1/24         10     P2P    1/1
R1#
```

Note: The **show ip ospf interface brief** command is not supported in Packet Tracer.

Labs and Activities

Command Reference

In Table 2-5, record the command, including the correct router or switch prompt, that fits each description.

Table 2-5   Commands for Chapter 2, "Single-Area OSPFv2 Configuration"

Command	Description
	Configure R1 OSPFv2 with router ID 1.1.1.1.
	Configure R1 for OSPFv2 routing using process ID 20.
	Configure R1 OSPFv2 to advertise network 10.10.10.128/27. Use the wildcard mask argument.
	Configure R1 OSPFv2 to advertise the network attached to interface 10.10.10.33. Use the quad-zero mask argument.
	Configure R1 with OSPFv2 process 10 for area 0 on the interface.
	Configure the R1 OSPV2 process to not send routing messages out the Gigabit Ethernet 0/0/0 interface.
	Configure R1's LAN interface to be the DR with a priority of 10.
	Configure the R1 OSPFv2 routing process to set the cost of Gigabit Ethernet interfaces to 10.
	Configure the cost of R1's LAN interface to be 30.
	On R1, set the OSPFv2 Hello interval to 60 seconds.
	On R1, set the OSPFv2 Dead interval to 240 seconds.
	Configure R1 with an IPv4 default route pointing out the Gigabit Ethernet 0/1/1 interface.
	Propagate the default route in the OSPFv2 routing process on R1.

2.2.13 Packet Tracer—Point-to-Point Single-Area OSPFv2 Configuration

Addressing Table

Device	Interface	IP Address	Subnet Mask
R1	G0/0/0	192.168.10.1	/24
	S0/1/0	10.1.1.1	/30
	S0/1/1	10.1.1.5	/30
R2	G0/0/0	192.168.20.1	/24
	S0/1/0	10.1.1.2	/30
	S0/1/1	10.1.1.9	/30
R3	G0/0/0	192.168.30.1	/24
	S0/1/0	10.1.1.10	/30
	S0/1/1	10.1.1.6	/30
PC1	NIC	192.168.10.10	/24
PC2	NIC	192.168.20.10	/24
PC3	NIC	192.168.30.10	/24

Objectives

Part 1: Configure Router IDs.

Part 2: Configure Networks for OSPF Routing.

Part 3: Configure Passive Interfaces.

Part 4: Verify OSPF configuration.

Background

In this activity, you will activate OSPF routing using network statements and wildcard masks, configuring OSPF routing on interfaces, and using network statements quad-zero masks. In addition, you will configure explicit router IDs and passive interfaces.

Instructions

Part 1: Configure Router IDs

a. Start the OSPF routing process on all three routers. Use process ID **10**.

```
Router(config)# router ospf process-id
```

b. Use the **router-id** command to set the OSPF IDs of the three routers as follows

- R1: **1.1.1.1**

- R2: **2.2.2.2**

- R3: **3.3.3.3**

Use the following command:

```
Router(config-router)# router-id rid
```

Part 2: Configure Networks for OSPF Routing

Step 1: Configure networks for OSPF routing using network commands and wildcard masks.

Questions:

How many statements are required to configure OSPF to route all the networks attached to router R1?

_____

The LAN attached to router R1 has a /24 mask. What is the equivalent of this mask in dotted decimal representation?

_____

Subtract the dotted decimal subnet mask from 255.255.255.255. What is the result?

_____

What is the dotted decimal equivalent of the /30 subnet mask?

_____

Subtract the dotted decimal representation of the /30 mask from 255.255.255.255. What is the result?

_____

a. Configure the routing process on R1 with the network statements and wildcard masks that are required to activate OSPF routing for all the attached networks. The network statement values should be the network or subnet addresses of the configured networks.

```
Router(config-router)# network network-address wildcard-mask area
area-id
```

b. Verify that OSPF has been configured properly by the displaying the running configuration. If you find an error, delete the network statement using the **no** command and reconfigure it.

Step 2: Configure networks for OSPF routing using interface IP addresses and quad-zero masks.

On router R2, configure OSPF using network commands with the IP addresses of the interfaces and quad-zero masks. The syntax of the network command is the same as was used above.

Step 3: Configure OSPF routing on router interfaces

On router R3, configure the required interfaces with OSPF.

Question:

Which interfaces on R3 should be configured with OSPF?

_____

Configure each interface using the command syntax shown below:

```
Router(config-if)# ip ospf process-id area area-id
```

Part 3: Configure Passive Interfaces

OSPF will send its protocol traffic out of all interfaces that are participating in the OSPF process. On links that are not configured to other networks, such as LANs, this unnecessary traffic consumes resources. The passive-interface command will prevent the OSPF process from sending unnecessary routing protocol traffic out LAN interfaces.

Question:

Which interfaces on R1, R2, and R3 are a LAN interfaces?

_____

Configure the OSPF process on each of the three routers with the **passive-interface** command.

```
Router(config-router)# passive-interface interface
```

Part 4: Verify OSPF Configuration

Use **show** commands to verify the network and passive interface configuration of the OSPF process on each router.

2.3.11 Packet Tracer—Determine the DR and BDR

Addressing Table

Device	Interface	IP Address	Subnet Mask
RA	G0/0	192.168.1.1	255.255.255.0
	Lo0	192.168.31.11	255.255.255.255
RB	G0/0	192.168.1.2	255.255.255.0
	Lo0	192.168.31.22	255.255.255.255
RC	G0/0	192.168.1.3	255.255.255.0
	Lo0	192.168.31.33	255.255.255.255

Objectives

Part 1: Examine DR and BDR Changing Roles

Part 2: Modify OSPF Priority and Force Elections

Scenario

In this activity, you will examine DR and BDR roles and watch the roles change when there is a change in the network. You will then modify the priority to control the roles and force a new election. Finally, you will verify routers are filling the desired roles.

Instructions

Part 1: Examine DR and BDR Changing Roles

Step 1: Wait until the amber link lights turn green.

When you first open the file in Packet Tracer, you may notice that the link lights for the switch are amber. These link lights will stay amber for 50 seconds while the STP protocol on the switch makes sure that one of the routers is not another switch. Alternatively, you can click **Fast Forward Time** to bypass this process.

Step 2: Verify the current OSPF neighbor states.

Use the appropriate command on each router to examine the current DR and BDR. If a router shows FULL/DROTHER it means that the router is not a DR or a BDR.

```
RA# show ip ospf neighbor

Neighbor ID     Pri  State         Dead Time   Address       Interface
192.168.31.33    2   FULL/DR       00:00:35    192.168.1.3   gabitEthernet0/0
192.168.31.22    1   FULL/BDR      00:00:35    192.168.1.2   GigabitEthernet0/0


RB# show ip ospf neighbor

Neighbor ID     Pri  State         Dead Time   Address       Interface
192.168.31.11    1   FULL/DROTHER  00:00:36    192.168.1.1   gabitEthernet0/0
192.168.31.33    2   FULL/DR       00:00:36    192.168.1.3   igabitEthernet0/0
```

```
RC# show ip ospf neighbor

Neighbor ID     Pri  State         Dead Time  Address       Interface
192.168.31.11    1   FULL/DROTHER  00:00:39   192.168.1.1   GigabitEthernet0/0
192.168.31.22    1   FULL/BDR      00:00:38   192.168.1.2
GigabitEthernet0/0
```

Questions:

Which router is the DR?

_____

Which router is the BDR?

_____

What is the OSPF state of router RA?

_____

Step 3: Turn on IP OSPF adjacency debugging.

You can monitor the DR and BDR election process with a **debug** command. On **RA** and **RB**, enter the following command.

```
RA# debug ip ospf adj
RB# debug ip ospf adj
```

Step 4: Disable the Gigabit Ethernet 0/0 interface on RC.

a. Use the **shutdown** command to disable the link between **RC** and the switch to cause roles to change.

b. Wait about 30 seconds for the dead timers to expire on **RA** and **RB**.

Question:

According to the debug output, which router was elected DR and which router was elected BDR?

_____

Step 5: Restore the Gigabit Ethernet 0/0 interface on RC.

a. Re-enable the link between **RC** and the switch.

b. Wait for the new DR/BDR elections to occur.

Question:

Did DR and BDR roles change? Explain.

_____

c. Verify the DR and BDR assignments using the **show ip ospf neighbor** command on router **RC**.

```
RC# show ip ospf neighbor

Neighbor ID     Pri  State     Dead Time  Address       Interface
192.168.31.22    1   FULL/DR   00:00:34   192.168.1.2   GigabitEthernet0/0
192.168.31.11    1   FULL/BDR  00:00:34   192.168.1.1   GigabitEthernet0/0
```

Note: If the **show ip ospf neighbor** command does not return RB as the DR and RA as the BDR, turn off debugging on RA and RB with the **undebug all** command and retry steps 4 and 5.

Step 6: Disable the GigabitEthernet0/0 interface on RB.

    a. Disable the link between **RB** and the switch to cause roles to change.

    b. Wait about 30 seconds for the holddown timers to expire on **RA** and **RC**.

    Question:

    According to the debug output on RA, which router was elected DR and which router was elected BDR?

Step 7: Restore the GigabitEthernet0/0 interface on RB.

    a. Re-enable the link between **RB** and the switch.

    Question:

    Wait for the new DR/BDR elections to occur. Did DR and BDR roles change? Explain.

    b. Use the **show ip ospf interface** command on router RC.

    Question:

    What is the status of router RC now?

Step 8: Turn off Debugging.

Enter the command **undebug all** on **RA** and **RB** to disable debugging.

Part 2: Modify OSPF Priority and Force Elections

Step 1: Configure OSPF priorities on each router.

    a. To change the DR and BDR, use the **ip ospf priority** command to configure the GigabitEthernet 0/0 port of each router with the following OSPF interface priorities:

- RA: 200
- RB: 100
- RC: 1 (This is the default priority)

```
RA(config)# interface g0/0
RA(config-if)# ip ospf priority 200
```

    b. Set the priority on router **RB** and **RC**.

Step 2: Force an election by resetting the OSPF process on the routers.

Starting with router **RA**, issue the **clear ip ospf process** on each router to reset the OSPF process.

Step 3: Verify DR and BDR elections were successful.

Wait long enough for OSPF to converge and for the DR/BDR election to occur. This should take a few minutes. You can click **Fast Forward Time** to speed up the process.

Question:

According to output from the **show ip ospf neighbor** command on the routers, which router is now DR and which router is now BDR?

_____

_____

Note: If the routers do not elect the correct DR and BDR after setting the OSPF priorities, try restarting Packet Tracer.

**Packet Tracer
☐ Activity**

2.4.11 Packet Tracer—Modify Single-Area OSPFv2

Addressing Table

Devicess	Interface	IPv4 Address	Subnet Mask	Default Gateway
R1	G0/0	172.16.1.1	255.255.255.0	N/A
	S0/0/0	172.16.3.1	255.255.255.252	
	S0/0/1	192.168.10.5	255.255.255.252	
R2	G0/0	172.16.2.1	255.255.255.0	N/A
	S0/0/0	172.16.3.2	255.255.255.252	
	S0/0/1	192.168.10.9	255.255.255.252	
	S0/1/0	209.165.200.225	255.255.255.224	
R3	G0/0	192.168.1.1	255.255.255.0	N/A
	S0/0/0	192.168.10.6	255.255.255.252	
	S0/0/1	192.168.10.10	255.255.255.252	
PC1	NIC	172.16.1.2	255.255.255.0	172.16.1.1
PC2	NIC	172.16.2.2	255.255.255.0	172.16.2.1
PC3	NIC	192.168.1.2	255.255.255.0	192.168.1.1
Web Server	NIC	64.100.1.2	255.255.255.0	64.100.1.1

Objectives

Part 1: Modify OSPF Default Settings

Part 2: Verify Connectivity

Scenario

In this activity, OSPF is already configured and all end devices currently have full connectivity. You will modify the default OSPF routing configurations by changing the hello and dead timers and adjusting the bandwidth of a link. Then you will verify that full connectivity is restored for all end devices.

Instructions

Part 1: Modify OSPF Default Settings

Step 1:   Test connectivity between all end devices.

Before modifying the OSPF settings, verify that all PCs can ping the web server and each other.

Step 2:   Adjust the hello and dead timers between R1 and R2.

   a.   Enter the following commands on **R1**.

```
R1(config)# interface s0/0/0
R1(config-if)# ip ospf hello-interval 15
R1(config-if)# ip ospf dead-interval 60
```

   b.   After a short period of time, the OSPF connection with **R2** will fail, as shown in the router output.

```
00:02:40: %OSPF-5-ADJCHG: Process 1, Nbr 209.165.200.225 on Serial0/0/0
from FULL to DOWN, Neighbor Down: Dead timer expired


00:02:40: %OSPF-5-ADJCHG: Process 1, Nbr 209.165.200.225 on Serial0/0/0
from FULL to DOWN, Neighbor Down: Interface down or detached
```

Both sides of the connection need to have the same timer values for the adjacency to be maintained. Identify the interface on R2 that is connected to R1. Adjust the timers on the R2 interface to match the settings on R1.

After a brief period of time, you should see a status message that indicates that the OSPF adjacency has been reestablished.

```
00:21:52: %OSPF-5-ADJCHG: Process 1, Nbr 192.168.10.5 on Serial0/0/0
from LOADING to FULL, Loading Done
```

Step 3:   Adjust the bandwidth setting on R1.

   a.   Trace the path between **PC1** and the web server located at 64.100.1.2. Notice that the path from **PC1** to 64.100.1.2 is routed through **R2**. OSPF prefers the lower cost path.

```
C:\> tracert 64.100.1.2


Tracing route to 64.100.1.2 over a maximum of 30 hops:


1 1 ms 0 ms 8 ms 172.16.1.1
2 0 ms 1 ms 0 ms 172.16.3.2
3 1 ms 9 ms 2 ms 209.165.200.226
4 * 1 ms 0 ms 64.100.1.2


Trace complete.
```

   b.   On the **R1** Serial 0/0/0 interface, set the bandwidth to 64 Kb/s. This does not change the actual port speed, only the metric that the OSPF process on **R1** will use to calculate best routes.

```
R1(config-if)# bandwidth 64
```

   c.   Trace the path between **PC1** and the web server located at 64.100.1.2. Notice that the path from **PC1** to 64.100.1.2 is redirected through **R3**. OSPF prefers the lower cost path.

```
C:\> tracert 64.100.1.2


Tracing route to 64.100.1.2 over a maximum of 30 hops:
```

```
1  1 ms  0 ms  3 ms  172.16.1.1
2  8 ms  1 ms  1 ms  192.168.10.6
3  2 ms  0 ms  2 ms  172.16.3.2
4  2 ms  3 ms  1 ms  209.165.200.226
5  2 ms  11 ms  11 ms  64.100.1.2

Trace complete.
```

Part 2: Verify Connectivity

Verify that all PCs can ping the web server and each other.

Packet Tracer
☐ Activity

2.5.3 Packet Tracer—Propagate a Default Route in OSPFv2

Addressing Table

Device	Interface	IPv4 Address	Subnet Mask	Default Gateway
R1	G0/0	172.16.1.1	255.255.255.0	N/A
	S0/0/0	172.16.3.1	255.255.255.252	
	S0/0/1	192.168.10.5	255.255.255.252	
R2	G0/0	172.16.2.1	255.255.255.0	N/A
	S0/0/0	172.16.3.2	255.255.255.252	
	S0/0/1	192.168.10.9	255.255.255.252	
	S0/1/0	209.165.200.225	255.255.255.224	
R3	G0/0	192.168.1.1	255.255.255.0	N/A
	S0/0/0	192.168.10.6	255.255.255.252	
	S0/0/1	192.168.10.10	255.255.255.252	
PC1	NIC	172.16.1.2	255.255.255.0	172.16.1.1
PC2	NIC	172.16.2.2	255.255.255.0	172.16.2.1
PC3	NIC	192.168.1.2	255.255.255.0	192.168.1.1
Web Server	NIC	64.100.1.2	255.255.255.0	64.100.1.1

Objectives

Part 1: Propagate a Default Route

Part 2: Verify Connectivity

Background

In this activity, you will configure an IPv4 default route to the Internet and propagate that default route to other OSPF routers. You will then verify the default route is in downstream routing tables and that hosts can now access a web server on the Internet.

Instructions

Part 1: Propagate a Default Route

Step 1:   Test connectivity to the Web Server

    a. From PC1, PC2, and PC3, attempt to ping the Web Server IP address, 64.100.1.2.

    Questions:

    Were any of the pings successful?

_____

    What message did you receive, and which device issued the message?

_____

b. Examine the routing tables on routers R1, R2, and R3.

Question:

What statement is present in the routing tables that indicates that the pings to the Web Server will fail?

_____

Step 2: Configure a default route on R2.

Configure **R2** with a directly attached default route to the Internet.

```
R2(config)# ip route 0.0.0.0 0.0.0.0 Serial0/1/0
```

Note: Router will give a warning that if this interface is not a point-to-point connection, it may impact performance. You can ignore this warning because it is a point-to-point connection.

Step 3: Propagate the route in OSPF.

Configure OSPF to propagate the default route in OSPF routing updates.

```
R2(config)# router ospf 1
R2(config-router)# default-information originate
```

Step 4: Examine the routing tables on R1 and R3.

Examine the routing tables of **R1** and **R3** to verify that the route has been propagated.

```
R1> show ip route
<output omitted>
Gateway of last resort is 172.16.3.2 to network 0.0.0.0
<output omitted>
O*E2 0.0.0.0/0 [110/1] via 172.16.3.2, 00:00:08, Serial0/0/0
!------------------
R3> show ip route
<output omitted>
Gateway of last resort is 192.168.10.9 to network 0.0.0.0
<output omitted>
O*E2 0.0.0.0/0 [110/1] via 192.168.10.9, 00:08:15, Serial0/0/1
```

Part 2: Verify Connectivity

Verify that **PC1**, **PC2**, and **PC3** can ping the web server.

2.6.6 Packet Tracer—Verify Single-Area OSPFv2

Addressing Table

Device	Interface	IP Address	Subnet Mask	Default Gateway
R1	G0/0	172.16.1.1	255.255.255.0	N/A
	G0/1	64.100.54.6	255.255.255.252	
	S0/0/0	172.16.3.1	255.255.255.252	
	S0/0/1	192.168.10.5	255.255.255.252	
R2	G0/0	172.16.2.1	255.255.255.0	N/A
	S0/0/0	172.16.3.2	255.255.255.252	
	S0/0/1	192.168.10.9	255.255.255.252	
R3	G0/0	192.168.1.1	255.255.255.0	N/A
	G0/1	192.168.11.1	255.255.255.0	
	S0/0/0	192.168.10.6	255.255.255.252	
	S0/0/1	192.168.10.10	255.255.255.252	
R4	G0/0/0	192.168.1.2	255.255.255.0	N/A
	G0/0/1	192.168.11.1	255.255.255.0	
ISP Router	NIC	64.100.54.5	255.255.255.252	N/A
PC1	NIC	172.16.1.2	255.255.255.0	172.16.1.1
PC2	NIC	172.16.2.2	255.255.255.0	172.16.2.1
PC3	NIC	192.168.1.2	255.255.255.0	192.168.1.1
Laptop	NIC	DHCP	DHCP	DHCP

Objectives

In this lab, you will use the CLI commands to verify the operation of an existing OSPFv2 network. In Part 2, you will add a new LAN to the configuration and verify connectivity.

- Identify and verify the status of OSPF neighbors.

- Determine how the routes are being learned in the network.

- Explain how the neighbor state is determined.

- Examine the settings for the OSPF process ID.

- Add a new LAN into an existing OSPF network and verify connectivity.

Background / Scenario

You are the network administrator for a branch office of a larger organization. Your branch is adding a new wireless network into an existing branch office LAN. The existing network is configured to exchange routes using OSPFv2 in a single-area configuration. Your task is to verify the operation of the existing OSPFv2 network before adding in the new LAN. When you are sure that the current OSPFv2 LAN is operating correctly, you will connect the new LAN and verify that OSPF routes are being propagated for the new LAN. As branch office network administrator, you have full access to the IOS on routers R3 and R4. You only have read access to the enterprise LAN routers R1 and R2, using the username **BranchAdmin**, and the password **Branch1234**.

Instructions

Part 1: Verify the Existing OSPFv2 Network Operation.

The following commands will help you find the information needed to answer the questions:

```
show ip interface brief
show ip route
show ip route ospf
show ip ospf neighbor
show ip protocols
show ip ospf
show ip ospf interface
```

Step 1: Verify OSPFv2 operation.

Wait until STP has converged on the network. You can click the Packet Tracer Fast Forward Time button to speed up the process. Continue only when all link lights are green.

a. Log into router **R1** using the username **BranchAdmin** and the password **Branch1234**. Execute the **show ip route** command.

```
R1# show ip route
--- output omitted ----

Gateway of last resort is 172.16.3.2 to network 0.0.0.0

      172.16.0.0/16 is variably subnetted, 5 subnets, 3 masks
C        172.16.1.0/24 is directly connected, GigabitEthernet0/0
L        172.16.1.1/32 is directly connected, GigabitEthernet0/0
O        172.16.2.0/24 [110/65] via 172.16.3.2, 00:02:18, Serial0/0/0
C        172.16.3.0/30 is directly connected, Serial0/0/0
L        172.16.3.1/32 is directly connected, Serial0/0/0
O     192.168.1.0/24 [110/65] via 192.168.10.6, 00:02:18, Serial0/0/1
      192.168.10.0/24 is variably subnetted, 3 subnets, 2 masks
C        192.168.10.4/30 is directly connected, Serial0/0/1
L        192.168.10.5/32 is directly connected, Serial0/0/1
O        192.168.10.8/30 [110/128] via 172.16.3.2, 00:02:18, Serial0/0/0
                         [110/128] via 192.168.10.6, 00:02:18,
Serial0/0/1
O*E2 0.0.0.0/0 [110/1] via 172.16.3.2, 00:02:18, Serial0/0/0
```

Questions:

How did router **R1** receive the default route?

_____

From which router did **R1** receive the default route?

_____

How can you filter the output of **show ip route** to show only the routes learned through OSPF?

_____

b. Execute the **show ip ospf neighbor** command on **R1**.

Questions:

Which routers have formed adjacencies with router **R1**?

_____

What are the router IDs and state of the routers shown in the command output?

_____

Are all of the adjacent routers shown in the output?

_____

c. Using the command prompt on **PC1**, ping the address of the **ISP Router** shown in the Address Table. Is it successful? If not, do a **clear ospf process** command on the routers and repeat the ping command.

Step 2:   Verify OSPFv2 operation on R2.

a. Log into router **R2** using the username **BranchAdmin** and the password **Branch1234**. Execute the **show ip route** command. Verify that routes to all the networks in the topology are shown in the routing table.

Question:

How did router R2 learn the default route to the ISP?

_____

b. Enter the **show ip ospf interface g0/0** on router **R2**.

Questions:

What type of OSPF network is attached to this interface?

_____

Are OSPF hello packets being sent out this interface? Explain.

_____

c. Using the command prompt on **PC2**, ping the S0/0/1 address on router **R3**.

Question:

Is it successful?

_____

Step 3:   Verify OSPFv2 operation on R3.

a. Execute the **show ip protocols** command on router R3.

Question:

Router R3 is routing for which networks?

_____

    b. Execute the **show ip ospf neighbor detail** command on router **R3**.

        Question:

        What is the neighbor priority shown for the OSPF neighbor routers? This value is the default.

    c. Using the command prompt on **PC3**, ping the address of the **ISP Router** shown in the Address Table.

        Question:

        Is it successful?

Part 2: Add the New Branch Office LAN to the OSPFv2 Network.

You will now add the preconfigured Branch Office LAN to the OSPFv2 network.

Step 1:   Verify the OSPFv2 configuration on router R4.

        Execute a **show run | begin router ospf** command on router **R4**. Verify that the network statements are present for the networks that are configured on the router.

        Which interface is configured to not send OSPF update packets?

Step 2:   Connect the Branch Office router R4 to the OSPFv2 network.

    a. Using the correct Ethernet cable, connect the G0/0/0 interface on router **R4** to the G0/1 interface on switch **S3**. Use the **show ip ospf neighbor** command to verify that router **R4** is now adjacent with router **R3**.

        Question:

        What state is displayed for router **R3**?

    b. Using the **show ip ospf neighbor** command on **R3**, determine the state of router **R4**. There may be a delay while OSPF converges.

        Question:

        Why is the state of router R4 different than the state of R1 and R2?

    c. Using the command prompt on Laptop, ping the address of PC2.

        Question:

        Is it successful?

2.7.1 Packet Tracer—Single-Area OSPFv2 Configuration

Addressing Table

Device	Interface	IP Address / Prefix
P2P-1	S0/1/0	10.0.0.1/30
	S0/1/1	10.0.0.9/30
	S0/2/0	10.0.0.13/30
P2P-2	S0/1/0	10.0.0.2/30
	S0/1/1	10.0.0.5/30
	G0/0/0	192.168.1.1/24
	G0/0/1	192.168.2.1/24
P2P-3	S0/1/0	10.0.0.6/30
	S0/1/1	10.0.0.10/30
	G0/0/0	192.168.3.1/28
BC-1	S0/1/0	10.0.0.14/30
	S0/1/1	64.0.100.2/30
	G0/0/0	10.0.1.1/29
BC-2	G0/0/0	192.168.4.1/30
	G0/0/1	10.0.1.2/29
BC-3	G0/0/0	192.168.5.1/24
	G0/0/1	10.0.1.3/29
Internet Server	NIC	203.0.113.100/24
PC 1	NIC	192.168.1.10/24
Laptop 1	NIC	192.168.2.20/24
Workgroup Server	NIC	192.168.3.14/28
PC 2	NIC	192.168.4.40/24
PC 3	NIC	192.168.5.50/24

Objectives

Implement single-area OSPFv2 in both point-to-point and broadcast multiaccess networks.

Background

You are helping a network engineer test an OSPF set up by building the network in the lab where you work. You have interconnected the devices and configured the interfaces and have connectivity within the local LANs. Your job is to complete the OSPF configuration according to the requirements left by the engineer.

Use the information provided and the list of requirements to configure the test network. When the task has been successfully completed, all hosts should be able to ping the internet server.

Instructions

Configure the network to meet the requirements.

Requirements

Use process ID 10 for OSPF activation on all routers.

- Activate OSPF using network statements and inverse masks on the routers in the Headquarters network.

- Activate OSPF by configuring the interfaces of the network devices in the Data Service network, where required.

- Configure router IDs on the multiaccess network routers as follows:

  - BC-1: 6.6.6.6

  - BC-2: 5.5.5.5

  - BC-3: 4.4.4.4

- Configure OSPF so that routing updates are not sent into networks where they are not required.

- Configure router BC-1 with the highest OSPF interface priority so that it will always be the designated router of the multiaccess network.

- Configure a default route to the ISP cloud using the exit interface command argument.

- Automatically distribute the default route to all routers in the network.

- Configure the OSPF routers so that the Gigabit Ethernet interface cost will be 10 and the Fast Ethernet cost will be 100.

- Configure the OSPF cost value of P2P-1 interface Serial0/1/1 to 50.

- Configure the hello and dead timer values on the interfaces that connect P2P-1 and BC-1 to be twice the default values.

2.7.2 Lab—Configure Single-Area OSPFv2

Topology

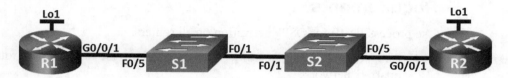

Addressing Table

Device	Interface	IP Address	Subnet Mask
R1	G0/0/1	10.53.0.1	255.255.255.0
	Loopback1	172.16.1.1	255.255.255.0
R2	G0/0/1	10.53.0.2	255.255.255.0
	Loopback1	192.168.1.1	255.255.255.0

Objectives

Part 1: Build the Network and Configure Basic Device Settings

Part 2: Configure and Verify Single-Area OSPFv2 for Basic Operation

Part 3: Optimize and Verify the Single-Area OSPFv2 Configuration

Background / Scenario

You have been tasked with configuring a small company's network using OSPFv2. R1 will be hosting an internet connection (simulated by interface Loopback 1) and sharing the default route information to R2. After the initial configuration, the organization has asked for the configuration to be optimized to reduce protocol traffic and ensure that R1 remains in control of routing.

Note: The static routing approach used in this lab is to assess your ability to configure and adjust OSPFv2 in a single-area configuration. This approach used in this lab may not reflect networking best practices.

Note: The routers used with CCNA hands-on labs are Cisco 4221 with Cisco IOS XE Release 16.9.4 (universalk9 image). The switches used in the labs are Cisco Catalyst 2960s with Cisco IOS Release 15.2(2) (lanbasek9 image). Other routers, switches, and Cisco IOS versions can be used. Depending on the model and Cisco IOS version, the commands available and the output produced might vary from what is shown in the labs. Refer to the Router Interface Summary Table at the end of the lab for the correct interface identifiers.

Note: Ensure that the routers and switches have been erased and have no startup configurations. If you are unsure contact your instructor.

Required Resources

- 2 Routers (Cisco 4221 with Cisco IOS XE Release 16.9.4 universal image or comparable)
- 2 Switches (Cisco 2960 with Cisco IOS Release 15.2(2) lanbasek9 image or comparable)
- 1 PC (Windows with a terminal emulation program, such as Tera Term)
- Console cables to configure the Cisco IOS devices via the console ports
- Ethernet cables as shown in the topology

Instructions

Part 1: Build the Network and Configure Basic Device Settings.

Step 1: Cable the network as shown in the topology.

Attach the devices as shown in the topology diagram, and cable as necessary.

Step 2: Configure basic settings for each router.

    a. Assign a device name to each router.

    b. Disable DNS lookup to prevent the router from attempting to translate incorrectly entered commands as though they were host names.

    c. Assign **class** as the privileged EXEC encrypted password.

    d. Assign **cisco** as the console password and enable login.

    e. Assign **cisco** as the VTY password and enable login.

    f. Encrypt the plaintext passwords.

    g. Create a banner that warns anyone accessing the device that unauthorized access is prohibited.

    h. Save the running configuration to the startup configuration file.

Step 3: Configure basic settings for each switch.

    a. Assign a device name to each switch.

    b. Disable DNS lookup to prevent the router from attempting to translate incorrectly entered commands as though they were host names.

    c. Assign **class** as the privileged EXEC encrypted password.

    d. Assign **cisco** as the console password and enable login.

    e. Assign **cisco** as the VTY password and enable login.

    f. Encrypt the plaintext passwords.

g. Create a banner that warns anyone accessing the device that unauthorized access is prohibited.

h. Save the running configuration to the startup configuration file.

Part 2: Configure and Verify Single-Area OSPFv2 for Basic Operation.

Step 1:   Configure interface addresses and basic OSPFv2 on each router.

a. Configure interface addresses on each router as shown in the Addressing Table above.

b. Enter OSPF router configuration mode using process ID 56.

c. Configure a static router ID for each router (1.1.1.1 for R1, 2.2.2.2 for R2).

d. Configure a network statement for the network between R1 and R2 placing it in area 0.

e. On R2 only, add the configuration necessary to advertise the Loopback 1 network into OSPF area 0.

f. Verify OSPFv2 is operational between the routers. Issue the command to verify R1 and R2 have formed an adjacency.

Question:

Which router is identified as the DR? Which is the BDR? What was the selection criteria?

_____

g. On R1, issue the **show ip route ospf** command to verify that the R2 Loopback1 network is present in the routing table. Notice the default behavior of OSPF is to advertise a loopback interface as a host route using a 32 bit mask.

h. Ping the R2 Loopback 1 interface address from R1. The ping should succeed.

Part 3: Optimize the Single-Area OSPFv2 Configuration.

Step 1:   Implement various optimizations on each router.

a. On R1, configure the interface G0/0/1 OSPF priority to 50 to ensure R1 is the Designated Router.

b. Configure the OSPF timers on the G0/0/1 of each router for a hello timer of 30 seconds.

c. On R1, configure a default static route that uses interface Loopback 1 as the exit interface. Then, propagate the default route into OSPF. Note the console message after setting the default route.

d. On R2 only, add the configuration necessary for OSPF to treat R2 Loopback 1 like a point-to-point network. This results in OSPF advertising Loopback 1 using the interface subnet mask.

e. On R2 only, add the configuration necessary to prevent OSPF advertisements from being sent to the Loopback 1 network.

     f. Change the reference bandwidth on each router to 1Gbs. After this configuration, restart OSPF using the **clear ip ospf process** command. Note the console message after setting the new reference bandwidth.

Step 2: Verify OSPFv2 optimizations are in place.

     a. Issue the **show ip ospf interface g0/0/1** command on R1 and verify that the interface priority has been set to 50 and that the time intervals are Hello 30, Dead 120, and the default Network Type is Broadcast.

     b. On R1, issue the **show ip route ospf** command to verify that the R2 Loopback1 network is present in the routing table. Note the difference in the metric between this output and the previous output. Also note the mask is now 24 bits as opposed to the 32 bits previously advertised.

     c. On R2, issue the **show ip route ospf** command. The only OSPF route information should be the default route R1 is propagating.

     d. Ping the R1 Loopback 1 interface address from R2. The ping should succeed.

     Question:

     Why is the OSPF cost for the default route different than the OSPF cost at R1 for the 192.168.1.0/24 network?

Router Interface Summary Table

Router Model	Ethernet Interface #1	Ethernet Interface #2	Serial Interface #1	Serial Interface #2
1800	Fast Ethernet 0/0 (F0/0)	Fast Ethernet 0/1 (F0/1)	Serial 0/0/0 (S0/0/0)	Serial 0/0/1 (S0/0/1)
1900	Gigabit Ethernet 0/0 (G0/0)	Gigabit Ethernet 0/1 (G0/1)	Serial 0/0/0 (S0/0/0)	Serial 0/0/1 (S0/0/1)
2801	Fast Ethernet 0/0 (F0/0)	Fast Ethernet 0/1 (F0/1)	Serial 0/1/0 (S0/1/0)	Serial 0/1/1 (S0/1/1)
2811	Fast Ethernet 0/0 (F0/0)	Fast Ethernet 0/1 (F0/1)	Serial 0/0/0 (S0/0/0)	Serial 0/0/1 (S0/0/1)
2900	Gigabit Ethernet 0/0 (G0/0)	Gigabit Ethernet 0/1 (G0/1)	Serial 0/0/0 (S0/0/0)	Serial 0/0/1 (S0/0/1)
4221	Gigabit Ethernet 0/0/0 (G0/0/0)	Gigabit Ethernet 0/0/1 (G0/0/1)	Serial 0/1/0 (S0/1/0)	Serial 0/1/1 (S0/1/1)
4300	Gigabit Ethernet 0/0/0 (G0/0/0)	Gigabit Ethernet 0/0/1 (G0/0/1)	Serial 0/1/0 (S0/1/0)	Serial 0/1/1 (S0/1/1)

Note: To find out how the router is configured, look at the interfaces to identify the type of router and how many interfaces the router has. There is no way to effectively list all the combinations of configurations for each router class. This table includes identifiers for the possible combinations of Ethernet and Serial interfaces in the device. The table does not include any other type of interface, even though a specific router may contain one. An example of this might be an ISDN BRI interface. The string in parenthesis is the legal abbreviation that can be used in Cisco IOS commands to represent the interface.

CHAPTER 3

Network Security Concepts

The "Study Guide" portion of this chapter uses a variety of exercises to test your knowledge about how vulnerabilities, threats, and exploits can be mitigated to enhance network security. The "Labs and Activities" portion of this chapter includes all the online curriculum lab instructions. There are no Packet Tracer activities for this chapter.

As you work through this chapter, use Chapter 3 in *Enterprise Networking, Security, and Automation v7 Companion Guide* or use the corresponding Module 3 in the Enterprise Networking, Security, and Automation online curriculum for assistance.

Study Guide

Current State of Cybersecurity

In this section, you will review the current state of cybersecurity and vectors of data loss.

Current State of Affairs

Cybercriminals now have the expertise and tools necessary to take down critical infrastructure and systems. Maintaining a secure network ensures the safety of network users and protects commercial interests.

Assets must be identified and protected. Vulnerabilities must be addressed before they become threats and are exploited. Mitigation techniques are required to reduce risk. Briefly describe each of the security terms in Table 3-1.

Table 3-1   Common Security Terms

Security Term	Description
Asset	
Vulnerability	
Threat	
Exploit	
Mitigation	
Risk	

Vectors of Network Attacks

An attack vector is a path by which a threat actor can gain access to a server, host, or network. Attack vectors originate from inside or outside the corporate network, as shown in Figure 3-1.

Figure 3-1   External and Internal Threats

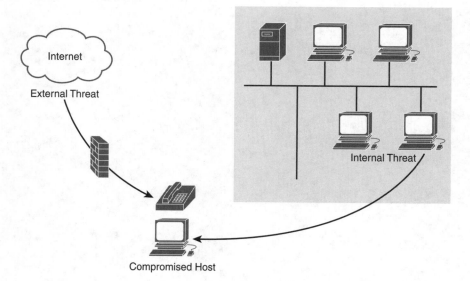

Internet

External Threat

Internal Threat

Compromised Host

Data Loss

Data loss or data exfiltration occurs when data is intentionally or unintentionally lost, stolen, or leaked to the outside world. In Table 3-2, briefly describe each common data loss vector.

Table 3-2   Common Data Loss Vectors

Data Loss Vector	Description
Email/social networking	
Unencrypted devices	
Cloud storage devices	
Removable media	
Hard copy	
Improper access control	

Check Your Understanding—Current State of Cybersecurity

Check your understanding of the current state of cybersecurity by choosing the BEST answer to each of the following questions.

1. Which security term is used to describe anything of value to an organization, including people, equipment, resources, and data?

   a. Vulnerability

   b. Exploit

   c. Asset

   d. Risk

2. Which security term is used to describe a weakness in a system or its design that could be exploited by a threat?

   a. Vulnerability

   b. Asset

   c. Risk

   d. Mitigation

3. Which security term is used to describe a potential danger to a company's assets, data, or network functionality?

   a. Vulnerability

   b. Exploit

   c. Threat

   d. Risk

4. Which security term is used to describe a mechanism that takes advantage of a vulnerability?

   a. Exploit

   b. Threat

   c. Risk

   d. Mitigation

5. Which security term is used to describe countermeasure for a potential threat or risk?

   a. Vulnerability

   b. Exploit

   c. Asset

   d. Mitigation

6. Which security term is used to describe the likelihood of a threat to exploit the vulnerability of an asset, with the aim of negatively affecting an organization?

   a. Vulnerability

   b. Exploit

   c. Threat

   d. Risk

Threat Actors

In this section, you will review the threat actors who exploit networks.

The Hacker

Hacker is a common term used to describe a threat actor. The terms *white hat hacker*, *black hat hacker*, and *gray hat hacker* are often used to describe types of hackers, as shown in Table 3-3.

Table 3-3   Three Hacker Types

Hacker Type	Description
White hat hackers	These are ethical hackers who use their programming skills for good, ethical, and legal purposes. White hat hackers may perform network penetration tests in an attempt to compromise networks and systems by using their knowledge of computer security systems to discover network vulnerabilities. Security vulnerabilities are reported to developers so they can fix them before the vulnerabilities can be exploited.
Gray hat hackers	These are individuals who commit crimes and do arguably unethical things but not for personal gain or to cause damage. Gray hat hackers may disclose a vulnerability to the affected organization after having compromised the network.
Black hat hackers	These are unethical criminals who compromise computer and network security for personal gain or for malicious reasons, such as attacking networks.

Evolution of Hackers

In Table 3-4, briefly describe each hacking term.

Table 3-4   Hacking Terms

Hacking Term	Description
Script kiddies	
Vulnerability brokers	
Hacktivists	
Cybercriminals	
State-sponsored hackers	

Check Your Understanding—Threat Actors

Check your understanding of threat actors by choosing the BEST type of threat actor for each scenario.

1. After hacking into ATMs remotely using a laptop, this type of hacker worked with ATM manufacturers to resolve the security vulnerabilities that he discovered.

   a. White hat

   b. Gray hat

   c. Black hat

2. From her laptop, this hacker transferred $10 million to her bank account, using victim account numbers and PINs after viewing recordings of victims entering the numbers.

   a. White hat

   b. Gray hat

   c. Black hat

3. This hacker's job is to identify weaknesses in his company's network.

   a. White hat

   b. Gray hat

   c. Black hat

4. This type of hacker used malware to compromise several corporate systems to steal credit card information and then sold that information to the highest bidder.

   a. White hat

   b. Gray hat

   c. Black hat

5. During her research for security exploits, this hacker stumbled across a security vulnerability on a corporate network that she was authorized to access.

   a. White hat

   b. Gray hat

   c. Black hat

6. It this hacker's job to work with technology companies to fix a flaw with DNS.

    a. White hat

    b. Gray hat

    c. Black hat

Threat Actor Tools

In this section, you will review how threat actors use tools to exploit networks.

Video—Threat Actor Tools

Be sure you review the video in the online curriculum, which shows how to do the following:

- Explain penetration testing tools
- Explain attack types

Evolution of Security Tools

Ethical hacking involves using many different types of tools to test a network and keep its data secure. Table 3-5 highlights categories of common penetration testing tools. For more details, refer to the online course or *Enterprise Networking, Security, and Automation v7 Companion Guide.*

Table 3-5   Types of Penetration Testing Tools

Penetration Testing Tool	Description
Password crackers	Password cracking tools, often referred to as password recovery tools, can be used to crack or recover a password by repeatedly making guesses.
Wireless hacking tools	Wireless hacking tools are used to intentionally hack into a wireless network to detect security vulnerabilities.
Network scanning and hacking tools	Network scanning tools are used to probe network devices, servers, and hosts for open TCP or UDP ports.
Packet crafting tools	These tools are used to probe and test a firewall's robustness using specially crafted forged packets.
Packet sniffers	These tools are used to capture and analyze packets in traditional Ethernet LANs or WLANs.
Rootkit detectors	These are directory and file integrity checkers that are used by white hat hackers to detect installed rootkits.
Fuzzers to search vulnerabilities	Fuzzers are tools threat actors use to discover a computer's security vulnerabilities.
Forensic tools	These tools are used by white hat hackers to sniff out any trace of evidence existing in a computer.
Debuggers	These tools are used by black hat hackers to reverse engineer binary files when writing exploits. They are also used by white hat hackers when analyzing malware.

Penetration Testing Tool	Description
Hacking operating systems	These specially designed operating systems are preloaded with tools optimized for hacking.
Encryption tools	Encryption tools use algorithm schemes to encrypt data to prevent unauthorized access to that data.
Vulnerability exploitation tools	These tools identify whether a remote host is vulnerable to a security attack.
Vulnerability scanners	These tools scan a network or system to identify open ports. They can also be used to scan for known vulnerabilities and scan VMs, BYOD devices, and client databases.

Attack Types

Table 3-6 describes some common types of attacks. However, this list of attacks is not exhaustive as new attack vulnerabilities are constantly being created and discovered.

Table 3-6   Common Types of Attacks

Attack Type	Description
Eavesdropping attack	A threat actor captures and "listens" to network traffic. This attack is also referred to as sniffing or snooping.
Data modification attack	If threat actors have captured enterprise traffic, they can alter the data in the packet without the knowledge of the sender or receiver.
IP address spoofing attack	A threat actor constructs an IP packet that appears to originate from a valid address inside the corporate intranet.
Password-based attacks	If threat actors discover a valid user account, they have the same rights as the real user. Threat actors could use that valid account to obtain lists of other users and network information, change server and network configurations, and modify, reroute, or delete data.
Denial-of-service (DoS) attack	A DoS attack prevents normal use of a computer or network by valid users. A DoS attack can flood a computer or an entire network with traffic until a shutdown occurs because of the overload. A DoS attack can also block traffic, which results in a loss of access to network resources by authorized users.
Man-in-the-middle attack	This attack occurs when threat actors have positioned themselves between a source and a destination. They can use their position to actively monitor, capture, and control the communication transparently.
Compromised-key attack	If a threat actor obtains a secret key, that key is referred to as a compromised key. A compromised key can be used to gain access to a secured communication without the sender or receiver being aware of the attack.
Sniffer attack	A sniffer is an application or a device that can read, monitor, and capture network data exchanges and read network packets. If the packets are not encrypted, a sniffer provides a full view of the data inside the packet.

Check Your Understanding—Threat Actor Tools

Check your understanding of threat actor tools by choosing the BEST answer to each of the following questions.

1. Which penetration testing tools use algorithm schemes to encode the data, which then prevents access to the data?

   a. Packet sniffers

   b. Encryption tools

   c. Vulnerability exploitation tools

   d. Forensic tools

   e. Debuggers

2. Which penetration testing tools do white hat hackers use to analyze malware and black hat hackers use to reverse-engineer binary files when writing exploits?

   a. Packet crafting tools

   b. Rootkit detectors

   c. Vulnerability exploitation tools

   d. Forensic tools

   e. Debuggers

3. Which penetration testing tools are used to probe and test a firewall's robustness?

   a. Packet crafting tools

   b. Encryption tools

   c. Rootkit detectors

   d. Forensic tools

   e. Debuggers

4. Which penetration testing tools do white hat hackers use to sniff out any trace of evidence existing in a computer?

   a. Fuzzers to search vulnerabilities

   b. Encryption tools

   c. Packet sniffers

   d. Forensic tools

   e. Debuggers

5. Which penetration testing tools identify whether a remote host is susceptible to a security attack?

   a. Packet sniffers

   b. Encryption tools

   c. Vulnerability exploitation tools

   d. Forensic tools

   e. Debuggers

Malware

In this section, you will review malware types.

Viruses and Trojan Horses

A virus is malware that executes a specific unwanted, and often harmful, function on a computer. Modern viruses are developed for specific intent. Briefly describe each type of virus in Table 3-7.

Table 3-7   Types of Viruses

Type of Virus	Description
Boot sector virus	
Firmware virus	
Macro virus	
Program virus	
Script virus	

A Trojan horse is a non-self-replicating type of malware. Trojans often contain malicious code that is designed to look like something else, such as a legitimate application or file. When an infected application or file is downloaded and opened, the Trojan horse can attack the end device from within.

Briefly describe each type of Trojan horse in Table 3-8.

Table 3-8   Types of Trojan Horses

Type of Trojan Horse	Description
Remote access	
Data sending	
Destructive	
Proxy	
FTP	
Security software disabler	
Denial of service (DoS)	
Keylogger	

Other Types of Malware

Table 3-9 shows details about other types of malware.

Table 3-9   Other Types of Malware

Malware	Description
Adware	■ Adware is usually distributed through online software downloads. ■ Adware can display unsolicited advertising using pop-up web browser windows or new toolbars, or it can unexpectedly redirect a web page to a different website. ■ Pop-up windows may be difficult to control as new windows can pop up faster than the user can close them.
Ransomware	■ Ransomware typically denies a user access to his or her files by encrypting the files and then displaying a message demanding a ransom for the decryption key. ■ Users without up-to-date backups must pay the ransom to decrypt their files. ■ Payment is usually made using wire transfer or cryptocurrencies such as bitcoin.
Rootkit	■ Rootkits are used by threat actors to gain administrator account-level access to a computer. ■ They are very difficult to detect because they can alter firewall, antivirus protection, system files, and even OS commands to conceal their presence. ■ A rootkit can provide a backdoor to give a threat actor access to the PC, allowing the threat actor to upload files and install new software to be used in a DDoS attack. ■ Special rootkit removal tools must be used to remove rootkits, or a complete OS reinstall may be required.
Spyware	■ Spyware is similar to adware but is used to gather information about the user and send it to threat actors without the user's consent. ■ Spyware can be a low threat, gathering browsing data, or it can be a high threat, capturing personal and financial information.
Worm	■ A worm is a self-replicating program that propagates automatically without user actions by exploiting vulnerabilities in legitimate software. ■ It uses the network to search for other victims with the same vulnerability. ■ The intent of a worm is usually to slow or disrupt network operations.

Check Your Understanding—Malware

Check your understanding of malware by choosing the BEST answer to each of the following questions.

1. Which of the following executes arbitrary code and installs copies of itself in the memory of the infected computer? The main purpose of this malware is to automatically replicate from system to system across the network.

   a. Adware

   b. Rootkit

   c. Spyware

   d. Virus

   e. Worm

2. Which of the following is a non-self-replicating type of malware that often contains malicious code that is designed to look like something else, such as a legitimate application or file.

   a. Adware

   b. Rootkit

   c. Spyware

   d. Trojan horse

   e. Worm

3. Which of the following is used to gather information about a user and then, without the user's consent, sends the information to another entity?

   a. Adware

   b. Rootkit

   c. Spyware

   d. Virus

   e. Ransomware

4. Which of the following typically displays annoying pop-ups to generate revenue for its author?

   a. Adware

   b. Rootkit

   c. Spyware

   d. Virus

   e. Worm

5. Which of the following attempts to convince people to divulge sensitive information?

   a. Phishing

   b. Rootkit

   c. Spyware

   d. Virus

   e. Worm

6. Which of the following is installed on a compromised system and provides privileged access to the threat actor?

   a. Adware

   b. Virus

   c. Spyware

   d. Rootkit

   e. Worm

7. Which of the following denies access to the infected computer system and demands payment before the restriction is removed?

    a. Adware

    b. Rootkit

    c. Spyware

    d. Virus

    e. Ransomware

Common Network Attacks

In this section, you will review common network attacks.

Overview of Network Attacks

Networks are susceptible to the following types of attacks:

- Reconnaissance attacks
- Access attacks
- DoS attacks

Video—Reconnaissance Attacks

Be sure you review the video in the online curriculum, which shows how to do the following:

- Perform an information query on a target
- Initiate a ping sweep of the target network
- Initiate a port scan of active IP addresses
- Run vulnerability scanners
- Run exploitation tools

Reconnaissance Attacks

Reconnaissance is information gathering. Threat actors use reconnaissance attacks to do unauthorized discovery and mapping of systems, services, or vulnerabilities. Briefly describe each reconnaissance attack technique listed in Table 3-10.

Table 3-10   Reconnaissance Attack Techniques

Technique	Description
Perform an information query of a target	
Initiate a ping sweep of the target network	
Initiate a port scan of active IP addresses	
Run vulnerability scanners	
Run exploitation tools	

Video—Access and Social Engineering Attacks

Be sure you review the video in the online curriculum, which covers the following:

- Techniques used in access attacks (password attacks, spoofing attacks, trust exploitations, port redirections, man-in-the-middle attacks, buffer overflow attacks)
- Techniques used in social engineering attacks (pretexting, phishing, spear phishing, spam, something for something, baiting, impersonation, tailgating, shoulder surfing, dumpster diving)

Access Attacks

Access attacks exploit known vulnerabilities in authentication services, FTP services, and web services. The purpose of these types of attacks is to gain entry to web accounts, confidential databases, and other sensitive information. In a password attack, the threat actor attempts to discover critical system passwords using various methods. Password attacks are very common and can be launched using a variety of password cracking tools. Briefly describe each of the access attacks in Table 3-11.

Table 3-11   Types of Access Attacks

Access Attack	Description
Spoofing attack	
Trust exploitation attack	
Port redirection attack	
Man-in-the-middle attack	
Buffer overflow attack	

Social Engineering Attacks

Social engineering is an access attack that attempts to manipulate individuals into performing actions or divulging confidential information. Briefly describe each type of social engineering attack in Table 3-12.

Table 3-12   Types of Social Engineering Attacks

Social Engineering Attack	Description
Pretexting	
Phishing	
Spear phishing	
Spam	
Something for something	
Baiting	
Impersonation	
Tailgating	
Shoulder surfing	
Dumpster diving	

Video—Denial of Service Attacks

Be sure you review the video in the online curriculum, which covers the following:

- Techniques used in denial-of-service attacks (overwhelming quantity of traffic, maliciously formatted packets)
- Techniques used in distributed denial-of-service attacks (zombies)

DoS and DDoS Attacks

A denial-of-service (DoS) attack creates some sort of interruption of network services to users, devices, or applications. There are two major types of DoS attacks:

- **Overwhelming quantity of traffic:** The threat actor sends an enormous quantity of data at a rate that the network, host, or application cannot handle. This causes transmission and response times to slow down. It can also crash a device or service.
- **Maliciously formatted packets:** The threat actor sends a maliciously formatted packet to a host or an application, and the receiver is unable to handle it. This causes the receiving device to run very slowly or crash.

Briefly describe the difference between a DoS attack and a DDoS attack.

Check Your Understanding—Common Network Attacks

Check your understanding of common network attacks by choosing the BEST classification for each attack type.

1. What type of attack is tailgating?

   a. Reconnaissance

   b. Access

   c. DoS

   d. Social engineering

2. What type of attack is a password attack?

   a. Reconnaissance

   b. Access

   c. DoS

   d. Social engineering

3. What type of attack is port scanning?

   a. Reconnaissance

   b. Access

   c. DoS

   d. Social engineering

4. What type of attack is a man-in-the-middle attack?

   a. Reconnaissance

   b. Access

   c. DoS

   d. Social engineering

5. What type of attack is address spoofing?

   a. Reconnaissance

   b. Access

   c. DoS

   d. Social engineering

IP Vulnerabilities and Threats

In this section, you will review how IP vulnerabilities are exploited by threat actors.

Video—Common IP and ICMP Attacks

Be sure you review the video in the online curriculum, which covers the following:

- Techniques used in IP attacks (ICMP attacks, amplification and reflection attacks, address spoofing attacks, man-in-the-middle attacks, session hijacking)

- Techniques used in ICMP attacks (ICMP echo requests and echo replies, ICMP unreachable, ICMP mask reply, ICMP redirects, ICMP router discovery)

IPv4 and IPv6

IP does not validate whether the source IP address contained in a packet actually came from that source. For this reason, threat actors can send packets using a spoofed source IP address. Threat actors can also tamper with the other fields in the IP header to carry out their attacks. Briefly describe how threat actors use each IP attack technique in Table 3-13.

Table 3-13 Types of IP Attacks

IP Attack Technique	Description
Internet Control Message Protocol (ICMP) attacks	
Amplification and reflection attacks	
Address spoofing attacks	
Man-in-the-middle attack	
Session hijacking	

ICMP Attacks

Threat actors use ICMP for reconnaissance and scanning attacks. They can launch information-gathering attacks to map out a network topology, discover which hosts are active (reachable), identify the host operating system (OS fingerprinting), and determine the state of a firewall. Threat actors also use ICMP for DoS attacks. Table 3-14 lists ICMP messages that threat actors commonly use in their attacks.

Table 3-14   ICMP Messages Used by Hackers

ICMP Message	Description
ICMP echo request and echo reply	Used to perform host verification and DoS attacks.
ICMP unreachable	Used to perform network reconnaissance and scanning attacks.
ICMP mask reply	Used to map an internal IP network.
ICMP redirects	Used to lure a target host into sending all traffic through a compromised device and create an MITM attack.
ICMP router discovery	Used to inject bogus route entries into the routing table of a target host.

Video—Amplification, Reflection, and Spoofing Attacks

Be sure you review the video in the online curriculum. It explains amplification, reflection, and spoofing attacks and gives examples of each.

Amplification and Reflection Attacks

Threat actors often use amplification and reflection techniques to create DoS attacks. Figure 3-2 illustrates an amplification and reflection attack, which works as follows:

Figure 3-2   Example of an Amplification and Reflection Attack

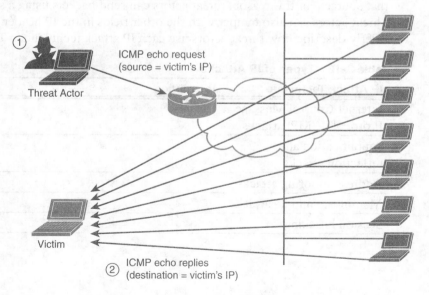

1. **Amplification:** The threat actor forwards ICMP echo request messages to many hosts. These messages contain the source IP address of the victim.

2. **Reflection:** These hosts all reply to the spoofed IP address of the victim to overwhelm it.

Address Spoofing Attacks

IP address spoofing attacks occur when a threat actor creates packets with false source IP address information to either hide the identity of the sender or to pose as another legitimate user.

Spoofing attacks can be non-blind or blind. Briefly describe each.

- **Non-blind spoofing:** _____
  _____
  _____

- **Blind spoofing:** _____
  _____

MAC address spoofing attacks are used when threat actors have access to the internal network. Threat actors alter the MAC address of the host to match another known MAC address of a target host, as shown in Figures 3-3 and 3-4.

Figure 3-3   Threat Actor Spoofs a Server's MAC Address

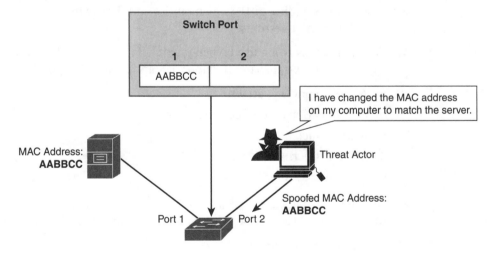

Figure 3-4   Switch Updates CAM Table with Spoofed Address

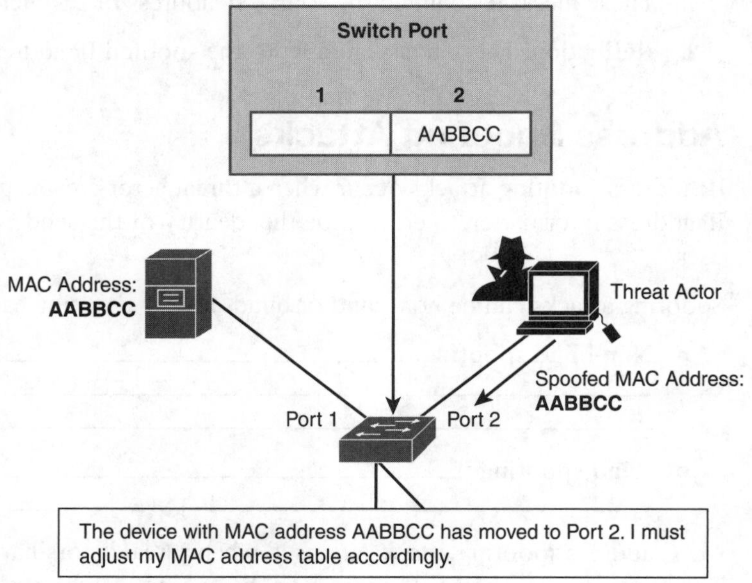

Check Your Understanding—IP Vulnerabilities and Threats

Check your understanding of IP vulnerabilities and threats by choosing the BEST answer to each of the following questions.

1. Which attack is being used when threat actors position themselves between a source and a destination to transparently monitor, capture, and control the communication?

   a. Address spoofing attack

   b. Amplification and reflection attack

   c. ICMP attack

   d. MITM attack

   e. Session hijacking

2. Which attack is being used when threat actors gain access to the physical network and then use an MITM attack to capture and manipulate a legitimate user's traffic?

   a. Address spoofing attack

   b. Amplification and reflection attack

   c. ICMP attack

   d. Session hijacking

3. Which attack is being used when threat actors initiate a simultaneous, coordinated attack from multiple source machines?

   a. Address spoofing attack

   b. Amplification and reflection attack

   c. ICMP attack

   d. MITM attack

   e. Session hijacking

4. Which attack is being used when threat actors use pings to discover subnets and hosts on a protected network, to generate flood attacks, and to alter host routing tables?

   a. Address spoofing attack

   b. Amplification and reflection attack

   c. ICMP attack

   d. MITM attack

   e. Session hijacking

5. In which type of attack does a threat actor create packets with false source IP address information to either hide the identity of the sender or to pose as another legitimate user?

   a. Address spoofing attack

   b. Amplification and reflection attack

   c. ICMP attack

   d. MITM attack

   e. Session hijacking

TCP and UDP Vulnerabilities

In this section, you will review how Transport Control Protocol (TCP) and User Datagram Protocol (UDP) vulnerabilities are exploited by threat actors.

TCP Segment Header

TCP segment information appears immediately after the IP header. The following are the six control bits of the TCP segment, which control the operation of the three-way handshake:

- **URG:** Urgent pointer field significant

- **ACK:** Acknowledgment field significant

- **PSH:** Push function

- **RST:** Reset the connection

- **SYN:** Synchronize sequence numbers

- **FIN:** No more data from sender

TCP Services

List and briefly describe the three TCP services.

- _____

- _____

- _____

- _____

Figure 3-5 illustrates the three-way handshake. Below the figure, briefly describe the three steps.

Figure 3-5   TCP Three-Way Handshake

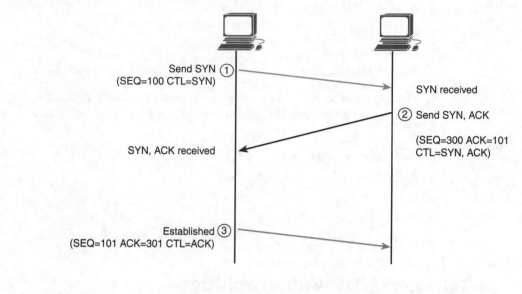

_____

_____

_____

_____

TCP Attacks

A TCP SYN flood attack exploits the TCP three-way handshake. Figure 3-6 shows how it works:

Figure 3-6   TCP SYN Flood Attack

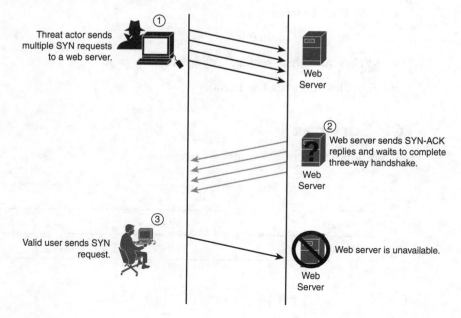

Step 1.   The threat actor sends multiple SYN requests to a web server.

Step 2.   The web server replies with SYN-ACKs for each SYN request and waits to complete the three-way handshake. The threat actor does not respond to the SYN-ACKs.

Step 3.   A valid user cannot access the web server because the web server has too many half-opened TCP connections.

A TCP reset attack can be used to terminate TCP communications between two hosts. Figure 3-7 shows how TCP uses a four-way exchange to close the TCP connection using a pair of FIN and ACK segments from each TCP endpoint:

Figure 3-7   Terminating a TCP Connection

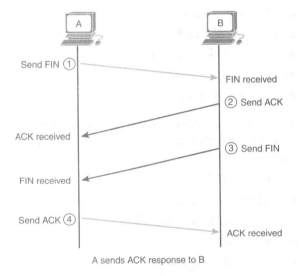

Step 1.   When the client has no more data to send in the stream, it sends a segment with the FIN flag set.

Step 2.   The server sends an ACK to acknowledge the receipt of the FIN to terminate the session from client to server.

Step 3.   The server sends a FIN to the client to terminate the server-to-client session.

Step 4.   The client responds with an ACK to acknowledge the FIN from the server.

Check Your Understanding—TCP and UDP Vulnerabilities

Check your understanding of TCP and UDP vulnerabilities by choosing the BEST answer to each of the following questions.

1.   Which attack exploits the three-way handshake?

   a. TCP reset attack

   b. UDP flood attack

   c. TCP SYN flood attack

   d. DoS attack

   e. TCP session hijacking

2. Which attack uses a four-way exchange to close the connection using a pair of FIN and ACK segments from each endpoint?

   a. TCP reset attack

   b. UDP flood attack

   c. TCP SYN flood attack

   d. DoS attack

   e. TCP session hijacking

3. Which attack is being used when the threat actor spoofs the IP address of one host, predicts the next sequence number, and sends an ACK to the other host?

   a. TCP reset attack

   b. UDP flood attack

   c. TCP SYN flood attack

   d. DoS attack

   e. TCP session hijacking

4. Which attack is being used when a program sweeps through all the known ports, trying to find closed ports, causing the server to reply with an ICMP port unreachable message?

   a. TCP reset attack

   b. UDP flood attack

   c. TCP SYN flood attack

   d. DoS attack

   e. TCP session hijacking

IP Services

In this section, you will review how IP services are exploited by threat actors.

ARP Vulnerabilities

Hosts broadcast an ARP Request to other hosts on the segment to determine the MAC address of a host with a particular IP address. Any client can send an unsolicited ARP Reply, called a "gratuitous ARP." This feature of ARP also means that any host can claim to be the owner of any IP or MAC address. Threat actors can position themselves in between the victim and all other systems outside the local subnet.

For example, in Figure 3-8, the threat actor sends two spoofed gratuitous ARP Reply messages, using its own MAC address for the indicated destination IP addresses. PC-A updates its ARP cache with its default gateway, which is now pointing to the threat actor's host MAC address. R1 also updates its ARP cache with the IP address of PC-A pointing to the threat actor's MAC address.

Figure 3-8   ARP Cache Poisoning

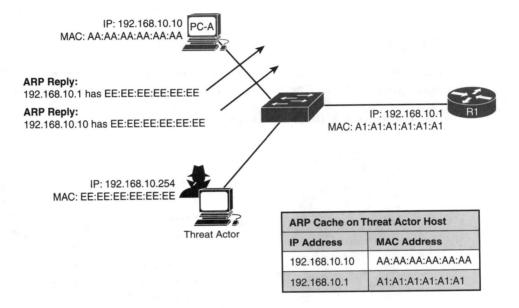

ARP Cache on PC-A	
IP Address	MAC Address
192.168.10.1	EE:EE:EE:EE:EE:EE

ARP Cache on R1	
IP Address	MAC Address
192.168.10.10	EE:EE:EE:EE:EE:EE

ARP Cache on Threat Actor Host	
IP Address	MAC Address
192.168.10.10	AA:AA:AA:AA:AA:AA
192.168.10.1	A1:A1:A1:A1:A1:A1

Video—ARP Spoofing

Be sure you review the video in the online curriculum. It uses Packet Tracer to demonstrate ARP spoofing.

DNS Attacks

The Domain Name System (DNS) protocol defines an automated service that matches resource names, such as www.cisco.com, with the required numeric network address, such as the IPv4 or IPv6 address.

Securing DNS is often overlooked. However, DNS is crucial to the operation of a network and should be secured accordingly. When not secured, DNS is vulnerable to a number of attacks. Briefly describe each of the following attacks:

- DNS open resolver attack: _____
  _____
  _____

- DNS stealth attack: _____
  _____
  _____
  _____

- DNS domain shadowing attack: _____

  _____

  _____

  _____

- DNS tunneling attack: _____

  _____

  _____

  _____

DHCP

Recall that Dynamic Host Configuration Protocol (DHCP) servers provide IP configuration information to clients. The normal DHCP operation is shown in Figure 3-9.

Figure 3-9   Normal DHCP Operation

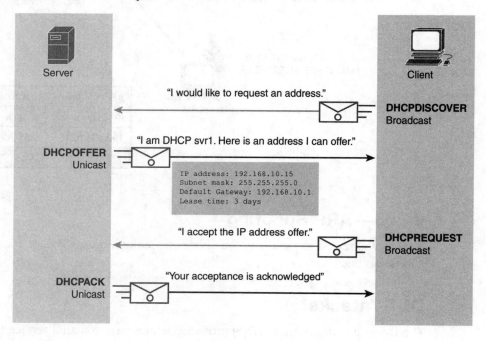

DCHP Spoofing Attacks

A DHCP spoofing attack occurs when a rogue DHCP server is connected to the network and provides false IP configuration parameters to legitimate clients. A rogue server can provide a variety of misleading information:

- **Wrong default gateway:** The threat actor provides an invalid gateway or the IP address of its host to create an MITM attack. This may go entirely undetected as the intruder intercepts the data flow through the network.

- **Wrong DNS server:** The threat actor provides an incorrect DNS server address that points the user to a malicious website.

- **Wrong IP address:** The threat actor provides an invalid IP address, invalid default gateway IP address, or both. The threat actor then creates a DoS attack on the DHCP client.

Network Security Best Practices

In this section, you will review best practices for protecting a network.

Confidentiality, Integrity, and Availability (CIA)

Briefly describe each element of the CIA information security triad:

- Confidentiality: _____
  _____
  _____

- Integrity: _____
  _____

- Availability: _____
  _____

The Defense-in-Depth Approach

Most organizations employ a defense-in-depth approach to security, which requires a combination of networking devices and services working together, as shown in Figure 3-10.

Figure 3-10   Protecting Against Network Attacks

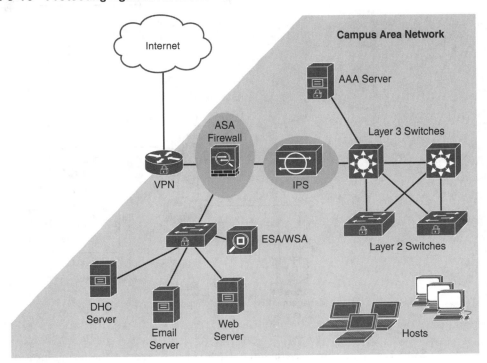

Devices in Figure 3-10 include the following:

- **VPN:** A router is used to provide secure virtual private network (VPN) services with corporate sites and remote access support for remote users using secure encrypted tunnels.

- **ASA firewall:** A Cisco Adaptive Security Appliance (ASA) firewall is a dedicated device that provides stateful firewall services. It ensures that internal traffic can go out and come back but external traffic cannot initiate connections to inside hosts.

- **IPS:** An intrusion prevention system (IPS) monitors incoming and outgoing traffic, looking for malware, network attack signatures, and more. If it recognizes a threat, it can immediately stop it.

- **ESA/WSA:** A Cisco Email Security Appliance (ESA) filters spam and suspicious emails. A Cisco Web Security Appliance (WSA) filters known and suspicious Internet malware sites.

- **AAA server:** An authentication, authorization, and accounting (AAA) server contains a secure database of who is authorized to access and manage network devices. Network devices authenticate administrative users by using this database.

IPS

Figure 3-11 shows how an IPS handles denied traffic. It works as follows:

Figure 3-11   IPS Operation

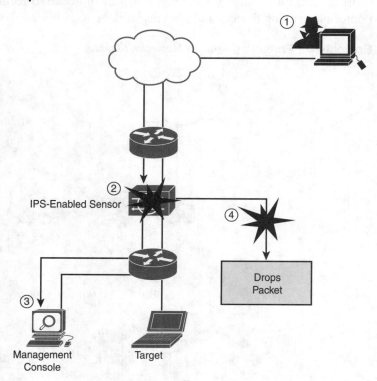

Step 1.   The threat actor sends a packet destined for the target laptop.

Step 2.   The IPS intercepts the traffic and evaluates it against known threats and the configured policies.

Step 3.   The IPS sends a log message to the management console.

Step 4.   The IPS drops the packet.

Content Security Appliances

Content security appliances, such as the Cisco ESA and Cisco WSA, provide fine-grained control over email and web browsing for an organization's users.

Figure 3-12 shows how an ESA protects against a phishing attack:

Figure 3-12 ESA Operation

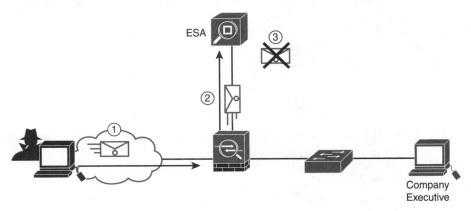

Step 1.   The threat actor sends a phishing attack to an important host on the network.

Step 2.   The firewall forwards all email to the ESA.

Step 3.   The ESA analyzes the email, logs it, and discards it.

Figure 3-13 shows how a WSA protects a user from accessing a blacklisted site:

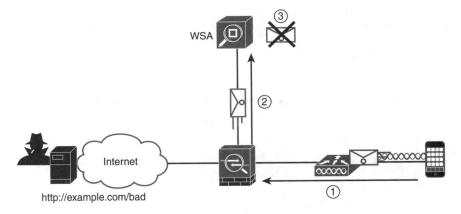

Figure 3-13 WSA Operation

Step 1.   A user attempts to connect to a website.

Step 2.   The firewall forwards the website request to the WSA.

Step 3.   The WSA evaluates the URL and determines that it is a known blacklisted site. The WSA discards the packet and sends an access denied message to the user.

Check Your Understanding—Network Security Best Practices

Check your understanding of network security best practices by choosing the BEST answer to each of the following questions.

1. Which network security device ensures that internal traffic can go out and come back but external traffic cannot initiate connections to inside hosts?

   a. VPN

   b. ASA firewall

   c. IPS

   d. ESA/WSA

   e. AAA server

2. Which network security device contains a secure database of who is authorized to access and manage network devices?

   a. VPN

   b. ASA firewall

   c. IPS

   d. ESA/WSA

   e. AAA server

3. Which network security device filters known and suspicious Internet malware sites?

   a. VPN

   b. ASA firewall

   c. IPS

   d. ESA/WSA

   e. AAA server

4. Which network security device is used to provide secure services with corporate sites and remote access support for remote users using secure encrypted tunnels?

   a. VPN

   b. ASA firewall

   c. IPS

   d. ESA/WSA

   e. AAA server

5. Which network security device monitors incoming and outgoing traffic, looking for malware and network attack signatures, and stops any threats that it recognizes?

   a. VPN

   b. ASA firewall

   c. IPS

   d. ESA/WSA

   e. AAA server

Cryptography

In this section, you will review common cryptographic processes used to protect data in transit.

Video—Cryptography

Be sure you review the video in the online curriculum. It demonstrates securing data using hashing and encryption.

Securing Communications

Briefly describe the following four elements of secure communications:

- Data integrity: _____

  _____

- Origin authentication: _____

  _____

- Data confidentiality: _____

  _____

- Data nonrepudiation: _____

  _____

Data Integrity

Hash functions are used to ensure the integrity of a message. They guarantee that message data has not changed accidentally or intentionally. Figure 3-14 shows how hashing can protect the integrity of a message. In the figure, the receiver knows that the message has been compromised because the starting and ending hashes do not match.

Figure 3-14   Hashing Example

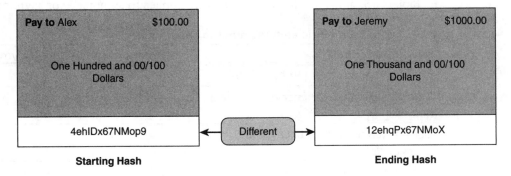

Hashing functions include Message Digest version 5 (MD5) or Secure Hash Algorithm (SHA) hash-generating algorithms. SHA-1 has known flaws and is considered legacy. Although the curriculum shows SHA-2 as the recommended next-generation family of hashing algorithms, the National Institute of Standards and Technology (NIST) now recommends the SHA-3 family of next-generation algorithms.

Origin Authentication

To add authentication to integrity assurance, use a keyed hash message authentication code (HMAC), which uses an additional secret key as input to the hash function. An HMAC is calculated using a cryptographic algorithm that combines a cryptographic hash function with a secret key, as shown in Figure 3-15. Only the sender and the receiver know the secret key, and the output of the hash function depends on the input data and the secret key.

Figure 3-15 Generating an HMAC Code

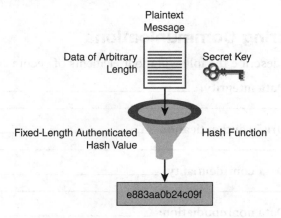

Data Confidentiality

Two classes of encryption are used to provide data confidentiality: symmetric and asymmetric.

Symmetric encryption algorithms, which are based on the premise that each communicating party knows the pre-shared key, include Triple Data Encryption Standard (3DES) and Advanced Encryption Standard (AES).

Asymmetric algorithms include Rivest, Shamir, and Adleman (RSA) and public key infrastructure (PKI).

In Table 3-15, indicate whether each feature applies to symmetric or asymmetric algorithms.

Table 3-15 Symmetric and Asymmetric Features

Algorithm Feature	Symmetric Encryption	Asymmetric Encryption
Key lengths are short (40 bits–256 bits).		
Uses the same key to encrypt and decrypt data.		
Uses different keys to encrypt and decrypt data.		
Commonly used for quick data transactions such as when accessing bank data.		
Faster of the two encryption types.		
Computationally taxing and therefore slower than the other encryption type.		
Key lengths are long (512 bits–4096 bits).		
Commonly used for encrypting bulk data, such as in VPN traffic.		

Symmetric Encryption

Symmetric algorithms use the same pre-shared key to encrypt and decrypt data. A pre-shared key, also called a secret key, is known by the sender and receiver before any encrypted communications can take place. Well-known symmetric encryption algorithms are described in Table 3-16.

Table 3-16   Symmetric Encryption Algorithms

Symmetric Encryption Algorithm	Description
Data Encryption Standard (DES)	This is a legacy symmetric encryption algorithm and should not be used.
3DES (Triple DES)	The replacement for DES, 3DES repeats the DES algorithm process three times. It should be avoided if possible because it is scheduled to be retired in 2023. If implemented, use very short key lifetimes.
Advanced Encryption Standard (AES)	AES is a popular and recommended symmetric encryption algorithm. It offers combinations of 128-, 192-, or 256-bit keys to encrypt data blocks that are 128, 192, or 256 bits long.
Software-Optimized Encryption Algorithm (SEAL)	SEAL is a faster symmetric encryption algorithm than AES. It uses a 160-bit encryption key and has a lower impact on the CPU compared to other software-based algorithms.
Rivest Cipher (RC) series algorithms	RC includes several versions developed by Ron Rivest. RC4 was used to secure web traffic.

Asymmetric Encryption

Asymmetric algorithms, also called public key algorithms, are designed so that the key that is used for encryption is different from the key that is used for decryption.

The following are examples of protocols that use asymmetric key algorithms:

- **Internet Key Exchange (IKE):** This is a fundamental component of IPsec VPNs.

- **Secure Socket Layer (SSL):** This is now implemented as the IETF standard Transport Layer Security (TLS).

- **Secure Shell (SSH):** This protocol provides a secure remote access connection to network devices.

- **Pretty Good Privacy (PGP):** This computer program provides cryptographic privacy and authentication. It is often used to increase the security of email communications.

Table 3-17 describes common examples of asymmetric encryption algorithms.

Table 3-17   Asymmetric Encryption Algorithms

Asymmetric Encryption Algorithm	Key Length	Description
Diffie-Hellman (DH)	512, 1024, 2048, 3072, 4096	The Diffie-Hellman algorithm allows two parties to agree on a key that they can use to encrypt messages they want to send to each other. The security of this algorithm depends on the assumption that it is easy to raise a number to a certain power but difficult to compute which power was used, given the number and the outcome.
Digital Signature Standard (DSS) and Digital Signature Algorithm (DSA)	512–1024	DSS specifies DSA as the algorithm for digital signatures. DSA is a public key algorithm based on the ElGamal signature scheme. Speed of signature creation is similar to that of RSA, but the speed is 10 to 40 times slower for verification.
Rivest, Shamir, and Adleman (RSA) encryption algorithms	512–2048	RSA is for public key cryptography that is based on the current difficulty of factoring very large numbers. It is the first algorithm known to be suitable for signing as well as encryption. It is widely used in electronic commerce protocols and is believed to be secure, given sufficiently long keys and the use of up-to-date implementations.
ElGamal	512–1024	An asymmetric key encryption algorithm for public key cryptography that is based on the Diffie-Hellman key agreement. A disadvantage of the ElGamal system is that the encrypted message becomes very big—about twice the size of the original message—and for this reason it is used only for small messages such as secret keys.
Elliptic curve techniques	224	Elliptic curve cryptography can be used to adapt many cryptographic algorithms, such as Diffie-Hellman or ElGamal. The main advantage of elliptic curve cryptography is that the keys can be much smaller.

Diffie-Hellman

Diffie-Hellman (DH) is an asymmetric mathematical algorithm in which two computers generate an identical shared secret key without having communicated before. The new shared key is never actually exchanged between the sender and receiver. However, because both parties know it, the key can be used by an encryption algorithm to encrypt traffic between the two systems. Figure 3-16 illustrates how DH algorithms work.

Figure 3-16 Illustration of DH Operation

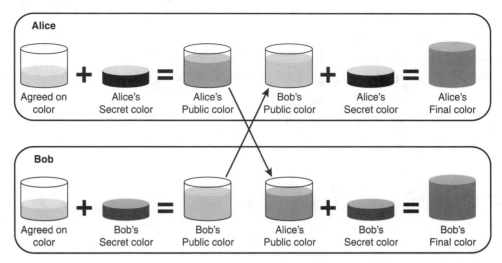

Check Your Understanding—Cryptography

Check your understanding of cryptography by choosing the BEST answer to each of the following questions.

1. Which encryption method repeats an algorithm process three times and is considered very trustworthy when implemented using very short key lifetimes?

   a. Rivest Cipher

   b. Triple DES

   c. Block Cipher

   d. Data Encryption Standard

   e. Stream Cipher

2. Which encryption method encrypts plaintext 1 byte or 1 bit at a time?

   a. Rivest Cipher

   b. Block Cipher

   c. Data Encryption Standard

   d. Software Encryption algorithm

   e. Stream Cipher

3. Which encryption method uses the same key to encrypt and decrypt data?

   a. Triple DES

   b. Symmetric

   c. Block Cipher

   d. Data Encryption Standard

   e. Asymmetric

4. Which encryption method is a stream cipher and is used to secure web traffic in SSL and TLS?

   a. Rivest Cipher

   b. Triple DES

   c. Symmetric

   d. Block Cipher

   e. Data Encryption Standard

Labs and Activities

 ## 3.5.7 Lab—Social Engineering

Objective

In this lab, you will research examples of social engineering and identify ways to recognize and prevent it.

Resources

- Computer with Internet access

Instructions

Step 1:   Research Social Engineering Examples

Social engineering, as it relates to information security, is used to describe the techniques used by a person (or persons) who manipulate people to access or compromise information about an organization or its computer systems. A social engineer is usually difficult to identify and may claim to be a new employee, a repair person, or researcher. The social engineer might even offer credentials to support that identity. By gaining trust and asking questions, he or she may be able to piece together enough information to infiltrate an organization's network.

Question:

Use any Internet browser to research incidents of social engineering. Summarize three examples found in your research.

_____

Step 2:   Recognize the Signs of Social Engineering

Social engineers are nothing more than thieves and spies. Instead of hacking their way into your network via the Internet, they attempt to gain access by relying on a person's desire to be accommodating. Although not specific to network security, the scenario below, described in Christopher Hadnagy's book, *The Art of Human Hacking*, illustrates how an unsuspecting person can unwittingly give away confidential information.

"The cafe was relatively quiet as I, dressed in a suit, sat at an empty table. I placed my briefcase on the table and waited for a suitable victim. Soon, just such a victim arrived with a friend and sat at the table next to mine. She placed her bag on the seat beside her, pulling the seat close and keeping her hand on the bag at all times.

After a few minutes, her friend left to find a restroom. The mark [target] was alone, so I gave Alex and Jess the signal. Playing a couple, Alex and Jess asked the mark if she would take a picture of them both. She was happy to do so. She removed her hand from her bag to take the camera and snap a picture of the "happy couple" and, while distracted, I reached over, took her bag, and locked it inside my briefcase. My victim had yet to notice her purse was missing as Alex and Jess left the café. Alex then went to a nearby parking garage.

It didn't take long for her to realize her bag was gone. She began to panic, looking around frantically. This was exactly what we were hoping for so, I asked her if she needed help.

She asked me if I had seen anything. I told her I hadn't but convinced her to sit down and think about what was in the bag. A phone. Make-up. A little cash. And her credit cards. Bingo!

I asked who she banked with and then told her that I worked for that bank. What a stroke of luck! I reassured her that everything would be fine, but she would need to cancel her credit card right away. I called the "help-desk" number, which was actually Alex, and handed my phone to her.

Alex was in a van in the parking garage. On the dashboard, a CD player was playing office noises. He assured the mark that her card could easily be canceled but, to verify her identity, she needed to enter her PIN on the keypad of the phone she was using. My phone and my keypad.

When we had her PIN, I left. If we were real thieves, we would have had access to her account via ATM withdrawals and PIN purchases. Fortunately for her, it was just a TV show."

Remember: "Those who build walls think differently than those who seek to go over, under, around, or through them." Paul Wilson—The Real Hustle

Question:

Research ways to recognize social engineering. Describe three examples found in your research.

_____

Step 3:   Research Ways to Prevent Social Engineering

Questions:

Does your company or school have procedures in place to help to prevent social engineering?

_____

If so, what are some of those procedures?

_____

Use the Internet to research procedures that other organizations use to prevent social engineers from gaining access to confidential information. List your findings.

_____

3.8.8 Lab—Explore DNS Traffic

Objectives

Part 1: Capture DNS Traffic

Part 2: Explore DNS Query Traffic

Part 3: Explore DNS Response Traffic

Background / Scenario

Wireshark is an open-source packet capture and analysis tool. Wireshark gives a detailed breakdown of the network protocol stack. Wireshark allows you to filter traffic for network troubleshooting, investigate security issues, and analyze network protocols. Because Wireshark allows you to view the packet details, it can be used as a reconnaissance tool for an attacker.

In this lab, you will install Wireshark on a Windows system and use Wireshark to filter for DNS packets and view the details of both DNS query and response packets.

Required Resources

- One Windows PC with Internet access and Wireshark installed

Instructions

Step 1:   Capture DNS traffic.

a. Open **Wireshark** and start a Wireshark capture by double-clicking a network interface with traffic.

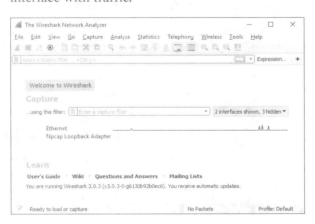

b. At the command prompt, enter **ipconfig /flushdns** clear the DNS cache.

```
C:\Users\Student> ipconfig /flushdns

Windows IP Configuration

Successfully flushed the DNS Resolver Cache.
```

c. Enter **nslookup** at the prompt to enter the nslookup interactive mode.

d. Enter the domain name of a website. The domain name www.cisco.com is used in this example. Enter **www.cisco.com** at the > prompt.

```
C:\Users\Student> nslookup
Default Server:  UnKnown
Address:  68.105.28.16


> www.cisco.com
Server:  UnKnown
Address:  68.105.28.16


Non-authoritative answer:
Name:     e2867.dsca.akamaiedge.net
Addresses: 2001:578:28:68d::b33
           2001:578:28:685::b33
           96.7.79.147
Aliases:  www.cisco.com
          www.cisco.com.akadns.net
          wwwds.cisco.com.edgekey.net
          wwwds.cisco.com.edgekey.net.globalredir.akadns.net
```

e. Enter **exit** when finished to exit the nslookup interactive mode. Close the command prompt.

f. Click **Stop capturing packets** to stop the Wireshark capture.

Step 2:   Explore DNS Query Traffic

a. Observe the traffic captured in the Wireshark Packet List pane. Enter **udp.port == 53** in the filter box and click the arrow (or press enter) to display only DNS packets.

b. Select the DNS packet labeled **Standard query 0x0002 A www.cisco.com.**

In the Packet Details pane, notice this packet has Ethernet II, Internet Protocol Version 4, User Datagram Protocol and Domain Name System (query).

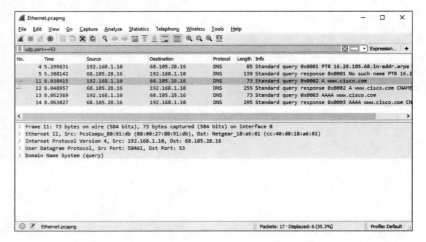

c. Expand **Ethernet II** to view the details. Observe the source and destination fields.

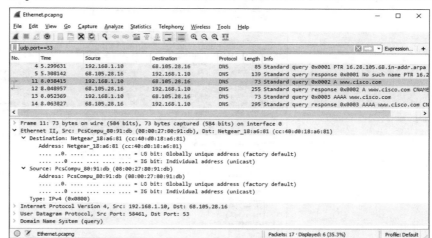

Question:

What are the source and destination MAC addresses? Which network interfaces are these MAC addresses associated with?

d. Expand **Internet Protocol Version 4**. Observe the source and destination IPv4 addresses.

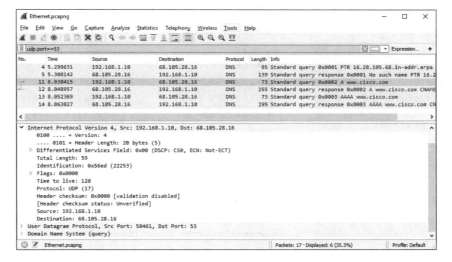

Question:

What are the source and destination IP addresses? Which network interfaces are these IP addresses associated with?

e. Expand the **User Datagram Protocol**. Observe the source and destination ports.

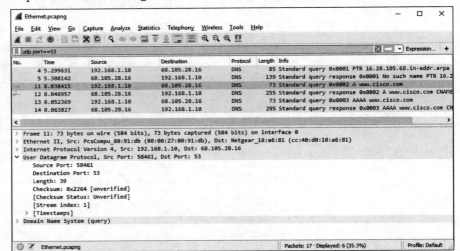

Question:

What are the source and destination ports? What is the default DNS port number?

---

f. Open a command prompt and enter **arp –a** and **ipconfig /all** to record the MAC and IP addresses of the PC.

```
C:\Users\Student> arp -a


Interface: 192.168.1.10 --- 0x4
    Internet Address        Physical Address        Type
    192.168.1.1             cc-40-d0-18-a6-81       dynamic
    192.168.1.122           b0-a7-37-46-70-bb       dynamic
    192.168.1.255           ff-ff-ff-ff-ff-ff       static
    224.0.0.22              01-00-5e-00-00-16       static
    224.0.0.252             01-00-5e-00-00-fc       static
    239.255.255.250         01-00-5e-7f-ff-fa       static
    255.255.255.255         ff-ff-ff-ff-ff-ff       static


C:\Users\Studuent> ipconfig /all


Windows IP Configuration


    Host Name . . . . . . . . . . . . : DESKTOP
    Primary Dns Suffix  . . . . . . . :
    Node Type . . . . . . . . . . . . : Hybrid
    IP Routing Enabled. . . . . . . . : No
    WINS Proxy Enabled. . . . . . . . : No


Ethernet adapter Ethernet:


    Connection-specific DNS Suffix  . :
```

```
Description . . . . . . . . . . . : Intel(R) PRO/1000 MT Desktop
                                    Adapter
Physical Address. . . . . . . . . : 08-00-27-80-91-DB
DHCP Enabled. . . . . . . . . . . : Yes
Autoconfiguration Enabled . . . . : Yes
Link-local IPv6 Address . . . . . : fe80::d829:6d18:e229:a705%4
                                    (Preferred)
IPv4 Address. . . . . . . . . . . : 192.168.1.10(Preferred)
Subnet Mask . . . . . . . . . . . : 255.255.255.0
Lease Obtained. . . . . . . . . . : Tuesday, August 20, 2019
                                    5:39:51 PM
Lease Expires . . . . . . . . . . : Wednesday, August 21, 2019
                                    5:39:50 PM
Default Gateway . . . . . . . . . : 192.168.1.1
DHCP Server . . . . . . . . . . . : 192.168.1.1
DHCPv6 IAID . . . . . . . . . . . : 50855975
DHCPv6 Client DUID. . . . . . . . : 00-01-00-01-24-21-BA-64-08-00-27
                                    -80-91-DB
DNS Servers . . . . . . . . . . . : 68.105.28.16
                                    68.105.29.16
NetBIOS over Tcpip. . . . . . . . : Enabled
```

Question:

Compare the MAC and IP addresses in the Wireshark results to the results from the **ipconfig /all** results. What is your observation?

_____

g.   Expand **Domain Name System (query)** in the Packet Details pane. Then expand the **Flags** and **Queries**.

Observe the results. The flag is set to do the query recursively to query for the IP address to www.cisco.com.

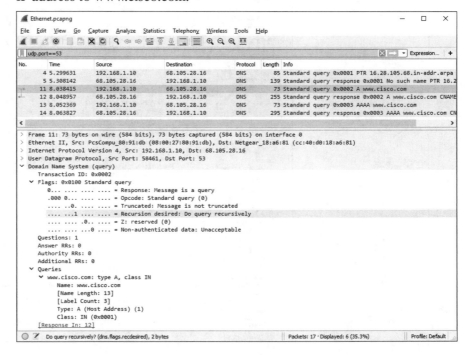

Step 3:   Explore DNS Response Traffic

a.   Select the corresponding response DNS packet labeled **Standard query response 0x0002 A www.cisco.com.**

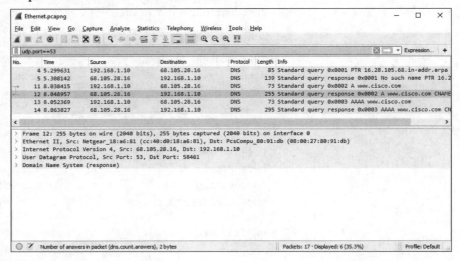

Questions:

What are the source and destination MAC and IP addresses and port numbers? How do they compare to the addresses in the DNS query packets?

_____

b.   Expand **Domain Name System (response).** Then expand the **Flags, Queries,** and **Answers.** Observe the results.

Question:

Can the DNS server do recursive queries?

_____

c. Observe the CNAME and A records in the answers details.

Question:

How do the results compare to nslookup results?

_____

Reflection Question

1. From the Wireshark results, what else can you learn about the network when you remove the filter?

_____

2. How can an attacker use Wireshark to compromise your network security?

_____

CHAPTER 4

ACL Concepts

The "Study Guide" portion of this chapter uses a variety of exercises to test your knowledge of how access control lists (ACLs) are used as part of a network security policy. The "Labs and Activities" portion of this chapter includes instructions for one Packet Tracer activity. There are no labs for this chapter.

As you work through this chapter, use Chapter 4 in *Enterprise Networking, Security, and Automation v7 Companion Guide* or use the corresponding Module 4 in the Enterprise Networking, Security, and Automation online curriculum for assistance.

Study Guide

Purpose of ACLs

In this section, you review how ACLs filter traffic.

ACL Operation

An ACL is a series of IOS commands that control whether a router forwards or drops packets, based on information found in the packet header. Each command is called an ACL statement or an access control entry (ACE). ACLs are among the most commonly used features of Cisco IOS software. The following are some router tasks that require the use of ACLs to identify traffic:

- Limit network traffic to increase network performance
- Provide traffic flow control
- Provide a basic level of security for network access
- Filter traffic based on traffic type
- Screen hosts to permit or deny access to network services
- Provide priority to certain classes of network traffic

Traffic that enters a router interface is routed solely based on information in the routing table. When an ACL is applied to the interface, the router performs the additional task of evaluating all network packets as they pass through the interface to determine whether the packet can be forwarded. This process is called *packet filtering*. Standard IP ACLs only filter at Layer 3. Extended IP ACLs filter at Layer 3 and Layer 4.

The last statement of an ACL is always an implicit deny. Because of this implicit deny, an ACL that does not have at least one permit statement will block all traffic.

ACLs can be configured to apply to inbound traffic and outbound traffic. For inbound traffic, packets are processed before they are routed. For outbound traffic, packets are processed after they are routed to the outbound interface.

IPv4 ACLs use a wildcard mask to determine which packets will be permitted.

Check Your Understanding—Purpose of ACLs

Check your understanding of the purpose of ACLs by choosing the BEST answer to each of the following questions.

1. What are the permit or deny statements in an ACL called?

    a. Access control entries

    b. Arbitrary statements

    c. Content control entries

    d. Control statements

2. Which packet filtering statement is true?

   a. Extended ACLs filter at Layer 3 only.

   b. Extended ACLs filter at Layer 4 only.

   c. Standard ACLs filter at Layer 3 only.

   d. Standard ACLs filter at Layer 4 only.

3. Which statement about the operation of a standard ACL is incorrect?

   a. The router extracts the source IPv4 address from the packet header.

   b. The router starts at the top of the ACL and compares the address to each ACE, in sequential order.

   c. When a match is made, the ACE either permits or denies the packet, and any remaining ACEs are not analyzed.

   d. If there are no matching ACEs in the ACL, the packet is forwarded because an implicit permit ACE is automatically applied to every ACL.

Wildcard Masks in ACLs

In this section, you review how ACLs use wildcard masks.

Wildcard Mask Overview

Wildcard masks use the following rules to match binary 1s and 0s:

- **Wildcard mask bit 0**: Match the corresponding bit value in the address.

- **Wildcard mask bit 1**: Ignore the corresponding bit value in the address.

Table 4-1 list some examples of wildcard masks and what they would identify.

Table 4-1   Examples of Wildcard Masks

Wildcard Mask	Last Octet (in Binary)	Meaning (0—match, 1—ignore)
0.0.0.0	00000000	■ Match all octets.
0.0.0.63	00111111	■ Match the first 3 octets. ■ Match the 2 leftmost bits of the last octet. ■ Ignore the last 6 bits.
0.0.0.15	00001111	■ Match the first 3 octets. ■ Match the 4 leftmost bits of the last octet. ■ Ignore the last 4 bits of the last octet.
0.0.0.248	11111100	■ Match the first 3 octets. ■ Ignore the 6 leftmost bits of the last octet. ■ Match the last 2 bits.
0.0.0.255	11111111	■ Match the first 3 octets. ■ Ignore the last octet.

Wildcard Mask Types

Refer to Tables 4-2, 4-3, and 4-4 to review how wildcard masks are used to filter traffic for one host, one subnet, and a range of IPv4 addresses.

Table 4-2 Wildcard Mask to Match a Host

	Decimal	Binary
IPv4 address	192.168.1.1	11000000.10101000.00000001.00000001
Wildcard mask	0.0.0.0	00000000.00000000.00000000.00000000
Permitted IPv4 address	192.168.1.1	**11000000.10101000.00000001.00000001**

Table 4-3 Wildcard Mask to Match an IPv4 Subnet

	Decimal	Binary
IPv4 address	192.168.1.1	11000000.10101000.00000001.00000001
Wildcard mask	0.0.0.255	00000000.00000000.00000000.11111111
Permitted IPv4 address	192.168.1.0/24	**11000000.10101000.00000001.00000000**

Table 4-4 Wildcard Mask to Match an IPv4 Address Range

	Decimal	Binary
IPv4 address	192.168.16.0	11000000.10101000.00010000.00000000
Wildcard mask	0.0.15.255	00000000.00000000.00001111.11111111
Permitted IPv4 address	192.168.16.0/24 to 192.168.31.0/24	**11000000.10101000.00010000.00000000** **11000000.10101000.00011111.00000000**

Wildcard Mask Calculation

The wildcard mask argument is simply the inverse of the subnet mask. Therefore, if you know the subnet mask, you can calculate the wildcard mask. For each of the ACL statements in Table 4-5, record the wildcard mask used to filter the specified IPv4 address or network.

Table 4-5 Determine the Correct Wildcard Mask

ACL Statement	Wildcard Mask
Permit all hosts from the 192.168.1.0/25 network	
Permit all hosts from the 10.0.0.0/16 network	
Deny all hosts from the 10.10.100.0/24 network	
Deny all hosts from the 10.20.30.128/26 network	
Permit all hosts from the 172.18.0.0/23 network	
Permit all hosts from the 192.168.5.0/27 network	
Deny host 172.18.33.1	
Deny all hosts from the 172.16.1.192/29 network	
Permit all hosts from the 172.31.64.0/18 network	
Permit host 10.10.10.1	

ACL Statement	Wildcard Mask
Deny all hosts from the 172.25.250.160/28 network	
Deny all hosts from the 172.30.128.0/20 network	
Deny all hosts from the 10.10.128.0/19 network	
Permit all hosts from the 172.18.0.0/16 network	
Permit all hosts from the 192.168.200.0/30 network	

Wildcard Mask Keywords

Keywords reduce ACL keystrokes and make it easier to read an ACE. The two keywords are:

- **host:** This keyword substitutes for the 0.0.0.0 mask. This mask states that all IPv4 address bits must match to filter just one host address.

- **any:** This keyword substitutes for the 255.255.255.255 mask. This mask says to ignore the entire IPv4 address or to accept any addresses.

Check Your Understanding—Wildcard Masks in ACLs

Check your understanding of wildcard masks in ACLs by choosing the BEST answer to each of the following questions.

1. Which wildcard mask would permit only host 10.10.10.1?

   a. 0.0.0.0

   b. 0.0.0.31

   c. 0.0.0.255

   d. 0.0.255.255

   e. 255.255.255.255

2. Which wildcard mask would permit only hosts from the 10.10.0.0/16 network?

   a. 0.0.0.0

   b. 0.0.0.31

   c. 0.0.0.255

   d. 0.0.255.255

   e. 255.255.255.255

3. Which wildcard mask would permit all hosts?

   a. 0.0.0.0

   b. 0.0.0.31

   c. 0.0.0.255

   d. 0.0.255.255

   e. 255.255.255.255

4. Which wildcard mask would permit all hosts from the 192.168.10.0/24 network?

    a. 0.0.0.0

    b. 0.0.0.31

    c. 0.0.0.255

    d. 0.0.255.255

    e. 255.255.255.255

Guidelines for ACL Creation

In this section, you review how to create ACLs.

Limited Number of ACLs per Interface

A router interface can have:

- One outbound IPv4 ACL

- One inbound IPv4 ACL

- One inbound IPv6 ACL

- One outbound IPv6 ACL

For example, R1 in Figure 4-1 has two interfaces. Therefore, it can have eight total ACLs applied to the interfaces.

Figure 4-1   Example of a Router with Two Interfaces and Eight Applied ACLs

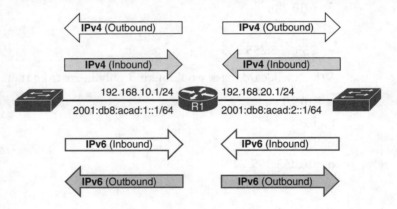

ACL Best Practices

Table 4-6 presents guidelines that form the basis of an ACL best practices list.

Table 4-6   ACL Best Practice Guidelines

Guideline	Benefit
Base ACLs on the organizational security policies.	This will ensure that you implement organizational security guidelines.
Write out what you want an ACL to do.	This will help you avoid inadvertently creating potential access problems.
Use a text editor to create, edit, and save all of your ACLs.	This will help you create a library of reusable ACLs.
Document the ACLs using the **remark** command.	This will help you (and others) understand the purpose of an ACE.
Test the ACLs on a development network before implementing them on a production network.	This will help you avoid costly errors.

Check Your Understanding—Guidelines for ACL Creation

Check your understanding of ACL creation by choosing the BEST answer to each of the following questions.

1. How many total ACLs (both IPv4 and IPv6) can be configured on an interface?

   a. 0

   b. 1

   c. 2

   d. 4

   e. 8

2. Which of the following is an ACL best practice?

   a. Always test ACLs on a production network.

   b. Create ACLs on a production router.

   c. Document ACLs by using the **description** ACL command.

   d. Write the ACL before configuring it on a router.

Types of IPv4 ACLs

In this section, you review standard and extended IPv4 ACLs.

Standard and Extended ACLs

There are two types of IPv4 ACLs:

- **Standard ACLs:** These ACLs permit or deny packets based only on the source IPv4 address.

- **Extended ACLs:** These ACLs permit or deny packets based on the source IPv4 address and destination IPv4 address, protocol type, source and destination TCP or UDP ports, and more.

Numbered and Named ACLs

An ACL can be numbered or named:

- **Numbered ACLs:** ACLs numbered 1 to 99 and 1300 to 1999 are standard ACLs, while ACLs numbered 100 to 199 and 2000 to 2699 are extended ACLs.

- **Named ACLs:** Named ACLs are preferred over numbered ACLs. Specifically, standard and extended ACLs can be named to provide information about the purpose of each ACL. For example, naming an extended ACL NAT-PERMIT is far better than numbering the ACL 10.

Standard and Extended ACL Placement

Every ACL should be placed where it has the greatest impact on efficiency. The basic rules are as follows:

- Locate standard ACLs as close as possible to the destination because these ACLs do not specify destination addresses.

- Locate extended ACLs as close as possible to the source of the traffic to be filtered.

Use the information shown in Figure 4-2 to determine the router, interface, and direction for each scenario in Table 4-7.

Figure 4-2   ACL Placement Topology

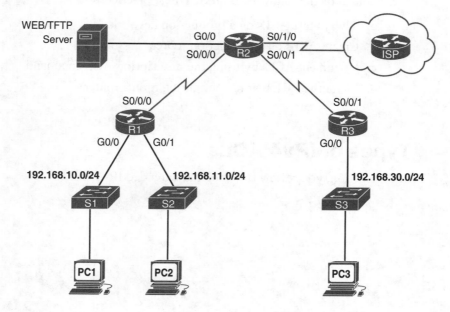

Table 4-7   ACL Placement Scenarios

Scenario	Router	Interface	Direction
Use a standard ACL to stop the 192.168.10.0/24 network from accessing the Internet through the ISP.			
Use a standard ACL to stop the 192.168.11.0/24 network from accessing the 192.168.10.0/24 network.			
Use an extended ACL to allow only TFTP and web traffic to access the web/TFTP server. The traffic could be from any source.			
Use an extended ACL to stop the 192.168.30.0/24 network from accessing the wen/TFTP server.			

Check Your Understanding—Types of IPv4 ACLs

Check your understanding of the types of IPv4 ACLs by choosing the BEST answer to each of the following questions.

1. Which type of ACL is capable of filtering based on TCP port number?

   a. Extended ACL

   b. Standard ACL

2. Which statement about ACLs is true?

   a. Extended ACLs are numbered 1300 to 2699.

   b. Named ACLs can be standard or extended.

   c. Numbered ACLs are preferred over numbered ACLs.

   d. Standard ACLs are numbered 1 to 199.

3. Where should standard ACLs be placed?

   a. Standard ACL location is not important.

   b. Standard ACLs should be placed as close to the destination as possible.

   c. Standard ACLs should be placed as close to the source as possible.

   d. Standard ACLs should be placed on serial interfaces.

4. Where should extended ACLs be placed?

   a. Extended ACL location is not important.

   b. Extended ACLs should be located as close to the destination as possible.

   c. Extended ACLs should be located as close to the source as possible.

   d. Extended ACLs should be located on serial interfaces.

Labs and Activities

4.1.4 Packet Tracer—Access Control List Demonstration

Objectives

Part 1: Verify Local Connectivity and Test Access Control List

Part 2: Remove Access Control List and Repeat Test

Background

In this activity, you will observe how an access control list (ACL) can be used to prevent a ping from reaching hosts on remote networks. After removing the ACL from the configuration, the pings will be successful.

Addressing Table

Device	Interface	IP Address / Prefix
R1	G0/0	192.168.10.1/24
	G0/1	192.168.11.1/24
	S0/0/0	10.1.1.1/30
R2	S0/0/0	10.10.1.2/30
	S0/0/1	10.10.1.5/30
R3	G0/0	192.168.30.1/24
	G0/1	192.168.31.1/24
	S0/0/1	10.10.1.6/24
PC1	NIC	192.168.10.10/24
PC2	NIC	192.168.10.11/24
PC3	NIC	192.168.11.10/24
PC4	NIC	192.168.30.12/24
DNS Server	NIC	192.168.31.12/24

Instructions

Part 1: Verify Local Connectivity and Test Access Control List

Step 1: Ping devices on the local network to verify connectivity.

   a. From the command prompt of **PC1**, ping **PC2**.

   b. From the command prompt of **PC1**, ping **PC3**.

   Question:

   Why were the pings successful?

Step 2: Ping devices on remote networks to test ACL functionality.

    a. From the command prompt of **PC1**, ping **PC4**.

    b. From the command prompt of **PC1**, ping the **DNS Server**.

    Question:

    Why did the pings fail? (**Hint:** Use simulation mode or view the router configurations to investigate.)

Part 2: Remove the ACL and Repeat the Test

Step 1: Use show commands to investigate the ACL configuration.

    a. Navigate to R1 CLI. Use the **show run** and **show access-lists** commands to view the currently configured ACLs. To quickly view the current ACLs, use **show access-lists**. Enter the **show access-lists** command, followed by a space and a question mark (**?**) to view the available options:

```
R1# show access-lists ?
  <1-199>   ACL number
  WORD      ACL name
  <cr>
```

If you know the ACL number or name, you can filter the **show** output further. However, **R1** only has one ACL; therefore, the **show access-lists** command will suffice.

```
R1# show access-lists
Standard IP access list 11
    10 deny 192.168.10.0 0.0.0.255
    20 permit any
```

The first line of the ACL blocks any packets that originate in the **192.168.10.0/24** network, which includes Internet Control Message Protocol (ICMP) echoes (ping requests). The second line of the ACL allows all other **ip** traffic from **any** source to transverse the router.

    c. For an ACL to impact router operation, it must be applied to an interface in a specific direction. In this scenario, the ACL is used to filter traffic exiting an interface. Therefore, all traffic leaving the specified interface of R1 will be inspected against ACL 11.

    Although you can view IP information with the **show ip interface** command, it may be more efficient in some situations to simply use the **show run** command. To obtain a complete list of interfaces that the ACL that may be applied to, and the list of all ACLs that are configured, use the following command:

```
R1# show run | include interface|access
interface GigabitEthernet0/0
interface GigabitEthernet0/1
interface Serial0/0/0
 ip access-group 11 out
interface Serial0/0/1
interface Vlan1
```

```
access-list 11 deny 192.168.10.0 0.0.0.255
access-list 11 permit any
```

The second pipe symbol (|) creates an OR condition that matches **interface** OR **access**. It is important that no spaces are included in the OR condition. Use one or both of these commands to find information about the ACL.

Question:

To which interface and in what direction is the ACL applied?

_____

Step 2:   Remove access list 11 from the configuration.

You can remove ACLs from the configuration by issuing the **no access list** [*number of the ACL*] command. The **no access-list** command when used without arguments deletes all ACLs configured on the router. The **no access-list** [*number of the ACL*] command removes only a specific ACL. Removing an ACL from a router does not remove the ACL from the interface. The command that applies the ACL to the interface must be removed separately.

a.   Under the Serial0/0/0 interface, remove access-list 11, which was previously applied to the interface as an **outgoing** filter:

```
R1(config)# interface s0/0/0
R1(config-if)# no ip access-group 11 out
```

b.   In global configuration mode, remove the ACL by entering the following command:

```
R1(config)# no access-list 11
```

c.   Verify that **PC1** can now ping the **DNS Server** and **PC4**.

CHAPTER 5

ACLs for IPv4 Configuration

The "Study Guide" portion of this chapter uses a variety of exercises to test your knowledge and skills related to implementing IPv4 access control lists (ACLs) to filter traffic and secure administrative access. The "Labs and Activities" portion of this chapter includes all the online curriculum labs and Packet Tracer activity instructions.

As you work through this chapter, use Chapter 5 in *Enterprise Networking, Security, and Automation v7 Companion Guide* or use the corresponding Module 5 in the Enterprise Networking, Security, and Automation online curriculum for assistance.

Study Guide

Configure Standard IPv4 ACLs

In this section, you review how to configure standard IPv4 ACLs to filter traffic to meet networking requirements.

Create an ACL

All ACLs must be planned. However, planning is especially important for ACLs requiring multiple access control entries (ACEs). When configuring a complex ACL, it is suggested that you

- Use a text editor and write out the specifics of the policy to be implemented.

- Add the IOS configuration commands to accomplish those tasks.

- Include remarks to document the ACL.

- Copy and paste the commands onto the device.

- Thoroughly test each ACL to ensure that it correctly applies the desired policy.

To use numbered or named standard ACLs on a Cisco router, you must first create the standard ACL. Then you must apply the ACL to one of the router's processes, such as an interface or Telnet lines.

Numbered Standard IPv4 ACLs

The full command syntax to configure a standard ACL is as follows:

```
Router(config)# access-list access-list-number {deny | permit | remark text} source
[source-wildcard] [log]
```

For example, the following ACL would first add a remark and then permit traffic from the 172.16.0.0/16 network:

```
R1(config)# access-list 1 remark Permit traffic from HR LAN, 172.16.0.0/16
```

```
R1(config)# access-list 1 permit 172.16.0.0 0.0.255.255
```

In this case, the remark is not very helpful. However, in more complex configuration scenarios, the **remark** option can help to quickly communicate the purpose of an ACL statement.

If a policy calls for filtering traffic for a specific host, you can use the host address and 0.0.0.0 as the wildcard mask. But if you do this, IOS drops the 0.0.0.0 and just uses the host address, as shown in Example 5-1.

Example 5-1   Filtering One IP Address

```
R1(config)# access-list 1 deny 172.16.1.10 0.0.0.0
R1(config)# do show access-lists
Standard IP access list 1
    10 deny   172.16.1.10
R1(config)#
```

If a policy calls for filtering traffic for all sources, you can configure 0.0.0.0 255.255.255.255 as the source address and wildcard mask. IOS converts it to the keyword **any**, as shown in Example 5-2.

Example 5-2   Filtering All Addresses

```
R1(config)# access-list 1 deny 172.16.1.10 0.0.0.0
R1(config)# access-list 1 permit 0.0.0.0 255.255.255.255
R1(config)# do show access-lists
Standard IP access list 1
    10 deny   172.16.1.10
    20 permit any
R1(config)#
```

Note: The sequence numbers before each statement can be used to edit the statement, as discussed later.

Apply a Standard IPv4 ACL

An ACL has no impact unless it is applied to some process. To filter inbound or outbound traffic, an ACL must be applied to an interface, and the direction of traffic must be specified. The command syntax to apply an ACL to an interface is as follows:

```
Router(config-if)# ip access-group { access-list-number | access-list-name }
{ in | out }
```

Named Standard IPv4 ACLs

Naming an ACL makes it easier to understand its function. For example, an ACL configured to deny FTP could be called NO_FTP. The command syntax to enter named ACL configuration mode is as follows:

```
Router(config)# ip access-list [ standard | extended ] name
```

where *name* can be any alphanumeric string that does not begin with a number. Once in named ACL configuration mode, the router prompt changes, depending on whether you chose **standard** or **extended**. The syntax for named standard ACL configuration mode is as follows:

```
Router(config-std-nacl)# [ permit | deny | remark ] { source [source-wildcard] }
[log}
```

So, to reconfigure Example 5-2 with a named standard ACL and a remark, we could use commands like the ones in Example 5-3.

Example 5-3   Named Standard IPv4 ACL

```
R1(config)# ip access-list standard NOT_BOB
R1(config-std-nacl)# remark Stop Bob
R1(config-std-nacl)# deny host 172.16.1.10
R1(config-std-nacl)# permit any
R1(config-std-nacl)# exit
R1(config)# interface g0/0
R1(config-if)# ip access-group NOT_BOB in
R1(config-if)# do show access-lists
Standard IP access list NOT_BOB
    10 deny host 172.16.1.10
    20 permit any
R1(config-if)#
```

Standard IPv4 ACL Scenarios

Use the information in Figure 5-1 to write ACL statements for the following two scenarios. Include the router prompts in your configurations. You can use numbered or named ACLs.

Figure 5-1   Topology for Standard ACL Configuration Scenarios

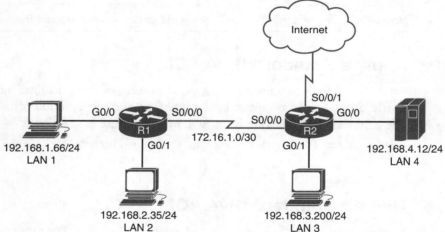

Standard ACL Scenario 1

Record the commands, including the router prompts, to configure and apply a standard ACL that filters traffic into the 192.168.1.0 LAN. The 192.168.3.200 host should not be able to access this LAN, but all other hosts on the 192.168.3.0 and 192.168.4.0 networks should be permitted. All other traffic should be blocked.

_____

_____

_____

_____
_____
_____
_____
_____

Standard ACL Scenario 2

Record the commands, including the router prompts, to configure and apply a standard ACL that filters traffic to host 192.168.4.12. Both the 192.168.1.66 host and all hosts in the 192.168.2.0 LAN should be permitted access to this host. All other networks should not be able to access the 192.168.4.12 host.

_____
_____
_____
_____
_____
_____

Modify IPv4 ACLs

To modify an ACL, you can use either a text editor or sequence numbers. Text editor modification involves basically copying the ACL to a text editor, modifying it, removing the old ACL, and pasting in the new one. In this section, you review how to use sequence numbers to edit existing standard IPv4 ACLs.

Sequence Numbers Method

IOS automatically adds a sequence number before the ACL statement, as you can see in the previous examples that used the show access-lists command. These sequence numbers can be used to delete an erroneous ACL statement and add back a correct ACL statement. The rules for using sequence numbers to edit a standard or extended numbered ACL are as follows:

- Enter named ACL configuration mode for the ACL, even if it is a numbered ACL.
- Delete the sequence number that is in error.
- Use the deleted sequence number to add the correct ACL statement.

Note: For standard and extended numbered ACLs, you cannot add a new sequence number statement in the middle of the ACL.

In Example 5-4, the wrong address is currently being denied. Enter the commands to delete the erroneous statement and add back a statement to deny 192.168.1.66.

Example 5-4   Standard Numbered ACL with Error

```
R1(config)# access-list 1 deny 192.168.1.65

R1(config)# access-list 1 permit any

R1(config)# do show access-lists

Standard IP access list 1

    10 deny   192.168.1.65

    20 permit any

R1(config)# _____

    _____

    _____

    _____

    _____

    _____

    _____

R1#
```

Secure VTY Ports with a Standard IPv4 ACL

In this section, you review how to configure a standard ACL to secure VTY access.

The access-class Command

Filtering Telnet or Secure Shell (SSH) traffic is usually considered an extended IP ACL function because it filters a higher-level protocol. However, because the access-class command is used to filter incoming or outgoing Telnet/SSH sessions by source address, you can use a standard ACL.

The command syntax of the access-class command is

```
Router(config-line)# access-class access-list-number { in [ vrf-also ] | out }
```

The parameter in restricts incoming connections between the addresses in the access list and the Cisco device, and the parameter out restricts outgoing connections between a particular Cisco device and the addresses in the access list.

Secure VTP Access Example

Record the commands to configure an ACL to permit host 192.168.2.35 and then apply the ACL to all Telnet lines.

```
R1(config)# _____

    _____

    _____
```

Configure Extended IPv4 ACLs

In this section, you review how to configure extended IPv4 ACLs to filter traffic according to networking requirements.

Extended ACLs

Like standard ACLs, extended ACLs can be created as either of the following:

- **Numbered extended ACL:** Created using the **access-list** *access-list-number* global configuration command.

- **Named extended ACL:** Created using the **ip access-list extended** *access-list-name*.

Numbered Extended IPv4 ACLs

The procedural steps for configuring extended ACLs are the same as for standard ACLs. The extended ACL is first configured, and then it is activated on an interface. However, the command syntax and parameters are more complex to support the additional features provided by extended ACLs. The command syntax for an extended ACL with some of the available options is as follows:

```
Router(config)# access-list access-list-number { deny | permit | remark } protocol
source [source-wildcard] destination [destination-wildcard] [operand] [port-number or
name] [established]
```

Use the *operand* to compare source or destination ports. Possible *operand* values are **lt** (less than), **gt** (greater than), **eq** (equal), **neq** (not equal), and **range**.

For example, to allow host 172.16.1.11 web access to 10.10.10.10, you might use the following ACL statement:

```
R1(config)# access-list 100 permit tcp host 172.16.1.11 host 10.10.10.10 eq 80
```

Note: You must either use the **host** keyword or **0.0.0.0** for the wildcard mask when configuring an extended ACL to filter one IP address.

The steps for configuring, applying, and editing named and numbered extended ACLs are the same as for standard ACLs.

Numbered Extended ACL Configuration Scenarios

Refer to the topology in Figure 5-2. Then use the bank of ACL statement components to construct an ACL statement for the following scenarios. Some components may be equivalent. Some components may not be used.

Figure 5-2   Topology for Extended ACL Configuration Scenarios

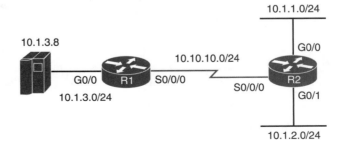

ACL Components					
10.1.3.0	50	udp	10.1.2.0	99	any
eq 21	0.0.0.0	eq 53	deny	host	10.1.3.8
101	150	ip	10.1.1.0	122	10.10.10.0
permit	eq 80	access-list	0.0.0.255	10.1.2.9	tcp

Extended ACL Scenario 1

Record the command to configure a numbered ACL statement that allows only users on the 10.1.1.0/24 network to have HTTP access to the web server on the 10.1.3.0/24 network. The ACL is applied to R2 G0/0 inbound.

Extended ACL Scenario 2

Record the command to configure a numbered ACL statement that blocks host 10.1.2.9 from having FTP access to the 10.1.1.0/24 network. The ACL is applied to R2 G0/1 inbound.

Extended ACL Scenario 3

Record the command to configure a numbered ACL statement that allows only host 10.1.3.8 on the 10.1.3.0/24 network to reach destinations beyond that network. The ACL is applied to R1 G0/0 inbound.

Evaluate Extended IPv4 ACL Statements

Refer to the topology in Figure 5-3. Each of the following scenarios applies an extended ACL to R1 G0/0 for inbound traffic. Evaluate the scenarios to determine whether the packets listed in the scenario's table would be permitted or denied. Each scenario is independent of the other two scenarios.

Figure 5-3 Evaluating an Extended ACL

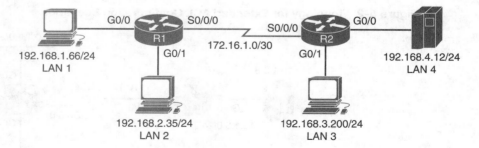

Extended ACL Evaluation Scenario 1

Use the following command output and the table that follows to indicate whether the source address will be permitted or denied.

```
R1# show access-lists
Extended IP access list 103
    permit ip host 192.168.1.66 host 192.168.4.12
    permit ip host 192.168.1.77 host 192.168.4.12
    deny ip 192.168.1.0 0.0.0.255 192.168.4.0 0.0.0.255
    permit ip 192.168.1.0 0.0.0.255 192.168.2.0 0.0.0.255
```

Source	Destination	Permit	Deny
192.168.1.66	192.168.3.51		
192.168.1.33	192.168.2.34		
192.168.1.88	192.168.4.39		
192.168.1.77	192.168.3.75		
192.168.1.88	192.168.2.51		
192.168.1.66	192.168.3.75		

Extended ACL Evaluation Scenario 2

Use the following command output and the table that follows to indicate whether the source address will be permitted or denied.

```
R1# show access-lists
Extended IP access list 104
    deny tcp host 192.168.1.66 host 192.168.4.12 eq www
    permit tcp host 192.168.1.77 host 192.168.3.75 eq 22
    deny ip 192.168.1.0 0.0.0.255 192.168.3.0 0.0.0.255
    permit ip 192.168.1.0 0.0.0.255 192.168.4.0 0.0.0.255
```

Source	Destination	Protocol	Permit	Deny
192.168.1.66	192.168.3.200	http		
192.168.1.88	192.168.2.75	http		
192.168.1.77	192.168.3.75	ssh		
192.168.1.77	192.168.3.75	http		
192.168.1.66	192.168.4.92	http		
192.168.1.66	192.168.4.75	ssh		

Extended ACL Evaluation Scenario 3

Use the following command output and the table that follows to indicate whether the source address will be permitted or denied.

```
R1# show access-lists
Extended IP access list 105
```

```
permit tcp 192.168.1.0 0.0.0.255 host 192.168.3.200 eq www

permit ip host 192.168.1.66 host 192.168.3.200

permit tcp 192.168.1.0 0.0.0.255 host 192.168.4.12 eq 22

permit tcp host 192.168.1.66 192.168.2.0 0.0.0.255 eq telnet
```

Source	Destination	Protocol	Permit	Deny
192.168.1.77	192.168.2.75	Telnet		
192.168.1.67	192.168.2.88	http		
192.168.1.66	192.168.3.200	Telnet		
192.168.1.66	192.168.2.75	Telnet		
192.168.1.77	192.168.3.75	http		
192.168.1.66	192.168.4.12	ssh		

Extended ACL Quiz

Refer to the topology in Figure 5-4 and the following scenario to answer the five questions.

Figure 5-4   Extended ACL Quiz Topology

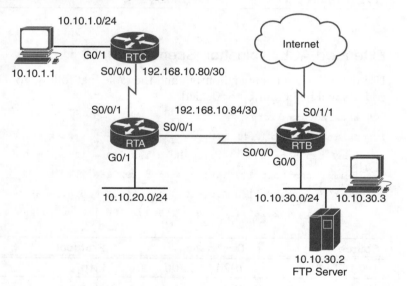

Scenario

A single access list needs to be created to deny the 10.10.1.0 /24 network and the 10.10.20.0 /24 network from reaching the 10.10.30.0 /24 network. The host 10.10.1.1 should have access to the FTP server only. The rest of the 10.0.0.0 network should have access to the 10.10.30.0 /24 network. All devices should be able to access the Internet.

Question 1

What should be the first line of the new access list in the practice scenario just described?

   a. `access-list 101 permit ip 10.10.1.1 0.0.0.0 10.10.30.0 0.0.0.255`

   b. `access-list 101 deny ip 10.10.1.0 0.0.0.255 10.10.30.0 0.0.0.255`

   c. `access-list 10 deny 10.10.1.0 0.0.0.255`

   d. `access-list 101 permit ip host 10.10.1.1 host 10.10.30.2`

Question 2

What should be the second line of the new access list in the practice scenario just described?

   a. `access-list 101 permit ip host 10.10.1.1  host 10.10.30.0 0.0.0.255`

   b. `access-list 101 deny ip 10.10.1.0 0.0.0.255 10.10.30.0 0.0.0.255`

   c. `access-list 101 deny ip 10.10.1.0 0.0.0.255 any`

   d. `access-list 101 permit ip host 10.10.1.1 host 10.10.30.1`

Question 3

What should be the third line of the new access list in the practice scenario just described?

   a. `access-list 101 deny ip 10.10.20.0 0.0.0.255 10.10.30.0 0.0.0.255`

   b. `access-list 101 permit ip host 10.10.1.1 10.10.30.0 0.0.0.255`

   c. `access-list 101 deny ip 10.20.1.0 0.0.0.255 any`

   d. `access-list 101 permit ip host 10.10.1.1  host 10.10.30.1 eq ftp`

Question 4

What should be the fourth line of the new access list in the practice scenario just described?

   a. `access-list 10 permit ip host 10.0.0.0 0.0.0.255`

   b. `access-list 101 permit ip 10.0.0.0 0.0.0.0 10.10.30.0 0.0.0.255`

   c. `access-list 101 deny ip 10.10.1.0 0.0.0.255 10.10.30.0 0.0.0.255 eq any`

   d. `access-list 101 permit ip any any`

Question 5

Where should the new access list in the practice scenario just described be placed to ensure its effectiveness?

   a. G 0/0 on RTB as an outbound list

   b. G 0/1 on RTA as an inbound list

   c. S 0/1/1 on RTB as an outbound list

   d. S 0/0/1 on RTA as an outbound list

Labs and Activities

Command Reference

In Table 5-1, record the command, including the correct router or switch prompt, that fits each description.

Table 5-1   Commands for Chapter 5, "ACLs for IPv4 Configuration"

Command	Description
	Configure the comment for ACL 10 "Allow only 10.1.1.10".
	Configure a standard ACL 10 statement to allow host 10.1.1.10.
	Configure a standard ACL 10 to block 10.1.1.0/24.
	Apply ACL 10 inbound on the interface.
	Configure a standard ACL 10 to block 10.1.1.0/24.
	Apply ACL 10 inbound on the interface.
	Name an extended ACL "NO_WEB".
	Configure an ACL statement for NO_WEB to block 172.16.1.0/24 from using WEB to access 10.1.1.0/24.
	List the command, other than **show run**, to view all the IPv4 and IPv6 ACLs configured on the router.
	List the command, other than **show run**, to view the placement of an IPv4 ACL.

5.1.8 Packet Tracer—Configure Numbered Standard IPv4 ACLs

Addressing Table

Device	Interface	IP Address	Subnet Mask	Default Gateway
R1	G0/0	192.168.10.1	255.255.255.0	N/A
	G0/1	192.168.11.1	255.255.255.0	
	S0/0/0	10.1.1.1	255.255.255.252	
	S0/0/1	10.3.3.1	255.255.255.252	
R2	G0/0	192.168.20.1	255.255.255.0	N/A
	S0/0/0	10.1.1.2	255.255.255.252	
	S0/0/1	10.2.2.1	255.255.255.252	
R3	G0/0	192.168.30.1	255.255.255.0	N/A
	S0/0/0	10.3.3.2	255.255.255.252	
	S0/0/1	10.2.2.2	255.255.255.252	
PC1	NIC	192.168.10.10	255.255.255.0	192.168.10.1
PC2	NIC	192.168.11.10	255.255.255.0	192.168.11.1
PC3	NIC	192.168.30.10	255.255.255.0	192.168.30.1
WebServer	NIC	192.168.20.254	255.255.255.0	192.168.20.1

Objectives

Part 1: Plan an ACL Implementation

Part 2: Configure, Apply, and Verify a Standard ACL

Background / Scenario

Standard access control lists (ACLs) are router configuration scripts that control whether a router permits or denies packets based on the source address. This activity focuses on defining filtering criteria, configuring standard ACLs, applying ACLs to router interfaces, and verifying and testing the ACL implementation. The routers are already configured, including IP addresses and Enhanced Interior Gateway Routing Protocol (EIGRP) routing.

Instructions

Part 1: Plan an ACL Implementation

Step 1:   Investigate the current network configuration.

Before applying any ACLs to a network, it is important to confirm that you have full connectivity. Verify that the network has full connectivity by choosing a PC and pinging other devices on the network. You should be able to successfully ping every device.

Step 2:   Evaluate two network policies and plan ACL implementations.

   a.   The following network policies are implemented on **R2**:

   - The 192.168.11.0/24 network is not allowed access to the **WebServer** on the 192.168.20.0/24 network.

   - All other access is permitted.

   To restrict access from the 192.168.11.0/24 network to the **WebServer** at 192.168.20.254 without interfering with other traffic, an ACL must be created on **R2**. The access list must be placed on the outbound interface to the **WebServer**. A second rule must be created on **R2** to permit all other traffic.

   b.   The following network policies are implemented on **R3**:

   - The 192.168.10.0/24 network is not allowed to communicate with the 192.168.30.0/24 network.

   - All other access is permitted.

   To restrict access from the 192.168.10.0/24 network to the 192.168.30/24 network without interfering with other traffic, an access list will need to be created on **R3**. The ACL must be placed on the outbound interface to **PC3**. A second rule must be created on **R3** to permit all other traffic.

Part 2: Configure, Apply, and Verify a Standard ACL

Step 1:   Configure and apply a numbered standard ACL on R2.

   a.   Create an ACL using the number **1** on **R2** with a statement that denies access to the 192.168.20.0/24 network from the 192.168.11.0/24 network.

   ```
   R2(config)# access-list 1 deny 192.168.11.0 0.0.0.255
   ```

   b.   By default, an access list denies all traffic that does not match any rules. To permit all other traffic, configure the following statement:

   ```
   R2(config)# access-list 1 permit any
   ```

   c.   Before applying an access list to an interface to filter traffic, it is a best practice to review the contents of the access list to verify that it will filter traffic as expected.

   ```
   R2# show access-lists
   Standard IP access list 1
        10 deny 192.168.11.0 0.0.0.255
        20 permit any
   ```

   d.   For the ACL to actually filter traffic, it must be applied to some router operation. Apply the ACL by placing it for outbound traffic on the GigabitEthernet 0/0 interface. Note: In an actual operational network, it is not a good practice to apply an untested access list to an active interface.

   ```
   R2(config)# interface GigabitEthernet0/0
   R2(config-if)# ip access-group 1 out
   ```

Step 2:   Configure and apply a numbered standard ACL on R3.

a.   Create an ACL using the number **1** on **R3** with a statement that denies access to the 192.168.30.0/24 network from the **PC1** (192.168.10.0/24) network.

```
R3(config)# access-list 1 deny 192.168.10.0 0.0.0.255
```

b.   By default, an ACL denies all traffic that does not match any rules. To permit all other traffic, create a second rule for ACL 1.

```
R3(config)# access-list 1 permit any
```

c.   Verify that the access list is configured correctly.

```
R3# show access-lists
Standard IP access list 1
       10 deny 192.168.10.0 0.0.0.255
       20 permit any
```

d.   Apply the ACL by placing it for outbound traffic on the GigabitEthernet 0/0 interface.

```
R3(config)# interface GigabitEthernet0/0
R3(config-if)# ip access-group 1 out
```

Step 3:   Verify ACL configuration and functionality.

a.   Enter the **show run** or **show ip interface gigabitethernet 0/0** command to verify the ACL placements.

b.   With the two ACLs in place, network traffic is restricted according to the policies detailed in Part 1. Use the following tests to verify the ACL implementations:

- A ping from 192.168.10.10 to 192.168.11.10 succeeds.

- A ping from 192.168.10.10 to 192.168.20.254 succeeds.

- A ping from 192.168.11.10 to 192.168.20.254 fails.

- A ping from 192.168.10.10 to 192.168.30.10 fails.

- A ping from 192.168.11.10 to 192.168.30.10 succeeds.

- A ping from 192.168.30.10 to 192.168.20.254 succeeds.

c.   Issue the **show access-lists** command again on routers **R2** and **R3**. You should see output that indicates the number of packets that have matched each line of the access list. Note: The number of matches shown for your routers may be different, due to the number of pings that are sent and received.

```
R2# show access-lists
Standard IP access list 1
       10 deny 192.168.11.0 0.0.0.255 (4 match(es))
       20 permit any (8 match(es))

R3# show access-lists
Standard IP access list 1
       10 deny 192.168.10.0 0.0.0.255 (4 match(es))
       20 permit any (8 match(es))
```

5.1.9 Packet Tracer—Configure Named Standard IPv4 ACLs

Addressing Table

Device	Interface	IP Address	Subnet Mask	Default Gateway
R1	F0/0	192.168.10.1	255.255.255.0	N/A
	F0/1	192.168.20.1	255.255.255.0	
	E0/0/0	192.168.100.1	255.255.255.0	
	E0/1/0	192.168.200.1	255.255.255.0	
File Server	NIC	192.168.200.100	255.255.255.0	192.168.200.1
Web Server	NIC	192.168.100.100	255.255.255.0	192.168.100.1
PC0	NIC	192.168.20.3	255.255.255.0	192.168.20.1
PC1	NIC	192.168.20.4	255.255.255.0	192.168.20.1
PC2	NIC	192.168.10.3	255.255.255.0	192.168.10.1

Objectives

Part 1: Configure and Apply a Named Standard ACL

Part 2: Verify the ACL Implementation

Background / Scenario

The senior network administrator has asked you to create a standard named ACL to prevent access to a file server. The file server contains the database for the web applications. Only the Web Manager workstation PC1 and the Web Server need to access the File Server. All other traffic to the File Server should be denied.

Instructions

Part 1: Configure and Apply a Named Standard ACL

Step 1:   Verify connectivity before the ACL is configured and applied.

All three workstations should be able to ping both the **Web Server** and **File Server**.

Step 2:   Configure a named standard ACL.

a.   Configure the following named ACL on **R1**.

```
R1(config)# ip access-list standard File_Server_Restrictions
R1(config-std-nacl)# permit host 192.168.20.4
R1(config-std-nacl)# permit host 192.168.100.100
R1(config-std-nacl)# deny any
```

Note: For scoring purposes, the ACL name is case-sensitive, and the statements must be in the same order as shown.

b. Use the **show access-lists** command to verify the contents of the access list before applying it to an interface. Make sure you have not mistyped any IP addresses and that the statements are in the correct order.

```
R1# show access-lists
Standard IP access list File_Server_Restrictions
10 permit host 192.168.20.4
20 permit host 192.168.100.100
30 deny any
```

Step 3:   Apply the named ACL.

a. Apply the ACL outbound on the Fast Ethernet 0/1 interface.

Note: In an actual operational network, applying an access list to an active interface is not a good practice and should be avoided if possible.

```
R1(config-if)# ip access-group File_Server_Restrictions out
```

b. Save the configuration.

Part 2: Verify the ACL Implementation

Step 1:   Verify the ACL configuration and application to the interface.

Use the **show access-lists** command to verify the ACL configuration. Use the **show run** or **show ip interface fastethernet 0/1** command to verify that the ACL is applied correctly to the interface.

Step 2:   Verify that the ACL is working properly.

All three workstations should be able to ping the **Web Server**, but only **PC1** and the **Web Server** should be able to ping the **File Server**. Repeat the **show access-lists** command to see the number of packets that matched each statement.

5.2.7 Packet Tracer—Configure and Modify Standard IPv4 ACLs

Addressing Table

Device	Interface	IP Address	Subnet Mask	Default Gateway
R1	G0/0/0	192.168.10.1	255.255.255.0	N/A
	G0/0/1	192.168.20.1	255.255.255.0	
	S0/1/0 (DCE)	10.1.1.1	255.255.255.252	
Edge	S0/1/0	10.1.1.2	255.255.255.252	N/A
	S0/1/1 (DCE)	10.2.2.2	255.255.255.252	
	S0/2/1	209.165.200.225	255.255.255.224	
R3	G0/0/0	192.168.30.1	255.255.255.0	N/A
	G0/0/1	192.168.40.1	255.255.255.0	
	S0/1/1	10.2.2.1	255.255.255.252	
S1	VLAN 1	192.168.10.11	255.255.255.0	192.168.10.1
S2	VLAN 1	192.168.20.11	255.255.255.0	192.168.20.1
S3	VLAN 1	192.168.30.11	255.255.255.0	192.168.30.1
S4	VLAN 1	192.168.40.11	255.255.255.0	192.168.40.1
PC-A	NIC	192.168.10.3	255.255.255.0	192.168.10.1
PC-B	NIC	192.168.20.3	255.255.255.0	192.168.20.1
PC-C	NIC	192.168.30.3	255.255.255.0	192.168.30.1
PC-D	NIC	192.168.40.3	255.255.255.0	192.168.40.1

Objectives

Part 1: Verify Connectivity

Part 2: Configure and Verify Standard Numbered and Named ACLs

Part 3: Modify a Standard ACL

Background / Scenario

Network security and traffic flow control are important issues when designing and managing IP networks. The ability to configure proper rules to filter packets, based on established security policies, is a valuable skill.

In this lab, you will set up filtering rules for two business locations that are represented by R1 and R3. Management has established some access policies between the LANs located at R1 and R3, which you must implement. The Edge router sitting between R1 and R3 has been provided by the ISP will not have any ACLs placed on it. You would not be allowed any administrative access to the Edge router because you can only control and manage your own equipment.

Instructions

Part 1: Verify Connectivity

In Part 1, you verify connectivity between devices.

Note: It is very important to test whether connectivity is working **before** you configure and apply access lists. You want to be sure that your network is properly functioning before you start to filter traffic.

Questions:

From PC-A, ping PC-C and PC-D. Were your pings successful?

From R1, ping PC-C and PC-D. Were your pings successful?

From PC-C, ping PC-A and PC-B. Were your pings successful?

From R3, ping PC-A and PC-B. Were your pings successful?

Can all of the PCs ping the server at 209.165.200.254?

Part 2: Configure and Verify Standard Numbered and Named ACLs

Step 1:   Configure a numbered standard ACL.

Standard ACLs filter traffic based on the source IP address only. A typical best practice for standard ACLs is to configure and apply the ACL as close to the destination as possible. For the first access list in this activity, create a standard numbered ACL that allows traffic from all hosts on the 192.168.10.0/24 network and all hosts on the 192.168.20.0/24 network to access all hosts on the 192.168.30.0/24 network. The security policy also states that an explicit **deny any** access control entry (ACE), also referred to as an ACL statement, should be present at the end of all ACLs.

Questions:

What wildcard mask would you use to allow all hosts on the 192.168.10.0/24 network to access the 192.168.30.0/24 network?

Following Cisco's recommended best practices, on which router would you place this ACL?

On which interface would you place this ACL? In what direction would you apply it?

a. Configure the ACL on R3. Use 1 for the access list number.

```
R3(config)# access-list 1 remark Allow R1 LANs Access
R3(config)# access-list 1 permit 192.168.10.0 0.0.0.255
R3(config)# access-list 1 permit 192.168.20.0 0.0.0.255
R3(config)# access-list 1 deny any
```

b. Apply the ACL to the appropriate interface in the proper direction.

```
R3(config)# interface g0/0/0
R3(config-if)# ip access-group 1 out
```

c. Verify a numbered ACL.

The use of various **show** commands can help you to verify both the syntax and placement of your ACLs in your router.

Questions:

To see access list 1 in its entirety with all ACEs, which command would you use?

_____

What command would you use to see where the access list was applied and in what direction?

_____

1) On R3, issue the **show access-lists 1** command.

```
R3# show access-list 1
Standard IP access list 1
    permit 192.168.10.0, wildcard bits 0.0.0.255
    permit 192.168.20.0, wildcard bits 0.0.0.255
    deny any
```

2) On R3, issue the **show ip interface g0/0/0** command.

```
R3# show ip interface g0/0/0
GigabitEthernet0/0/0 is up, line protocol is up (connected)
  Internet address is 192.168.30.1/24
  Broadcast address is 255.255.255.255
  Address determined by setup command
  MTU is 1500 bytes
  Helper address is not set
  Directed broadcast forwarding is disabled
  Outgoing access list is 1
  Inbound access list is not set
  <Output omitted>
```

Questions:

3) Test the ACL to see if it allows traffic from the 192.168.10.0/24 network to access the 192.168.30.0/24 network.

From the PC-A command prompt, ping the PC-C IP address. Were the pings successful?

_____

4) Test the ACL to see if it allows traffic from the 192.168.20.0/24 network access to the 192.168.30.0/24 network.

From the PC-B command prompt, ping the PC-C IP address. Were the pings successful?

_____

5) Should pings from PC-D to PC-C be successful? Ping from PC-D to PC-C to verify your answer.

_____

d. From the R1 prompt, ping PC-C's IP address again.

```
R1# ping 192.168.30.3
```

Question:

Was the ping successful? Explain.

_____

e. Issue the **show access-lists 1** command again. Note that the command output displays information for the number of times each ACE was matched by traffic that reached interface Gigabit Ethernet 0/0/0.

```
R3# show access-lists 1
Standard IP access list 1
    permit 192.168.10.0 0.0.0.255 (4 match(es))
    permit 192.168.20.0 0.0.0.255 (4 match(es))
    deny any (4 match(es))
```

Step 2:   Configure a named standard ACL.

Create a named standard ACL that conforms to the following policy: allow traffic from all hosts on the 192.168.40.0/24 network access to all hosts on the 192.168.10.0/24 network. Also, only allow host PC-C access to the 192.168.10.0/24 network. The name of this access list should be called BRANCH-OFFICE-POLICY.

Questions:

Following Cisco's recommended best practices, on which router would you place this ACL?

_____

On which interface would you place this ACL? In what direction would you apply it?

_____

a. Create the standard named ACL BRANCH-OFFICE-POLICY on R1.

```
R1(config)# ip access-list standard BRANCH-OFFICE-POLICY
R1(config-std-nacl)# permit host 192.168.30.3
R1(config-std-nacl)# permit 192.168.40.0 0.0.0.255
```

```
R1(config-std-nacl)# end
R1#
*Feb 15 15:56:55.707: %SYS-5-CONFIG_I: Configured from console by
console
```

Question:

Look at the first ACE in the access list. What is another way to write this?

_____

b. Apply the ACL to the appropriate interface in the proper direction.

```
R1# config t
R1(config)# interface g0/0/0
R1(config-if)# ip access-group BRANCH-OFFICE-POLICY out
```

c. Verify a named ACL.

1) On R1, issue the show access-lists command.

```
R1# show access-lists
Standard IP access list BRANCH-OFFICE-POLICY
    10 permit host 192.168.30.3
    20 permit 192.168.40.0 0.0.0.255
```

Question:

Is there any difference between this ACL on R1 and the ACL on R3? If so, what is it?

_____

2) On R1, issue the **show ip interface g0/0/0** command to verify that the ACL is configured on the interface.

```
R1# show ip interface g0/0/0
GigabitEthernet0/0/0 is up, line protocol is up (connected)
    Internet address is 192.168.10.1/24
    Broadcast address is 255.255.255.255
    Address determined by setup command
    MTU is 1500 bytes
    Helper address is not set
    Directed broadcast forwarding is disabled
    Outgoing access list is BRANCH-OFFICE-POLICY
    Inbound  access list is not set
<Output omitted>
```

Question:

Test the ACL. From the command prompt on PC-C, ping the IP address of PC-A. Were the pings successful?

_____

3) Test the ACL to ensure that only the PC-C host is allowed access to the 192.168.10.0/24 network. You must do an extended ping and use the G0/0/0 address on R3 as your source. Ping PC-A's IP address.

```
R3# ping
Protocol [ip]:
Target IP address: 192.168.10.3
```

```
Repeat count [5]:
Datagram size [100]:
Timeout in seconds [2]:
Extended commands [n]: y
Source address or interface: 192.168.30.1
Type of service [0]:
Set DF bit in IP header? [no]:
Validate reply data? [no]:
Data pattern [0xABCD]:
Loose, Strict, Record, Timestamp, Verbose[none]:
Sweep range of sizes [n]:
Type escape sequence to abort.
Sending 5, 100-byte ICMP Echos to 192.168.10.3, timeout is 2
seconds:
Packet sent with a source address of 192.168.30.1
U.U.U
```

Question:

Were the pings successful?

4) Test the ACL to see if it allows traffic from the 192.168.40.0/24 network access to the 192.168.10.0/24 network. From the PC-D command prompt, ping the PC-A IP address.

Question:

Were the pings successful?

Part 3: Modify a Standard ACL

It is common in business for security policies to change. For this reason, ACLs may need to be modified. In Part 3, you will change one of the ACLs you configured previously to match a new management policy that is being put in place.

Attempt to ping the server at 209.165.200.254 from PC-A. Notice that the ping is not successful. The ACL on R1 is blocking Internet traffic from returning to PC-A. This is because the source address in the packets that are returned is not in the range of permitted addresses.

Management has decided that traffic that is returning from the 209.165.200.224/27 network should be allowed full access to the 192.168.10.0/24 network. Management also wants ACLs on all routers to follow consistent rules. A **deny any** ACE should be placed at the end of all ACLs. You must modify the BRANCH-OFFICE-POLICY ACL.

You will add two additional lines to this ACL. There are two ways you could do this:

OPTION 1: Issue a **no ip access-list standard BRANCH-OFFICE-POLICY** command in global configuration mode. This would remove the ACL from the router. Depending upon the router IOS, one of the following scenarios would occur: all filtering of packets would be cancelled, and all packets would be allowed through the router; or, because you did not remove the **ip access-group** command from the G0/1 interface, filtering is still in place. Regardless, when the ACL is gone, you could retype the whole ACL, or cut and paste it in from a text editor.

OPTION 2: You can modify ACLs in place by adding or deleting specific lines within the ACL itself. This can come in handy, especially with ACLs that are long. The retyping of the whole ACL or cutting and pasting can easily lead to errors. Modifying specific lines within the ACL is easily accomplished.

For this activity, use Option 2.

Step 1:   Modify a named standard ACL.

   a.   From R1, issue the **show access-lists** command.

```
R1# show access-lists
Standard IP access list BRANCH-OFFICE-POLICY
    10 permit 192.168.30.3 (8 matches)
    20 permit 192.168.40.0 0.0.0.255 (5 matches)
```

   b.   Add two additional lines at the end of the ACL. From global config mode, modify the ACL, BRANCH-OFFICE-POLICY.

```
R1#(config)# ip access-list standard BRANCH-OFFICE-POLICY
R1(config-std-nacl)# 30 permit 209.165.200.224 0.0.0.31
R1(config-std-nacl)# 40 deny any
R1(config-std-nacl)# end
```

   c.   Verify the ACL.

   1)   On R1, issue the **show access-lists** command.

```
R1# show access-lists
Standard IP access list BRANCH-OFFICE-POLICY
    10 permit 192.168.30.3 (8 matches)
    20 permit 192.168.40.0, wildcard bits 0.0.0.255 (5 matches)
    30 permit 209.165.200.224, wildcard bits 0.0.0.31
    40 deny any
```

   Question:

   Do you have to apply the BRANCH-OFFICE-POLICY to the G0/1 interface on R1?

   _____

   2)   Test the ACL to see if it allows traffic from the 209.165.200.224/27 network access to return to the 192.168.10.0/24 network. From PC-A, ping the server at 209.165.200.254.

   Question:

   Were the pings successful?

   _____

Reflection Questions

1.   As you can see, standard ACLs are very powerful and work quite well. Why would you ever have the need for using extended ACLs?

_____

2.   More typing is typically required when using a named ACL as opposed to a numbered ACL. Why would you choose named ACLs over numbered?

_____

5.4.12 Packet Tracer—Configure Extended ACLs—Scenario 1

Addressing Table

Device	Interface	IP Address	Subnet Mask	Default Gateway
R1	G0/0	172.22.34.65	255.255.255.224	N/A
	G0/1	172.22.34.97	255.255.255.240	
	G0/2	172.22.34.1	255.255.255.192	
Server	NIC	172.22.34.62	255.255.255.192	172.22.34.1
PC1	NIC	172.22.34.66	255.255.255.224	172.22.34.65
PC2	NIC	172.22.34.98	255.255.255.240	172.22.34.97

Objectives

Part 1: Configure, Apply, and Verify an Extended Numbered ACL

Part 2: Configure, Apply, and Verify an Extended Named ACL

Background / Scenario

Two employees need access to services provided by the server. **PC1** only needs FTP access, while **PC2** only needs web access. Both computers need to be able to ping the server but not each other.

Instructions

Part 1: Configure, Apply, and Verify an Extended Numbered ACL

Step 1:   Configure an ACL to permit FTP and ICMP from PC1 LAN.

    a.   From global configuration mode on **R1**, enter the following command to determine the first valid number for an extended access list.

```
R1(config)# access-list ?
  <1-99>     IP standard access list
  <100-199>  IP extended access list
```

    b.   Add **100** to the command, followed by a question mark.

```
R1(config)# access-list 100 ?
  deny    Specify packets to reject
  permit  Specify packets to forward
  remark  Access list entry comment
```

    c.   To permit FTP traffic, enter **permit**, followed by a question mark.

```
R1(config)# access-list 100 permit ?
  ahp     Authentication Header Protocol
  eigrp   Cisco's EIGRP routing protocol
```

```
esp      Encapsulation Security Payload
gre      Cisco's GRE tunneling
icmp     Internet Control Message Protocol
ip       Any Internet Protocol
ospf     OSPF routing protocol
tcp      Transmission Control Protocol
udp      User Datagram Protocol
```

d. When configured and applied, this ACL should permit FTP and ICMP. ICMP is listed above, but FTP is not. This is because FTP is an application layer protocol that uses TCP at the transport layer. Enter TCP to further refine the ACL help.

```
R1(config)# access-list 100 permit tcp ?
A.B.C.D   Source address
any       Any source host
host      A single source host
```

e. The source address can represent a single device, such as PC1, by using the **host** keyword and then the IP address of PC1. Using the keyword **any** permits any host on any network. Filtering can also be done by a network address. In this case, it is any host that has an address belonging to the 172.22.34.64/27 network. Enter this network address, followed by a question mark.

```
R1(config)# access-list 100 permit tcp 172.22.34.64 ?
A.B.C.D   Source wildcard bits
```

f. Calculate the wildcard mask by determining the binary opposite of the /27 subnet mask.

```
11111111.11111111.11111111.11100000 = 255.255.255.224
00000000.00000000.00000000.00011111 = 0.0.0.31
```

g. Enter the wildcard mask, followed by a question mark.

```
R1(config)# access-list 100 permit tcp 172.22.34.64 0.0.0.31 ?
A.B.C.D   Destination address
any       Any destination host
eq        Match only packets on a given port number
gt        Match only packets with a greater port number
host      A single destination host
lt        Match only packets with a lower port number
neq       Match only packets not on a given port number
range     Match only packets in the range of port numbers
```

h. Configure the destination address. In this scenario, we are filtering traffic for a single destination, which is the server. Enter the host keyword followed by the server's IP address.

```
R1(config)# access-list 100 permit tcp 172.22.34.64 0.0.0.31 host
172.22.34.62 ?
dscp          Match packets with given dscp value
eq            Match only packets on a given port number
established   established
gt            Match only packets with a greater port number
lt            Match only packets with a lower port number
neq           Match only packets not on a given port number
precedence    Match packets with given precedence value
range         Match only packets in the range of port numbers
<cr>
```

i. Notice that one of the options is **<cr>** (carriage return). In other words, you can press **Enter** and the statement would permit all TCP traffic. However, we are only permitting FTP traffic; therefore, enter the **eq** keyword, followed by a question mark to display the available options. Then, enter **ftp** and press **Enter**.

```
R1(config)# access-list 100 permit tcp 172.22.34.64 0.0.0.31 host
172.22.34.62 eq ?
  <0-65535>   Port number
  ftp         File Transfer Protocol (21)
  pop3        Post Office Protocol v3 (110)
  smtp        Simple Mail Transport Protocol (25)
  telnet      Telnet (23)
  www         World Wide Web (HTTP, 80)
R1(config)# access-list 100 permit tcp 172.22.34.64 0.0.0.31 host
172.22.34.62 eq ftp
```

j. Create a second access list statement to permit ICMP (ping, etc.) traffic from PC1 to Server. Note that the access list number remains the same and a specific type of ICMP traffic does not need to be specified.

```
R1(config)# access-list 100 permit icmp 172.22.34.64 0.0.0.31 host
172.22.34.62
```

k. All other traffic is denied, by default.

l. Execute the **show access-list** command and verify that access list 100 contains the correct statements. Notice that the statement **deny any any** does not appear at the end of the access list. The default execution of an access list is that if a packet does not match a statement in the access list, it is not permitted through the interface.

```
R1# show access-lists
Extended IP access list 100
    10 permit tcp 172.22.34.64 0.0.0.31 host 172.22.34.62 eq ftp
    20 permit icmp 172.22.34.64 0.0.0.31 host 172.22.34.62
```

Step 2: Apply the ACL on the correct interface to filter traffic.

From **R1**'s perspective, the traffic that ACL 100 applies to is inbound from the network connected to the Gigabit Ethernet 0/0 interface. Enter interface configuration mode and apply the ACL.

Note: On an actual operational network, it is not a good practice to apply an untested access list to an active interface.

```
R1(config)# interface gigabitEthernet 0/0
R1(config-if)# ip access-group 100 in
```

Step 3: Verify the ACL implementation.

a. Ping from PC1 to Server. If the pings are unsuccessful, verify the IP addresses before continuing.

b. FTP from PC1 to Server. The username and password are both **cisco**.

```
PC> ftp 172.22.34.62
```

c. Exit the FTP service.

```
ftp> quit
```

    d. Ping from PC1 to PC2. The destination host should be unreachable, because the ACL did not explicitly permit the traffic.

Part 2: Configure, Apply, and Verify an Extended Named ACL

Step 1:   Configure an ACL to permit HTTP access and ICMP from PC2 LAN.

    a. Named ACLs start with the **ip** keyword. From global configuration mode of **R1**, enter the following command, followed by a question mark.

```
R1(config)# ip access-list ?
  extended  Extended Access List
  standard  Standard Access List
```

    b. You can configure named standard and extended ACLs. This access list filters both source and destination IP addresses; therefore, it must be extended. Enter **HTTP_ONLY** as the name. (For Packet Tracer scoring, the name is case-sensitive and the access list statements must be the correct order.)

```
R1(config)# ip access-list extended HTTP_ONLY
```

    c. The prompt changes. You are now in extended named ACL configuration mode. All devices on the **PC2** LAN need TCP access. Enter the network address, followed by a question mark.

```
R1(config-ext-nacl)# permit tcp 172.22.34.96 ?
  A.B.C.D  Source wildcard bits
```

    d. An alternative way to calculate a wildcard is to subtract the subnet mask from **255.255.255.255.**

```
  255.255.255.255
- 255.255.255.240
-----------------
=   0.  0.  0. 15
R1(config-ext-nacl)# permit tcp 172.22.34.96 0.0.0.15
```

    e. Finish the statement by specifying the server address as you did in Part 1 and filtering **www** traffic.

```
R1(config-ext-nacl)# permit tcp 172.22.34.96 0.0.0.15 host 172.22.34.62
eq www
```

    f. Create a second access list statement to permit ICMP (ping, etc.) traffic from **PC2** to **Server**.

Note: The prompt remains the same and a specific type of ICMP traffic does not need to be specified.

```
R1(config-ext-nacl)# permit icmp 172.22.34.96 0.0.0.15 host 172.22.34.62
```

    g. All other traffic is denied, by default. Exit extended named ACL configuration mode.

    h. Execute the **show access-list** command and verify that access list **HTTP_ONLY** contains the correct statements.

```
R1# show access-lists
Extended IP access list 100
10 permit tcp 172.22.34.64 0.0.0.31 host 172.22.34.62 eq ftp
20 permit icmp 172.22.34.64 0.0.0.31 host 172.22.34.62
```

```
Extended IP access list HTTP_ONLY
 10 permit tcp 172.22.34.96 0.0.0.15 host 172.22.34.62 eq www
 20 permit icmp 172.22.34.96 0.0.0.15 host 172.22.34.62
```

Step 2:   Apply the ACL on the correct interface to filter traffic.

From **R1**'s perspective, the traffic that access list **HTTP_ONLY** applies to is inbound from the network connected to the Gigabit Ethernet 0/1 interface. Enter interface configuration mode and apply the ACL.

Note: On an actual operational network, it is not a good practice to apply an untested access list to an active interface. It should be avoided if possible.

```
R1(config)# interface gigabitEthernet 0/1
R1(config-if)# ip access-group HTTP_ONLY in
```

Step 3:   Verify the ACL implementation.

   a.   Ping from **PC2** to **Server**. If the ping is unsuccessful, verify the IP addresses before continuing.

   b.   From PC2 open a web browser and enter the IP address of the Server. The web page of the Server should be displayed.

   c.   FTP from **PC2** to **Server**. The connection should fail. If not, troubleshoot the access list statements and the access-group configurations on the interfaces.

5.4.13 Packet Tracer—Configure Extended IPv4 ACLs—Scenario 2

Addressing Table

Device	Interface	IP Address	Subnet Mask	Default Gateway
RT1	G0/0	172.31.1.126	255.255.255.224	N/A
	S0/0/0	209.165.1.2	255.255.255.252	
PC1	NIC	172.31.1.101	255.255.255.224	172.31.1.126
PC2	NIC	172.31.1.102	255.255.255.224	172.31.1.126
PC3	NIC	172.31.1.103	255.255.255.224	172.31.1.126
Server1	NIC	64.101.255.254		
Server2	NIC	64.103.255.254		

Objectives

Part 1: Configure a Named Extended ACL

Part 2: Apply and Verify the Extended ACL

Background / Scenario

In this scenario, specific devices on the LAN are allowed to various services on servers located on the Internet.

Instructions

Part 1: Configure a Named Extended ACL

Configure one named ACL to implement the following policy:

- Block HTTP and HTTPS access from **PC1** to **Server1** and **Server2**. The servers are inside the cloud, and you only know their IP addresses.

- Block FTP access from **PC2** to **Server1** and **Server2**.

- Block ICMP access from **PC3** to **Server1** and **Server2**.

Note: For scoring purposes, you must configure the statements in the order specified in the following steps.

Step 1:   Deny PC1 access to HTTP and HTTPS services on Server1 and Server2.

a.   Create a named extended IP access list on router RT1 which will deny **PC1** access to the HTTP and HTTPS services of **Server1** and **Server2**. Four access control statements are required.

Question:

What is the command to begin the configuration of an extended access list with the name ACL?

b. Begin the ACL configuration with a statement that denies access from **PC1** to **Server1**, only for HTTP (port 80). Refer to the addressing table for the IP address of **PC1** and **Server1**.

```
RT1(config-ext-nacl)# deny tcp host 172.31.1.101 host 64.101.255.254
eq 80
```

c. Next, enter the statement that denies access from **PC1** to **Server1**, only for HTTPS (port 443).

```
RT1(config-ext-nacl)# deny tcp host 172.31.1.101 host 64.101.255.254
eq 443
```

d. Enter the statement that denies access from **PC1** to **Server2**, only for HTTP. Refer to the addressing table for the IP address of **Server 2**.

```
RT1(config-ext-nacl)# deny tcp host 172.31.1.101 host 64.103.255.254
eq 80
```

e. Enter the statement that denies access from **PC1** to **Server2**, only for HTTPS.

```
RT1(config-ext-nacl)# deny tcp host 172.31.1.101 host 64.103.255.254
eq 443
```

Step 2: Deny PC2 to access FTP services on Server1 and Server2.

Refer to the addressing table for the IP address of **PC2**.

a. Enter the statement that denies access from **PC2** to **Server1**, only for FTP (port 21 only).

```
RT1(config-ext-nacl)# deny tcp host 172.31.1.102 host 64.101.255.254
eq 21
```

b. Enter the statement that denies access from **PC2** to **Server2**, only for FTP (port 21 only).

```
RT1(config-ext-nacl)# deny tcp host 172.31.1.102 host 64.103.255.254
eq 21
```

Step 3: Deny PC3 to ping Server1 and Server2.

Refer to the addressing table for the IP address of **PC3**.

a. Enter the statement that denies ICMP access from **PC3** to **Server1**.

```
RT1(config-ext-nacl)# deny icmp host 172.31.1.103 host 64.101.255.254
```

b. Enter the statement that denies ICMP access from **PC3** to **Server2**.

```
RT1(config-ext-nacl)# deny icmp host 172.31.1.103 host 64.103.255.254
```

Step 4: Permit all other IP traffic.

By default, an access list denies all traffic that does not match any rule in the list. Enter the command that permits all traffic that does not match any of the configured access list statements.

Step 5: Verify the access list configuration before applying it to an interface.

Before any access list is applied, the configuration needs to be verified to make sure that there are no typographical errors and that the statements are in the correct order. To view the current configuration of the access list, use either the **show access-lists** or the **show running-config** command.

```
RT1# show access-lists
Extended IP access list ACL
    10 deny tcp host 172.31.1.101 host 64.101.255.254 eq www
    20 deny tcp host 172.31.1.101 host 64.101.255.254 eq 443
    30 deny tcp host 172.31.1.101 host 64.103.255.254 eq www
    40 deny tcp host 172.31.1.101 host 64.103.255.254 eq 443
    50 deny tcp host 172.31.1.102 host 64.101.255.254 eq ftp
    60 deny tcp host 172.31.1.102 host 64.103.255.254 eq ftp
    70 deny icmp host 172.31.1.103 host 64.101.255.254
    80 deny icmp host 172.31.1.103 host 64.103.255.254
    90 permit ip any any


RT1# show running-config | begin access-list
ip access-list extended ACL
    deny tcp host 172.31.1.101 host 64.101.255.254 eq www
    deny tcp host 172.31.1.101 host 64.101.255.254 eq 443
    deny tcp host 172.31.1.101 host 64.103.255.254 eq www
    deny tcp host 172.31.1.101 host 64.103.255.254 eq 443
    deny tcp host 172.31.1.102 host 64.101.255.254 eq ftp
    deny tcp host 172.31.1.102 host 64.103.255.254 eq ftp
    deny icmp host 172.31.1.103 host 64.101.255.254
    deny icmp host 172.31.1.103 host 64.103.255.254
    permit ip any any
```

Note: The difference between the output of the **show access-lists** command and the output of the **show running-config** command is that the **show access-lists** command includes the sequence numbers assigned to the configuration statements. These sequence numbers enable the editing, deleting, and inserting of single lines within the access list configuration. Sequence numbers also define the processing order of individual access control statements, starting with the lowest sequence number.

Part 2: Apply and Verify the Extended ACL

The traffic to be filtered is coming from the 172.31.1.96/27 network and is destined for remote networks. Appropriate ACL placement depends on the relationship of the traffic with respect to **RT1**. In general, extended access lists should be placed on the interface closest to the source of the traffic.

Step 1:   Apply the ACL to the correct interface and in the correct direction.

Note: In an actual operational network, an untested ACL should never be applied to an active interface. This is not a good practice and can disrupt network operation.

Question:

On which interface should the named ACL be applied, and in which direction?

Enter the configuration commands to apply the ACL to the interface.

Step 2:   Test access for each PC.

a. Access the websites of **Server1** and **Server2** using the web browser of **PC1**. Use both the HTTP and HTTPS protocols. Use the **show access-lists** command to view which access list statement permitted or denied the traffic. The output of the **show access-lists** command displays the number of packets that match each statement since the last time the counters were cleared, or the router rebooted.

Note: To clear the counters on an access list, use the **clear access-list counters** command.

```
RT1# show ip access-lists
Extended IP access list ACL
10 deny tcp host 172.31.1.101 host 64.101.255.254 eq www (12 match(es))
20 deny tcp host 172.31.1.101 host 64.101.255.254 eq 443 (12 match(es))
30 deny tcp host 172.31.1.101 host 64.103.255.254 eq www
40 deny tcp host 172.31.1.101 host 64.103.255.254 eq 443
50 deny tcp host 172.31.1.102 host 64.101.255.254 eq ftp
60 deny tcp host 172.31.1.102 host 64.103.255.254 eq ftp
70 deny icmp host 172.31.1.103 host 64.101.255.254
80 deny icmp host 172.31.1.103 host 64.103.255.254
90 permit ip any any
```

b. Access FTP of **Server1** and **Server2** using **PC1**. The username and password is **cisco**.

c. Ping **Server1** and **Server2** from **PC1**.

d. Repeat Step 2a to Step 2c with **PC2** and **PC3** to verify proper access list operation.

5.5.1 Packet Tracer—IPv4 ACL Implementation Challenge

Addressing Table

Device	Interface	IP Address
Branch	G0/0/0	192.168.1.1/26
	G0/0/1	192.168.1.65/29
	S0/1/0	192.0.2.1/30
	S0/1/1	192.168.3.1/30
HQ	G0/0/0	192.168.2.1/27
	G0/0/1	192.168.2.33/28
	S0/1/1	192.168.3.2/30
PC-1	NIC	192.168.1.10/26
PC-2	NIC	192.168.1.20/26
PC-3	NIC	192.168.1.30/26
Admin	NIC	192.168.1.67/29
Enterprise Web Server	NIC	192.168.1.70/29
Branch PC	NIC	192.168.2.17/27
Branch Server	NIC	192.168.2.45/28
Internet User	NIC	198.51.100.218/24
External Web Server	NIC	203.0.113.73/24

Objectives

- Configure a router with standard named ACLs.
- Configure a router with extended named ACLs.
- Configure a router with extended ACLs to meet specific communication requirements.
- Configure an ACL to control access to network device terminal lines.
- Configure the appropriate router interfaces with ACLs in the appropriate direction.
- Verify the operation of the configured ACLs.

Background / Scenario

In this activity, you will configure extended, standard named, and extended named ACLs to meet specified communication requirements.

Instructions

Step 1:   Verify Connectivity in the New Company Network

First, test connectivity on the network as it is before configuring the ACLs. All hosts should be able to ping all other hosts.

Step 2:   Configure Standard and Extended ACLs per Requirements.

Configure ACLs to meet the following requirements:

Important guidelines:

- Do **not** use explicit deny any statements at the end of your ACLs.

- Use shorthand (**host** and **any**) whenever possible.

- Write your ACL statements to address the requirements in the order that they are specified here.

- Place your ACLs in the most efficient location and direction.

ACL 1 Requirements

- Create ACL **101**.

- Explicitly block FTP access to the Enterprise Web Server from the Internet.

- No ICMP traffic from the Internet should be allowed to any hosts on HQ LAN 1.

- Allow all other traffic.

ACL 2 Requirements

- Use ACL number **111**

- No hosts on HQ LAN 1 should be able to access the Branch Server.

- All other traffic should be permitted.

ACL 3 Requirements

- Create a named standard ACL. Use the name **vty_block**. The name of your ACL must match this name exactly.

- Only addresses from the HQ LAN 2 network should be able to access the VTY lines of the HQ router.

ACL 4 Requirements

- Create a named extended ACL called **branch_to_hq**. The name of your ACL must match this name exactly.

- No hosts on either of the Branch LANs should be allowed to access HQ LAN 1. Use one access list statement for each of the Branch LANs.

- All other traffic should be allowed.

Step 3:   Verify ACL Operation.

a.   Perform the following connectivity tests between devices in the topology. Note whether they are successful.

Note: Use the **show ip access-lists** command to verify ACL operation. Use the **clear access list counters** command to reset the match counters.

Questions:

Send a ping request from Branch PC to the Enterprise Web Server. Was it successful? Explain.

Which ACL statement permitted or denied the ping between these two devices? List the access list name or number, the router on which it was applied, and the specific line that the traffic matched.

_____

Attempt to ping from PC-1 on the HQ LAN 1 to the Branch Server. Was it successful? Explain.

_____

Which ACL statement permitted or denied the ping between these two devices?

_____

Open a web browser on the External Server and attempt to bring up a web page stored on the Enterprise Web Server. Is it successful? Explain.

_____

Which ACL statement permitted or denied the ping between these two devices?

_____

b. Test connections to an internal server from the Internet.

Questions:

From the command line on the Internet User PC, attempt to make an FTP connection to the Branch Server. Is the FTP connection successful?

_____

Which access list should be modified to prevent users from the Internet to make FTP connections to the Branch Server?

_____

Which statement(s) should be added to the access list to deny this traffic?

_____

5.5.2 Lab—Configure and Verify Extended IPv4 ACLs

Topology

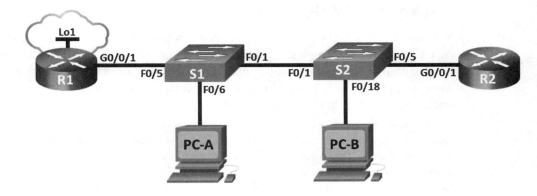

Addressing Table

Device	Interface	IP Address	Subnet Mask	Default Gateway
R1	G0/0/1	N/A	N/A	N/A
	G0/0/1.20	10.20.0.1	255.255.255.0	
	G0/0/1.30	10.30.0.1	255.255.255.0	
	G0/0/1.40	10.40.0.1	255.255.255.0	
	G0/0/1.1000	N/A	N/A	
	Loopback1	172.16.1.1	255.255.255.0	
R2	G0/0/1	10.20.0.4	255.255.255.0	N/A
S1	VLAN 20	10.20.0.2	255.255.255.0	10.20.0.1
S2	VLAN 20	10.20.0.3	255.255.255.0	10.20.0.1
PC-A	NIC	10.30.0.10	255.255.255.0	10.30.0.1
PC-B	NIC	10.40.0.10	255.255.255.0	10.40.0.1

VLAN Table

VLAN	Name	Interface Assigned
20	Management	S2: F0/5
30	Operations	S1: F0/6
40	Sales	S2: F0/18
999	ParkingLot	S1: F0/2-4, F0/7-24, G0/1-2
		S2: F0/2-4, F0/6-17, F0/19-24, G0/1-2
1000	Native	N/A

Objectives

Part 1: Build the Network and Configure Basic Device Settings

Part 2: Configure and Verify Extended Access Control Lists

Background / Scenario

You have been tasked with configuring access control lists on a small company's network. ACLs are one of the simplest and most direct means of controlling layer 3 traffic. R1 will be hosting an Internet connection (simulated by interface Loopback 1) and sharing the default route information to R2. After initial configuration is complete, the company has some specific traffic security requirements that you are responsible for implementing.

Note: The routers used with CCNA hands-on labs are Cisco 4221 with Cisco IOS XE Release 16.9.4 (universalk9 image). The switches used in the labs are Cisco Catalyst 2960s with Cisco IOS Release 15.2(2) (lanbasek9 image). Other routers, switches, and Cisco IOS versions can be used. Depending on the model and Cisco IOS version, the commands available and the output produced might vary from what is shown in the labs. Refer to the Router Interface Summary Table at the end of the lab for the correct interface identifiers.

Note: Ensure that the routers and switches have been erased and have no startup configurations. If you are unsure contact your instructor.

Required Resources

- Two routers (Cisco 4221 with Cisco IOS XE Release 16.9.4 universal image or comparable)
- Two switches (Cisco 2960 with Cisco IOS Release 15.2(2) lanbasek9 image or comparable)
- Two PCs (Windows with a terminal emulation program, such as Tera Term)
- Console cables to configure the Cisco IOS devices via the console ports
- Ethernet cables as shown in the topology

Instructions

Part 1: Build the Network and Configure Basic Device Settings.

Step 1:   Cable the network as shown in the topology.

Attach the devices as shown in the topology diagram, and cable as necessary.

Step 2:   Configure basic settings for each router.

   a.   Assign a device name to the router.

   b.   Disable DNS lookup to prevent the router from attempting to translate incorrectly entered commands as though they were host names.

   c.   Assign **class** as the privileged EXEC encrypted password.

   d.   Assign **cisco** as the console password and enable login.

   e.   Assign **cisco** as the VTY password and enable login.

    f.   Encrypt the plaintext passwords.

    g.   Create a banner that warns anyone accessing the device that unauthorized access is prohibited.

    h.   Save the running configuration to the startup configuration file.

Step 3:   Configure basic settings for each switch.

    a.   Assign a device name to the switch.

    b.   Disable DNS lookup to prevent the router from attempting to translate incorrectly entered commands as though they were host names.

    c.   Assign **class** as the privileged EXEC encrypted password.

    d.   Assign **cisco** as the console password and enable login.

    e.   Assign **cisco** as the VTY password and enable login.

    f.   Encrypt the plaintext passwords.

    g.   Create a banner that warns anyone accessing the device that unauthorized access is prohibited.

    h.   Save the running configuration to the startup configuration file.

Part 2: Configure VLANs on the Switches

Step 1:   Create VLANs on both switches.

    a.   Create and name the required VLANs on each switch from the table earlier in this lab.

    b.   Configure the management interface and default gateway on each switch using the IP address information in the Addressing Table.

    c.   Assign all unused ports on the switch to the Parking Lot VLAN, configure them for static access mode, and administratively deactivate them.

> **Note:** The interface range command is helpful to accomplish this task with as few commands as necessary.

Step 2:   Assign VLANs to the correct switch interfaces.

    a.   Assign used ports to the appropriate VLAN (specified in the VLAN table earlier in this lab) sswand configure them for static access mode.

    b.   Issue the **show vlan brief** command and verify that the VLANs are assigned to the correct interfaces.

Part 3: Configure Trunking

Step 1:   Manually configure trunk interface F0/1.

    a.   Change the switchport mode on interface F0/1 to force trunking. Make sure to do this on both switches.

    b.   As a part of the trunk configuration, set the native vlan to 1000 on both switches. You may see error messages temporarily while the two interfaces are configured for different native VLANs.

c. As another part of trunk configuration, specify that VLANs 10, 20, 30, and 1000, are allowed to cross the trunk.

d. Issue the **show interfaces trunk** command to verify trunking ports, the Native VLAN, and allowed VLANs across the trunk.

Step 2: Manually configure S1's trunk interface F0/5.

a. Configure S1's interface F0/5 with the same trunk parameters as F0/1. This is the trunk to the router.

b. Save the running configuration to the startup configuration file.

c. Issue the **show interfaces trunk** command to verify trunking.

Part 4: Configure Routing

Step 1: Configure Inter-VLAN Routing on R1.

a. Activate interface G0/0/1 on the router.

b. Configure sub-interfaces for each VLAN as specified in the IP addressing table. All sub-interfaces use 802.1Q encapsulation. Ensure the sub-interface for the native VLAN does not have an IP address assigned. Include a description for each sub-interface.

c. Configure interface Loopback 1 on R1 with addressing from the table earlier in this lab.

d. Use the **show ip interface brief** command to verify the sub-interfaces are operational.

Step 2: Configure the R2 interface g0/0/1 using the address from the table and a default route with the next hop 10.20.0.1.

Part 5: Configure Remote Access

Step 1: Configure all network devices for basic SSH support.

a. Create a local user with the username SSHadmin and the encrypted password $cisco123!

b. Use **ccna-lab.com** as the domain name.

c. Generate crypto keys using a 1024-bit modulus.

d. Configure the first five VTY lines on each device to support SSH connections only and to authenticate to the local user database.

Step 2: Enable secure, authenticated web services on R1.

a. Enable the HTTPS server on R1.

b. Configure R1 to authenticate users attempting to connect to the web server.

Part 6: Verify Connectivity

Step 1:   Configure PC hosts.

Refer to the Addressing Table for PC host address information.

Step 2:   Complete the following tests. All should be successful.

Note: You may have to disable the PC firewall for pings to be successful.

From	Protocol	Destination
PC-A	Ping	10.40.0.10
PC-A	Ping	10.20.0.1
PC-B	Ping	10.30.0.10
PC-B	Ping	10.20.0.1
PC-B	Ping	172.16.1.1
PC-B	HTTPS	10.20.0.1
PC-B	HTTPS	172.16.1.1
PC-B	SSH	10.20.0.1
PC-B	SSH	172.16.1.1

Part 7: Configure and Verify Extended Access Control Lists.

When basic connectivity is verified, the company requires the following security policies to be implemented:

Policy 1: The Sales Network is not allowed to SSH to the Management Network (but other SSH is allowed).

Policy 2: The Sales Network is not allowed to access IP addresses in the Management network using any web protocol (HTTP/HTTPS). The Sales Network is also not allowed to access R1 interfaces using any web protocol. All other web traffic is allowed (note – Sales can access the Loopback 1 interface on R1).

Policy 3: The Sales Network is not allowed to send ICMP echo-requests to the Operations or Management Networks. ICMP echo requests to other destinations are allowed.

Policy 4: The Operations network is not allowed to send ICMP echo-requests to the Sales network. ICMP echo requests to other destinations are allowed.

Step 1:   Analyze the network and the security policy requirements to plan ACL implementation.

Step 2:   Develop and apply extended access lists that will meet the security policy statements.

Step 3:   Verify security policies are being enforced by the deployed access lists.

Run the following tests. The expected results are shown in the table:

From	Protocol	Destination	Result
PC-A	Ping	10.40.0.10	Fail
PC-A	Ping	10.20.0.1	Success
PC-B	Ping	10.30.0.10	Fail
PC-B	Ping	10.20.0.1	Fail
PC-B	Ping	172.16.1.1	Success
PC-B	HTTPS	10.20.0.1	Fail
PC-B	HTTPS	172.16.1.1	Success
PC-B	SSH	10.20.0.4	Fail
PC-B	SSH	172.16.1.1	Success

CHAPTER 6

NAT for IPv4

The "Study Guide" portion of this chapter uses a variety of exercises to test your knowledge and skills related to configuring NAT services on the edge router to provide IPv4 address scalability. The "Labs and Activities" portion of this chapter includes all the online curriculum labs and Packet Tracer activity instructions.

As you work through this chapter, use Chapter 6 in *Enterprise Networking, Security, and Automation v7 Companion Guide* or use the corresponding Module 6 in the Enterprise Networking, Security, and Automation online curriculum for assistance.

Study Guide

NAT Characteristics

In the section, you review the purpose and function of NAT.

IPv4 Private Address Space

There are not enough public IPv4 addresses to assign a unique address to each device connected to the Internet. Networks are commonly implemented using private IPv4 addresses.

Fill in the table with the private addresses defined by RFC 1918.

Class	Address Range	CIDR Prefix
A		
B		
C		

NAT Terminology

Briefly explain the following terms:

- Inside local address: _____
- Inside global address: _____
- Outside global address: _____
- Outside local address: _____
  _____

In Figure 6-1, label each type of NAT address.

Figure 6-1   Identify NAT Address Types

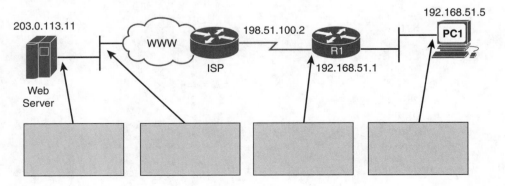

Check Your Understanding—NAT Characteristics

Refer to Figure 6-2 to answer the following questions.

Figure 6-2   Check Your Understanding Scenario

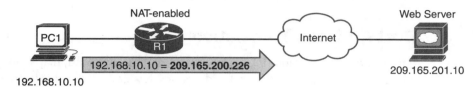

1. In Figure 6-2, what type of NAT address is the IP address of PC1 (that is, 192.168.10.10)?

   a. Outside local

   b. Inside local

   c. Outside global

   d. Inside global

2. In Figure 6-2, into what type of address has the IPv4 address for PC1 (that is, 209.165.200.226) been translated?

   a. Outside local

   b. Inside local

   c. Outside global

   d. Inside global

3. In Figure 6-2, what type of NAT address is the IP address of the web server (that is, 209.165.201.10)?

   a. Outside local

   b. Inside local

   c. Outside global

   d. Inside global

Types of NAT

In the section, you review the operation of different types of NAT.

Static NAT

Static NAT uses a one-to-one mapping of local and global addresses. These mappings are configured by the network administrator and remain constant. Static NAT is particularly useful for a web server or a device that must have a consistent address and is accessible from the Internet, such as a company web server. It is also useful for devices that must be accessible by authorized personnel when offsite but not by the general public on the Internet.

Dynamic NAT

Dynamic NAT uses a pool of public addresses and assigns them on a first-come, first-served basis. When an inside device requests access to an outside network, dynamic NAT assigns an available public IPv4 address from the pool.

Port Address Translation

Port Address Translation (PAT), also known as NAT overload, maps multiple private IPv4 addresses to a single public IPv4 address or a few addresses. This is possible because each private address is also tracked by a port number. PAT ensures that devices use a different TCP port number for each session with a server on the Internet. When a response comes back from the server, the source port number, which becomes the destination port number on the return trip, determines to which device the router forwards the packets. The PAT process also validates that the incoming packets were requested, thus adding a degree of security to the session.

NAT and PAT Comparison

Table 6-1 provides a summary of the differences between NAT and PAT.

Table 6-1   Differences Between NAT and PAT

NAT	PAT
One-to-one mapping between inside local and inside global addresses.	One inside global address can be mapped to many inside local addresses.
Uses only IPv4 addresses in the translation process.	Uses IPv4 addresses and TCP or UDP source port numbers in the translation process.
A unique inside global address is required for each inside host accessing the outside network.	A single unique inside global address can be shared by many inside hosts accessing the outside network.

NAT Advantages and Disadvantages

In the section, you review the advantages and disadvantages of NAT.

The following are the advantages of using NAT:

- It conserves the legally registered addressing scheme.
- It increases the flexibility of connections to the public network.
- It provides consistency for internal network addressing schemes.
- It provides network security.

The following are the disadvantages of using NAT:

- Performance is degraded.
- End-to-end functionality is degraded.
- End-to-end IP traceability is lost.

- Tunneling becomes more complicated.
- Initiating TCP connections can be disrupted.

Check Your Understanding—NAT Advantages and Disadvantages

Check your understanding of NAT advantages and disadvantages by choosing the BEST answer to each of the following questions.

1. True or false: A side effect of NAT is that it hides the inside local IP address of a host from the outside network.

   a. True

   b. False

2. True or false: With NAT overload, each inside local IP address is translated to a unique inside global IP address on a one-for-one basis.

   a. True

   b. False

3. True or false: The use of NAT makes end-to-end traceability between source and destination easier.

   a. True

   b. False

4. True or false: Tunneling protocols such as IPsec do not work well through NAT.

   a. True

   b. False

Static NAT

In the section, you review how to configure static NAT using the CLI.

Configure Static NAT

Use the following steps to configure static NAT:

Step 1. Create a map between the inside local IP address and the inside global IP address by using the **ip nat inside source static local-ip global-ip** global configuration command.

Step 2. Configure the inside interface of the LAN the device is attached to so it can participate in NAT by using the **ip nat inside** interface configuration command.

Step 3. Configure the outside interface where NAT translation will occur by using the **ip nat outside** interface configuration command.

Refer to the topology in Figure 6-3 to configure static NAT for this sample network.

Figure 6-3   Static NAT Configuration Topology

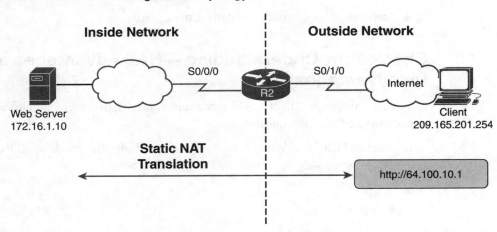

The web server uses the inside local address 172.16.1.10, which needs to be translated to the inside global address 64.100.10.1. Record the command, including the router prompt, to configure the static translation on R2.

_____

Record the commands, including the router prompts, to configure the inside interface.

_____

_____

Record the commands, including the router prompts, to configure the outside interface.

_____

_____

Packet Tracer Exercise 6-1: Configure Static NAT

Now you are ready to use Packet Tracer to apply your knowledge about static NAT configuration. Download the file LSG03-0601.pka from the companion website for this book and open it. Refer to the Introduction of this book for specifics on accessing files.

Note: The following instructions are also contained within the Packet Tracer Exercise.

In this Packet Tracer activity, you will configure and verify static NAT. Use the commands you documented in the "Configure Static NAT" section to help complete the activity.

Requirements

Use the following requirements and your documented commands from the "Configure Static NAT" section to configure this sample network:

- Configure R2 to use static NAT for the inside address 172.16.1.10 to the outside address 64.100.10.1.

- Configure the appropriate interfaces for NAT.

- Verify that the outside client can ping the web server at 64.100.10.1.

Your completion percentage should be 100%. If it is not, click Check Results to see which required components are not yet completed.

Dynamic NAT

In the section, you review how to configure dynamic NAT using the CLI.

Configure Dynamic NAT

Use the following steps to configure dynamic NAT:

Step 1.   Define the pool of addresses that will be used for dynamic translation by using the **ip nat pool** *name start-ip end-ip* {**netmask** *netmask* | **prefix-length** *prefix-length*} global configuration command.

Step 2.   Configure an ACL to specify which inside local addresses will be translated using a standard ACL.

Step 3.   Bind the NAT pool to the ACL by using the **ip nat inside source list** *ACL-number* **pool** *name* global configuration command.

Step 4.   Configure the inside interface of the LAN the device is attached to so it can participate in NAT by using the **ip nat inside** interface configuration command.

Step 5.   Configure the outside interface where NAT translation will occur by using the **ip nat outside** interface configuration command.

Refer to the topology in Figure 6-4 to configure dynamic NAT for this sample network.

Figure 6-4   Dynamic NAT Configuration Topology

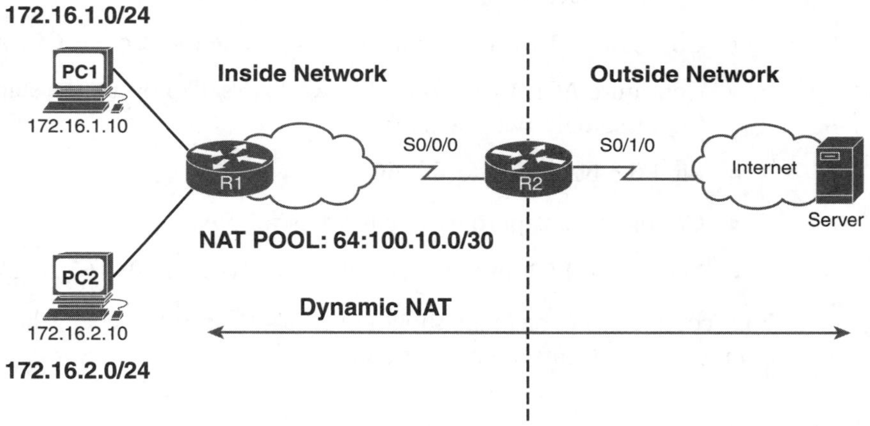

The pool of available addresses is 64.100.10.0/30. Record the command, including the router prompt, to configure the NAT pool with an appropriate name.

_____

The two LANs, 172.16.1.0/24 and 172.16.2.0/24, need to be translated. No other addresses are allowed. Record the command, including the router prompts, to configure a standard ACL number 1.

_____

_____

Record the command, including the router prompt, to bind the NAT pool to the ACL.

_____

Record the commands, including the router prompts, to configure the inside interface.

_____

_____

Record the commands, including the router prompts, to configure the outside interface.

_____

_____

Packet Tracer Exercise 6-2: Configure Dynamic NAT

Now you are ready to use Packet Tracer to apply your knowledge about static NAT configuration. Download the file LSG03-0602.pka from the companion website for this book and open it. Refer to the Introduction of this book for specifics on accessing files.

Note: The following instructions are also contained within the Packet Tracer Exercise.

In this Packet Tracer activity, you will configure and verify dynamic NAT. Use the commands you documented in the "Configure Dynamic NAT" section to help complete the activity.

Requirements

Use the following requirements and your documented commands from the "Configure Dynamic NAT" section to configure this sample network:

- Configure R2 with a pool named NAT. Use the address 64.100.10.0/30.
- Configure ACL 1 to permit the two LANs. Configure the statement for 172.16.1.0/24 first. Use only two statements.
- Bind the NAT pool to the ACL.
- Configure the appropriate interfaces for NAT.
- Verify that PC1 and PC2 can ping the server at 209.165.201.254.

Your completion percentage should be 100%. If it is not, click Check Results to see which required components are not yet completed.

PAT

In the section, you review how to configure Port Address Translation (PAT) by using the CLI.

Configure PAT

Configuring PAT is just like configuring dynamic NAT except that you add the keyword overload to your binding configuration:

```
Router(config)# ip nat inside source list ACL-number pool name overload
```

However, a more common solution in a small business enterprise network is to simply overload the IP address on the gateway router. In fact, this is what a home router does "out of the box."

To configure NAT to overload the public IP address on an interface, use the following command:

```
Router(config)# ip nat inside source list ACL-number interface type number overload
```

In this case, of course, there is no pool configuration.

Refer to the topology in Figure 6-5 to configure PAT for this sample network.

Figure 6-5   PAT Configuration Topology

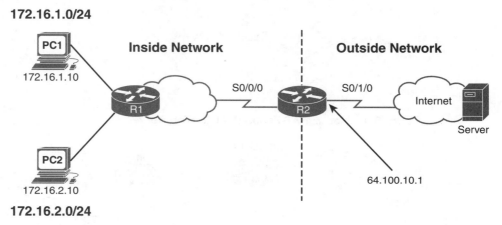

R2 is using the public IP address 64.100.10.1 on the Serial 0/1/0 interface. Record the command, including the router prompt, to bind the ACL you configured for dynamic NAT to the Serial 0/1/0 interface.

_____

That's it! The rest of the commands are the same as for dynamic NAT. However, the process of translating inbound and outbound packets is a bit more involved. PAT maintains a table of inside and outside addresses mapped to port numbers to track connections between the source and destination.

Figures 6-6 through 6-9 illustrate the PAT process overloading an interface address. Use the options in Table 6-2 to fill in the source address (SA), destination address (DA), and corresponding port numbers as the packet travels from source to destination and back.

Table 6-2   Addresses and Port Number Options

64.100.10.2	192.168.51.5	1268	209.165.201.11
1150	53	192.168.51.1	80

Figure 6-6   Hop 1: PC1 to NAT-Enabled R1

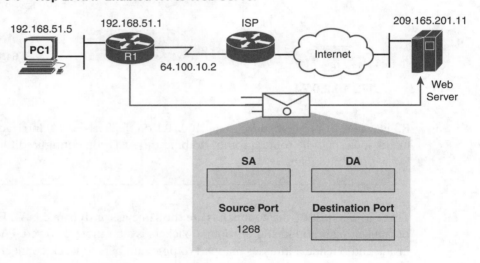

Figure 6-7   Hop 2: NAT-Enabled R1 to Web Server

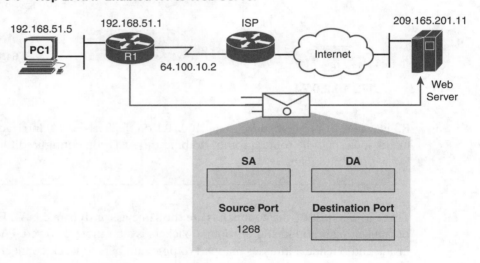

Figure 6-8   Hop 3: Web Server to NAT-Enabled R1

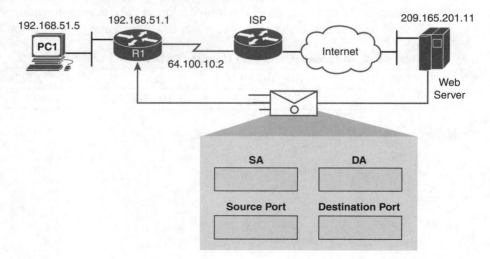

Figure 6-9   Hop 4: NAT-Enabled R1 to PC1

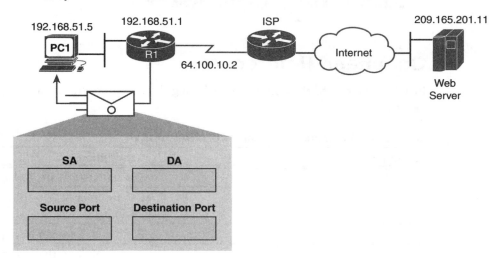

NAT64

NAT for IPv6 is used in a much different context than NAT for IPv4. The varieties of NAT for IPv6 are used to transparently provide access between IPv6-only and IPv4-only networks, as shown in Figure 6-10.

Figure 6-10   NAT64 and Native IPv6 Traffic Flows

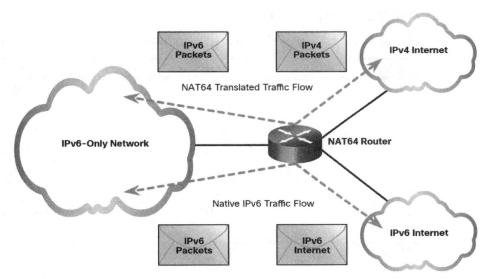

The Internet Engineering Task Force (IETF) has developed several transition techniques to accommodate a variety of IPv4-to-IPv6 scenarios, including the following:

- **Dual stack:** Devices can run protocols associated with both IPv4 and IPv6.

- **Tunneling:** Tunneling for IPv6 is the process of encapsulating an IPv6 packet inside an IPv4 packet.

- **Translation:** NAT64 is a NAT for IPv6 mechanism that can be used as a short-term strategy to assist in the migration from IPv4 to IPv6.

Labs and Activities

Command Reference

In Table 6-3, record the command, including the correct router or switch prompt, that fits each description.

Table 6-3   Commands for Chapter 6, "NAT for IPv4"

Command	Description
	Statically translate 10.10.10.10 to 192.0.2.1.
	Configure a NAT pool MYNAT for 192.0.2.8/29.
	Bind ACL 5 to MYNAT pool.
	Assign NAT to the internal interface.
	Assign NAT to the external interface.
	Bind NAT to ACL 5 and use the s0/0/0 interface with PAT.

6.2.7 Packet Tracer—Investigate NAT Operations

Addressing Table

The following table provides addressing for networking device interfaces only.

Device	Interface	IP Address and Prefix
R2	G0/0	10.255.255.245/30
	G0/1	10.255.255.249/30
	G0/2	10.10.10.1/24
	S0/0/0	64.100.100.2/27
	S0/0/1.1	64.100.200.2/30
R4	G0/0	172.16.0.1/24
	S0/0/0	64.100.150.1/30
	S0/0/1.1	64.100.200.1/30
WRS	LAN	192.168.0.1/24
	Internet	64.104.223.2/30

Objectives

Part 1: Investigate NAT Operation Across the Intranet

Part 2: Investigate NAT Operation Across the Internet

Part 3: Conduct Further Investigations

Scenario

As a frame travels across a network, the MAC addresses may change. IP addresses can also change when a packet is forwarded by a device configured with NAT. In this activity, we will investigate what happens to IP addresses during the NAT process.

Instructions

Part 1: Investigate NAT Operation Across the Intranet

Step 1: Wait for the network to converge.

It might take a few minutes for everything in the network to converge. You can speed the process up by clicking Fast Forward Time.

Step 2: Generate an HTTP request from any PC in the Central domain.

    a. Switch to **Simulation** mode and edit the filters to show only HTTP requests.

    b. Open the Web Browser of any PC in the **Central** domain and type the URL **http://branchserver.pka** and click **Go**. Minimize the browser window.

    c. Click **Capture / Forward** until the PDU is over **D1** or **D2**. Click on the most recent PDU in the Event List. Record the source and destination IP addresses.

    Question:

    To what devices do those addresses belong?

    _____

    d. Click **Capture / Forward** until the PDU is over **R2**. Record the source and destination IP addresses in the outbound packet.

    Question:

    To what devices do those addresses belong?

    _____

    e. Login to R2 from the CLI using the password **class** to enter privileged EXEC and issue the following command:

```
R2# show run | include pool
ip nat pool R2Pool 64.100.100.3 64.100.100.31 netmask 255.255.255.224
ip nat inside source list 1 pool R2Pool
```

    The address came from the NAT pool **R2Pool**.

f. Click **Capture / Forward** until the PDU is over **R4**. Record the source and destination IP addresses in the outbound packet.

Question:

To what devices do those addresses belong?

_____

g. Click **Capture / Forward** until the PDU is over **Branchserver.pka**. Record the source and destination TCP port addresses in the outbound segment.

_____

h. On both **R2** and **R4**, run the following command and match the IP addresses and ports recorded above to the correct line of output:

```
R2# show ip nat translations
R4# show ip nat translations
```

Questions:

What do the inside local IP addresses have in common?

_____

Did any private addresses cross the intranet?

_____

i. Click the Reset Simulation button and remain in Simulation Model.

Part 2: Investigate NAT Operation Across the Internet

Step 1:   Generate an HTTP request from any computer in the home office.

a. Open the Web Browser of any PC in the **Home Office** domain, type the URL **http://centralserver.pka**, and click **Go**.

b. Click Capture / Forward until the PDU is over WRS. Record the inbound source and destination IP addresses and the outbound source and destination addresses.

Question:

To what devices do those addresses belong?

_____

c. Click **Capture / Forward** until the PDU is over **R2**. Record the source and destination IP addresses in the outbound packet.

Question:

To what devices do those addresses belong?

_____

    d. On **R2**, run the following command and match the IP addresses and ports recorded above to the correct line of output:

```
R2# show ip nat translations
```

    e. Return to Realtime mode.

    Question:

    Did all of the web pages appear in the browsers?

Part 3: Conduct Further Investigations

Experiment with more packets, both HTTP and HTTPS and answer the following questions.

Questions:

Do the NAT translation tables grow?

Does WRS have a NAT pool of addresses?

Is this how the computers in the classroom connect to the Internet?

Why does NAT use four columns of addresses and ports?

Where are the networks are inside global and inside local?

On which devices are NAT services operating? What do they have in common?

6.4.5 Packet Tracer—Configure Static NAT

Objectives

Part 1: Test Access Without NAT

Part 2: Configure Static NAT

Part 3: Test Access with NAT

Scenario

In IPv4 configured networks, clients and servers use private addressing. Before packets with private addressing can cross the Internet, they need to be translated to public addressing. Servers that are accessed from outside the organization are usually assigned both a public and a private static IP address. In this activity, you will configure static NAT so that outside devices can access an inside server at its public address.

Instructions

Part 1: Test Access Without NAT

Step 1:   Attempt to connect to Server1 using Simulation mode.

    a. Switch to Simulation mode.

    b. From **PC1** or **L1**, use the Web Browser to attempt to connect to the **Server1** web page at 172.16.16.1. Continue to click the **Capture Forward** button, notice how the packets never leave the Internet cloud. The attempts should fail.

    c. Exit **Simulation** mode.

    d. From **PC1**, ping the **R1** S0/0/0 interface (209.165.201.2). The ping should succeed.

Step 2:   View R1 routing table and running-config.

    a. View the running configuration of **R1**. Note that there are no commands referring to NAT. An easy way to confirm this is to issue the following command:

```
R1# show run | include nat
```

    b. Verify that the routing table does not contain entries referring to the IP network addresses for **PC1** and **L1**.

    c. Verify that NAT is not being used by **R1**.

```
R1# show ip nat translations
```

Part 2: Configure Static NAT

Step 1:   Configure static NAT statements.

Refer to the Topology. Create a static NAT translation to map the **Server1** inside address to its outside address.

```
R1(config)# ip nat inside source static 172.16.16.1 64.100.50.1
```

Step 2:   Configure interfaces.

a.   Configure the **G0/0** interface as an inside interface.

```
R1(config)# interface g0/0
R1(config-if)# ip nat inside
```

b.   Configure the s0/0/0 public interface as an outside interface.

Part 3: Test Access with NAT

Step 1:   Verify connectivity to the Server1 web page.

a.   Open the command prompt on **PC1** or **L1**, attempt to ping the public address for **Server1**. Pings should succeed.

b.   Verify that both **PC1** and **L1** can now access the **Server1** web page.

Step 2:   View NAT translations.

Use the following commands to verify the static NAT configuration on **R1**:

```
show running-config
show ip nat translations
show ip nat statistics
```

6.5.6 Packet Tracer—Configure Dynamic NAT

Objectives

Part 1: Configure Dynamic NAT

Part 2: Verify NAT Implementation

Instructions

Part 1: Configure Dynamic NAT

Step 1:   Configure traffic that will be permitted.

On **R2**, configure one statement for ACL 1 to permit any address belonging to the 172.16.0.0/16 network.

Step 2:   Configure a pool of addresses for NAT.

Configure **R2** with a NAT pool that uses two addresses in the 209.165.200.228/30 address space.

Notice in the topology there are three network addresses that would be translated based on the ACL created.

Question:

What will happen if more than two devices attempt to access the Internet?

_____

Step 3:   Associate ACL 1 with the NAT pool.

Enter the command that associates ACL 1 with the NAT pool that you just created.

Step 4:   Configure the NAT interfaces.

Configure **R2** interfaces with the appropriate inside and outside NAT commands.

Part 2: Verify NAT Implementation

Step 1:   Access services across the Internet.

From the web browser of **L1**, **PC1**, or **PC2**, access the web page for **Server1**.

Step 2:   View NAT translations.

View the NAT translations on **R2**. Identify the internal source address of the PC and the translated address from the NAT pool in the command output.

```
R2# show ip nat translations
```

Packet Tracer
☐ Activity

6.6.7 Packet Tracer—Configure PAT

Objectives

Part 1: Configure Dynamic NAT with Overload

Part 2: Verify Dynamic NAT with Overload Implementation

Part 3: Configure PAT Using an Interface

Part 4: Verify PAT Interface Implementation

Part 1: Configure Dynamic NAT with Overload

Step 1: Configure traffic that will be permitted.

On **R1**, configure one statement for ACL 1 to permit any address belonging to 172.16.0.0/16.

```
R1(config)# access-list 1 permit 172.16.0.0 0.0.255.255
```

Step 2: Configure a pool of address for NAT.

Configure **R1** with a NAT pool that uses the two useable addresses in the 209.165.200.232/30 address space.

```
R1(config)# ip nat pool ANY_POOL_NAME 209.165.200.233 209.165.200.234
netmask 255.255.255.252
```

Step 3: Associate ACL 1 with the NAT pool and allow addresses to be reused.

```
R1(config)# ip nat inside source list 1 pool ANY_POOL_NAME overload
```

Step 4: Configure the NAT interfaces.

Configure **R1** interfaces with the appropriate inside and outside NAT commands.

```
R1(config)# interface s0/1/0
R1(config-if)# ip nat outside
R1(config-if)# interface g0/0/0
R1(config-if)# ip nat inside
R1(config-if)# interface g0/0/1
R1(config-if)# ip nat inside
```

Part 2: Verify Dynamic NAT with Overload Implementation

Step 1: Access services across the Internet.

From the web browser of each of the PCs that use **R1** as their gateway (**PC1**, **L1**, **PC2**, and **L2**), access the web page for **Server1**.

Question:

Were all connections successful?

Step 2:   View NAT translations.

View the NAT translations on **R1**.

```
R1# show ip nat translations
```

Notice that all four devices were able to communicate, and they are using just one address out of the pool. PAT will continue to use the same address until it runs out of port numbers to associate with the translation. Once that occurs, the next address in the pool will be used. While the theoretical limit would be 65,536 since the port number field is a 16-bit number, the device would likely run out of memory before that limit would be reached.

Part 3: Configure PAT Using an Interface

Step 1:   Configure traffic that will be permitted.

On **R2**, configure one statement for ACL 2 to permit any address belonging to 172.17.0.0/16.

Step 2:   Associate ACL 2 with the NAT interface and allow addresses to be reused.

Enter the **R2** NAT statement to use the interface connected to the Internet and provide translations for all internal devices.

```
R2(config)# ip nat inside source list 2 interface s0/1/1 overload
```

Step 3:   Configure the NAT interfaces.

Configure **R2** interfaces with the appropriate inside and outside NAT commands.

Part 4: Verify PAT Interface Implementation

Step 1:   Access services across the Internet.

From the web browser of each of the PCs that use **R2** as their gateway (**PC3**, **L3**, **PC4**, and **L4**), access the web page for **Server1**.

Question:

Were all connections successful?

_____

Step 2:   View NAT translations.

View the NAT translations on **R2**.

Step 3:   Compare NAT statistics on R1 and R2.

Compare the NAT statistics on the two devices.

Question:

Why doesn't **R2** list any dynamic mappings?

_____

Packet Tracer
☐ Activity

6.8.1 Packet Tracer—Configure NAT for IPv4

Addressing Table

Device	Interface	IP Address
R1	S0/0/0	10.1.1.1/30
	F0/0	192.168.10.1/24
R2	S0/0/0	10.1.1.2/30
	S0/0/1	10.2.2.1/30
	S0/1/0	209.165.200.225/27
	F0/0/0	192.168.20.1/24
R3	S0/0/1	10.2.2.2/30
	F0/0	192.168.30.1/24
PC1	NIC	192.168.10.10/24
PC2	NIC	192.168.30.10/24
local.pka	NIC	192.168.20.254/24
Outside PC	NIC	209.165.201.14/28
cisco.pka	NIC	209.165.201.30/28

Objectives

- Configure Dynamic NAT with PAT
- Configure Static NAT

Background / Scenario

In this lab, you will configure a router with dynamic NAT with PAT. This will translate addresses from the three internal LANs to a single outside address. In addition, you will configure static NAT to translate an internal server address to an outside address.

Instructions

In this activity you will only configure router R2.

- Use a named ACL to permit the addresses from LAN1, LAN2, and LAN3 to be translated. Specify the LANs in this order. Use the name **R2NAT**. The name you use must match this name exactly.

- Create a NAT pool named **R2POOL**. The pool should use the **first** address from the **209.165.202.128/30** address space. The pool name you use must match this name exactly. All translated addresses must use this address as their outside address.

- Configure NAT with the ACL and NAT pool that you have created.

- Configure static NAT to map the local.pka server inside address to the **second** address from the **209.165.202.128/30** address space.

- Configure the interfaces that will participate in NAT.

6.8.2 Lab—Configure NAT for IPv4

Topology

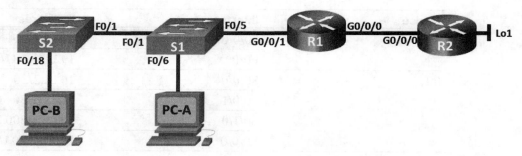

Addressing Table

Device	Interface	IP Address	Subnet Mask
R1	G0/0/0	209.165.200.230	255.255.255.248
	G0/0/1	192.168.1.1	255.255.255.0
R2	G0/0/0	209.165.200.225	255.255.255.248
	Lo1	209.165.200.1	255.255.255.224
S1	VLAN 1	192.168.1.11	255.255.255.0
S2	VLAN 1	192.168.1.12	255.255.255.0
PC-A	NIC	192.168.1.2	255.255.255.0
PC-B	NIC	192.168.1.3	255.255.255.0

Objectives

Part 1: Build the Network and Configure Basic Device Settings

Part 2: Configure and Verify NAT for IPv4

Part 3: Configure and Verify PAT for IPv4

Part 4: Configure and Verify Static NAT for IPv4

Background / Scenario

Network Address Translation (NAT) is the process where a network device, such as a Cisco router, assigns a public address to host devices inside a private network. The main reason to use NAT is to reduce the number of public IP addresses that an organization uses because the number of available IPv4 public addresses is limited.

An ISP has allocated the public IP address space of 209.165.200.224/29 to a company. This network is used to address the link between the ISP router (R2) and the company gateway (R1). The first address (209.165.200.225) is assigned to the g0/0/0 interface on R2 and the last address (209.165.200.230) is assigned to the g0/0/0 interface on R1. The remaining addresses (209.165.200.226-209.165.200.229) will be used to provide Internet access to the company hosts. A default route is used from R1 to R2. The Internet is simulated by a loopback address on R2.

In this lab, you will configure various types of NAT. You will test, view, and verify that the translations are taking place, and you will interpret the NAT/PAT statistics to monitor the process.

Note: The routers used with CCNA hands-on labs are Cisco 4221 with Cisco IOS XE Release 16.9.3 (universalk9 image). The switches used in the labs are Cisco Catalyst 2960s with Cisco IOS Release 15.2(2) (lanbasek9 image). Other routers, switches, and Cisco IOS versions can be used. Depending on the model and Cisco IOS version, the commands available and the output produced might vary from what is shown in the labs. Refer to the Router Interface Summary Table at the end of the lab for the correct interface identifiers.

Note: Ensure that the routers and switches have been erased and have no startup configurations. If you are unsure contact your instructor.

Required Resources

- Two routers (Cisco 4221 with Cisco IOS XE Release 16.9.4 universal image or comparable)
- Two switches (Cisco 2960 with Cisco IOS Release 15.2(2) lanbasek9 image or comparable)
- Two PCs (Windows with a terminal emulation program, such as Tera Term)
- Console cables to configure the Cisco IOS devices via the console ports
- Ethernet cables as shown in the topology

Instructions

Part 1: Build the Network and Configure Basic Device Settings

In Part 1, you will set up the network topology and configure basic settings on the PC hosts and switches.

Step 1:   Cable the network as shown in the topology.

Attach the devices as shown in the topology diagram and cable as necessary.

Step 2:   Configure basic settings for each router.

   a.   Assign a device name to the router.

   b.   Disable DNS lookup to prevent the router from attempting to translate incorrectly entered commands as though they were host names.

   c.   Assign **class** as the privileged EXEC encrypted password.

   d.   Assign **cisco** as the console password and enable login.

   e.   Assign **cisco** as the VTY password and enable login.

   f.   Encrypt the plaintext passwords.

   g.   Create a banner that warns anyone accessing the device that unauthorized access is prohibited.

   h.   Configure interface IP addressing as specified in the earlier table.

    i. Configure a default route to R2 from R1.

    j. Save the running configuration to the startup configuration file.

Step 2: Configure basic settings for each switch.

    a. Assign a device name to the switch.

    b. Disable DNS lookup to prevent the router from attempting to translate incorrectly entered commands as though they were host names.

    c. Assign **class** as the privileged EXEC encrypted password.

    d. Assign **cisco** as the console password and enable login.

    e. Assign **cisco** as the VTY password and enable login.

    f. Encrypt the plaintext passwords.

    g. Create a banner that warns anyone accessing the device that unauthorized access is prohibited.

    h. Shut down all interfaces that will not be used.

    i. Configure interface IP addressing as specified in the earlier table.

    j. Save the running configuration to the startup configuration file.

Part 2: Configure and Verify NAT for IPv4

In Part 2, you will configure and verify NAT for IPv4.

Step 1: Configure NAT on R1 using a pool of three addresses, 209.165.200.226-209.165.200.228.

    a. Configure a simple access list that defines what hosts are going to be allowed for translation. In this case, all devices on the R1 LAN are eligible for translation.

```
R1(config)# access-list 1 permit 192.168.1.0 0.0.0.255
```

    b. Create the NAT pool, and give it a name and a range of addresses to use.

```
R1(config)# ip nat pool PUBLIC_ACCESS 209.165.200.226 209.165.200.228
netmask 255.255.255.248
```

Note: The netmask parameter is not an IP address delimiter. It should be the correct subnet mask for the addresses being assigned, even if you are not using all the subnet addresses in the pool.

    c. Configure the translation, associating the ACL and Pool to the translation process.

```
R1(config)# ip nat inside source list 1 pool PUBLIC_ACCESS
```

Note: Three very important points. First, the word 'inside' is critical to the operation of this kind of NAT. If you omit it, NAT will not work. Second, the list number is the ACL number configured in a previous step. Third, the pool name is case-sensitive.

    d. Define the inside interface.

```
R1(config)# interface g0/0/1
R1(config-if)# ip nat inside
```

e. Define the outside interface.

```
R1(config)# interface g0/0/0
R1(config-if)# ip nat outside
```

Step 2: Test and verify the configuration.

a. From PC-B, ping the Lo1 interface (209.165.200.1) on R2. If the ping was unsuccessful, troubleshoot and correct the issues. On R1, display the NAT table on R1 with the command **show ip nat translations.**

```
R1# show ip nat translations
Pro   Inside global      Inside local     Outside local     Outside global
---   209.165.200.226    192.168.1.3      ---               ---
icmp 209.165.200.226:1  192.168.1.3:1    209.165.200.1:1   209.165.200.1:1
Total number of translations: 2
```

Questions:

What was the inside local address of PC-B translated to?

_____

What type of NAT address is the translated address?

_____

b. From PC-A, ping the Lo1 interface (**209.165.200.1**) on R2. If the ping was unsuccessful, troubleshoot and correct the issues. On R1, display the NAT table on R1 with the command **show ip nat translations.**

```
R1# show ip nat translations
Pro   Inside global      Inside local     Outside local     Outside global
---   209.165.200.227    192.168.1.2      ---               ---
---   209.165.200.226    192.168.1.3      ---               ---
icmp 209.165.200.227:1  192.168.1.2:1    209.165.200.1:1   209.165.200.1:1
icmp 209.165.200.226:1  192.168.1.3:1    209.165.200.1:1   209.165.200.1:1
Total number of translations: 4
```

c. Notice that the previous translation for PC-B is still in the table. From S1, ping the Lo1 interface (**209.165.200.1**) on R2. If the ping was unsuccessful, troubleshoot and correct the issues. On R1, display the NAT table on R1 with the command **show ip nat translations.**

```
R1# show ip nat translations
Pro   Inside global      Inside local     Outside local     Outside global
---   209.165.200.227    192.168.1.2      ---               ---
---   209.165.200.226    192.168.1.3      ---               ---
---   209.165.200.228    192.168.1.11     ---               ---
icmp 209.165.200.226:1  192.168.1.3:1    209.165.200.1:1   209.165.200.1:1
icmp 209.165.200.228:0  192.168.1.11:0   209.165.200.1:0   209.165.200.1:0
Total number of translations: 5
```

d. Now try to ping R2 Lo1 from S2. This time, the translations fail, and you get these messages (or similar) on the R1 console:

```
Sep 23 15:43:55.562: %IOSXE-6-PLATFORM: R0/0: cpp_cp: QFP:0.0 Thread:000
TS:00000001473688385900 %NAT-6-ADDR_ALLOC_FAILURE: Address allocation
failed; pool 1 may be exhausted [2]
```

e. This is an expected result, because only three addresses are allocated, and we tried to ping Lo1 from four devices. Recall that NAT is a one-to-one translation. So how long are the translations allocated? Issue the command **show ip nat translations verbose** and you will see that the answer is for 24 hours.

```
R1# show ip nat translations verbose
Pro  Inside global     Inside local    Outside local    Outside global
---  209.165.200.226   192.168.1.3     ---              ---
     create: 09/23/19 15:35:27, use: 09/23/19 15:35:27, timeout: 23:56:42
     Map-Id(In): 1
<output omitted>
```

f. Given that the pool is limited to three addresses, NAT to a pool of addresses is not adequate for our application. Clear the NAT translations and statistics and we will move on to PAT.

```
R1# clear ip nat translations *
R1# clear ip nat statistics
```

Part 3: Configure and Verify PAT for IPv4

In Part 3, you will configure replace NAT with PAT to a pool of addresses and then with PAT using an interface.

Step 1: Remove the translation command on R1.

The components of an Address Translation configuration are basically the same; something (an access-list) to identify addresses eligible to be translated, an optionally configured pool of addresses to translate them to, and the commands necessary to identify the inside and outside interfaces. From Part 1, our access-list (access-list 1) is still correct for the network scenario, so there is no need to re-create it. We are going to use the same pool of addresses, so there is no need to re-create that configuration either. Also, the inside and outside interfaces are not changing. To get started in Part 3, remove the command that ties the ACL and pool together.

```
R1(config)# no ip nat inside source list 1 pool PUBLIC_ACCESS
```

Step 2: Add the PAT command on R1.

Now, configure for PAT translation to a pool of addresses (remember, the ACL and Pool are already configured, so this is the only command we need to change from NAT to PAT).

```
R1(config)# ip nat inside source list 1 pool PUBLIC_ACCESS overload
```

Step 3: Test and verify the configuration.

a. Let's verify PAT is working. From PC-B, ping the Lo1 interface (209.165.200.1) on R2. If the ping was unsuccessful, troubleshoot and correct the issues. On R1, display the NAT table on R1 with the command **show ip nat translations**.

```
R1# show ip nat translations
```

```
Pro  Inside global      Inside local    Outside local    Outside global
icmp 209.165.200.226:1  192.168.1.3:1   209.165.200.1:1  209.165.200.1:1
Total number of translations: 1#
```

Questions:

What was the inside local address of PC-B translated to?

_____

What type of NAT address is the translated address?

_____

What is different about the output of the **show ip nat translations** command from the NAT exercise?

_____

b. From PC-A, ping the Lo1 interface (209.165.200.1) on R2. If the ping was unsuccessful, troubleshoot and correct the issues. On R1, display the NAT table on R1 with the command **show ip nat translations.**

```
R1# show ip nat translations
Pro  Inside global      Inside local    Outside local    Outside global
icmp 209.165.200.226:1  192.168.1.2:1   209.165.200.1:1  209.165.200.1:1
Total number of translations: 1
```

Notice that there is only one translation again. Send the ping once more, and quickly go back to the router and issue the command **show ip nat translations verbose** and you will see what happened.

```
R1# show ip nat translations verbose
Pro  Inside global      Inside local    Outside local    Outside global
icmp 209.165.200.226:1  192.168.1.2:1   209.165.200.1:1  209.165.200.1:1
   create: 09/23/19 16:57:22, use: 09/23/19 16:57:25, timeout: 00:01:00
<output omitted>
```

As you can see, the translation timeout has been dropped from 24 hours to 1 minute.

c. Generate traffic from multiple devices to observe PAT. On PC-A and PC-B, use the -t parameter with the ping command to send a nonstop ping to R2's Lo1 interface (**ping -t 209.165.200.1**), then go back to R1 and issue the **show ip nat translations** command:

```
R1# show ip nat translations
Pro  Inside global      Inside local    Outside local    Outside global
icmp 209.165.200.226:1  192.168.1.2:1   209.165.200.1:1  209.165.200.1:1
icmp 209.165.200.226:2  192.168.1.3:1   209.165.200.1:1  209.165.200.1:2
Total number of translations: 2
```

Notice that the inside global address is the same for both sessions.

Question:

How does the router keep track of what replies go where?

_____

d. PAT to a pool is a very effective solution for small-to-midsize organizations. However, there are unused IPv4 addresses involved in this scenario. We will move to PAT with interface overload to eliminate this waste of IPv4 addresses. Stop the pings on PC-A and PC-B with the Control-C key combination, then clear translations and translation statistics:

```
R1# clear ip nat translations *
R1# clear ip nat statistics
```

Step 4:   On R1, remove the nat pool translation commands.

Once again, our access-list (access-list 1) is still correct for the network scenario, so there is no need to re-create it. Also, the inside and outside interfaces are not changing. To get started with PAT to an interface, clean up the configuration by removing the NAT pool and the command that ties the ACL and pool together.

```
R1(config)# no ip nat inside source list 1 pool PUBLIC_ACCESS overload
R1(config)# no ip nat pool PUBLIC_ACCESS
```

Step 5:   Add the PAT overload command by specifying the outside interface.

Add the PAT command that will cause overload to the outside interface.

```
R1(config)# ip nat inside source list 1 interface g0/0/0 overload
```

Step 6:   Test and verify the configuration.

a. Let's verify PAT to the interface is working. From PC-B, ping the Lo1 interface (209.165.200.1) on R2. If the ping was unsuccessful, troubleshoot and correct the issues. On R1, display the NAT table on R1 with the command **show ip nat translations**.

```
R1# show ip nat translations
Pro   Inside global      Inside local    Outside local    Outside global
icmp 209.165.200.230:1  192.168.1.3:1   209.165.200.1:1  209.165.200.1:1
Total number of translations: 1
```

b. Generate traffic from multiple devices to observe PAT. On PC-A and PC-B, use the -t parameter with the ping command to send a nonstop ping to R2's Lo1 interface (**ping -t 209.165.200.1**). On S1 and S2, issue the privileged exec command ping 209.165.200.1 repeat 2000. Then go back to R1 and issue the **show ip nat translations** command.

```
R1# show ip nat translations
Pro   Inside global      Inside local    Outside local    Outside global
icmp 209.165.200.230:3  192.168.1.11:1 209.165.200.1:1  209.165.200.1:3
icmp 209.165.200.230:2  192.168.1.2:1  209.165.200.1:1  209.165.200.1:2
icmp 209.165.200.230:4  192.168.1.3:1  209.165.200.1:1  209.165.200.1:4
icmp 209.165.200.230:1  192.168.1.12:1 209.165.200.1:1  209.165.200.1:1
Total number of translations: 4
```

Now all the Inside Global addresses are mapped to the g0/0/0 interface IP address.

Stop all the pings. On PC-A and PC-B, using the CTRL-C key combination.

Part 4: Configure and Verify Static NAT for IPv4

In Part 4, you will configure static NAT so that PC-A is directly reachable from the Internet. PC-A will be reachable from R2 via the address 209.165.200.229.

Note: The configuration you are about to complete does not follow recommended practices for Internet-connected gateways. This lab completely omits what would be standard security practices to focus on successful configuration of static NAT. In a production environment, careful coordination between the network infrastructure and security teams would be fundamental to supporting this requirement.

Step 1:   On R1, clear current translations and statistics.

```
R1# clear ip nat translations *
R1# clear ip nat statistics
```

Step 2:   On R1, configure the NAT command required to statically map an inside address to an outside address.

For this step, configure a static mapping between 192.168.1.11 and 209.165.200.1 using the following command:

```
R1(config)# ip nat inside source static 192.168.1.2 209.165.200.229
```

Step 3:   Test and verify the configuration.

   a.   Let's verify the static NAT is working. On R1, display the NAT table on R1 with the command **show ip nat translations**, and you should see the static mapping.

```
R1# show ip nat translations
Pro   Inside global      Inside local    Outside local    Outside global
---   209.165.200.229    192.168.1.2     ---              ---
Total number of translations: 1
```

   b.   The translation table shows the static translation is in effect. Verify this by pinging from R2 to 209.165.200.229. The pings should work.

   Note: You may have to disable the PC firewall for the pings to work.

---

   c.   On R1, display the NAT table on R1 with the command **show ip nat translations**, and you should see the static mapping and the port-level translation for the inbound pings.

```
R1# show ip nat translations
Pro   Inside global      Inside local    Outside local     Outside global
---   209.165.200.229    192.168.1.2     ---               ---
icmp  209.165.200.229:3  192.168.1.2:3   209.165.200.225:3 209.165.200.225:3
Total number of translations: 2
```

This validates that the static NAT is working.

Router Interface Summary Table

Router Model	Ethernet Interface #1	Ethernet Interface #2	Serial Interface #1	Serial Interface #2
1800	Fast Ethernet 0/0 (F0/0)	Fast Ethernet 0/1 (F0/1)	Serial 0/0/0 (S0/0/0)	Serial 0/0/1 (S0/0/1)
1900	Gigabit Ethernet 0/0 (G0/0)	Gigabit Ethernet 0/1 (G0/1)	Serial 0/0/0 (S0/0/0)	Serial 0/0/1 (S0/0/1)
2801	Fast Ethernet 0/0 (F0/0)	Fast Ethernet 0/1 (F0/1)	Serial 0/1/0 (S0/1/0)	Serial 0/1/1 (S0/1/1)
2811	Fast Ethernet 0/0 (F0/0)	Fast Ethernet 0/1 (F0/1)	Serial 0/0/0 (S0/0/0)	Serial 0/0/1 (S0/0/1)
2900	Gigabit Ethernet 0/0 (G0/0)	Gigabit Ethernet 0/1 (G0/1)	Serial 0/0/0 (S0/0/0)	Serial 0/0/1 (S0/0/1)
4221	Gigabit Ethernet 0/0/0 (G0/0/0)	Gigabit Ethernet 0/0/1 (G0/0/1)	Serial 0/1/0 (S0/1/0)	Serial 0/1/1 (S0/1/1)
4300	Gigabit Ethernet 0/0/0 (G0/0/0)	Gigabit Ethernet 0/0/1 (G0/0/1)	Serial 0/1/0 (S0/1/0)	Serial 0/1/1 (S0/1/1)

Note: To find out how the router is configured, look at the interfaces to identify the type of router and how many interfaces the router has. There is no way to effectively list all the combinations of configurations for each router class. This table includes identifiers for the possible combinations of Ethernet and Serial interfaces in the device. The table does not include any other type of interface, even though a specific router may contain one. An example of this might be an ISDN BRI interface. The string in parenthesis is the legal abbreviation that can be used in Cisco IOS commands to represent the interface.

CHAPTER 7

WAN Concepts

The "Study Guide" portion of this chapter uses a variety of exercises to test your knowledge of how WAN access technologies can be used to satisfy business requirements. The "Labs and Activities" portion of this chapter includes all the online curriculum labs and Packet Tracer activity instructions.

As you work through this chapter, use Chapter 7 in *Enterprise Networking, Security, and Automation v7 Companion Guide* or use the corresponding Module 7 in the Enterprise Networking, Security, and Automation online curriculum for assistance.

Study Guide

Purpose of WANs

In this section, you review the purpose of a WAN.

LANs and WANs

Table 7-1 highlights differences between LANs and WANs.

Table 7-1   LAN and WAN Comparison

Local Area Networks (LANs)	Wide Area Networks (WANs)
LANs provide networking services within a small geographic area (for example, home network, office network, building network, or campus network).	WANs provide networking services over large geographic areas (for example, in and between cities, countries, and continents).
LANs are used to interconnect local computers, peripherals, and other devices.	WANs are used to interconnect remote users, networks, and sites.
A LAN is owned and managed by an organization or a home user.	WANs are owned and managed by Internet service, telephone, cable, and satellite providers.
Other than the network infrastructure costs, there is no fee to use a LAN.	WAN services are provided for a fee.
LANs provide high bandwidth speeds using wired Ethernet and Wi-Fi services.	WAN providers offer low to high bandwidth speeds over long distances, using complex physical networks.

WAN Topologies

WANs are implemented using the logical topologies shown in Figure 7-1. Label each topology with the correct topology type.

Figure 7-1   WAN Logical Topologies

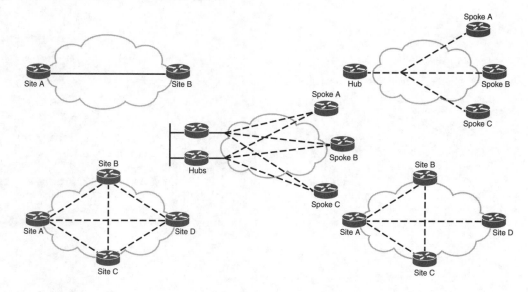

Evolving Networks

The WAN needs of a network depend greatly on the size of the network. These network types run the spectrum from small offices that really need only a broadband connection to the Internet all the way up to multinational enterprises that need a variety of WAN options to satisfy local, regional, and global restrictions.

In Table 7-1, indicate the network type that fits each of the descriptions. Some descriptions may apply to more than one network type.

Table 7-1   Identify the Network Type

Network Description	Small Office Network	Campus Network	Branch Network	Distributed Network
Outsourced IT support				
Very large-sized business				
Connectivity to the Internet				
Converged network and application services				
Hundreds of employees				
Home, branch, and regional offices, teleworkers, and a central office				
Limited number of employees				
In-house IT staff and network support				
Thousands of employees				
Several remote, branch, and regional offices (one central office)				
Small-sized business				
LAN focus of operations with broadband				
Small to medium-sized business				
Multiple campus LANs				
Medium-sized business				

Check Your Understanding—Purpose of WANs

Check your understanding of WANs by choosing the BEST answer to each of the following questions.

1. Which two options describe a WAN? (Choose two.)

    a. A WAN is owned and managed by an organization or a home user.

    b. A WAN provides networking services over large geographic areas.

    c. WAN services are provided for a fee.

    d. WAN providers offer low-bandwidth speeds over short distances.

    e. A WAN guarantees security between the endpoints.

2. Which topology type describes the virtual connection between source and destination?

    a. Cabling topology

    b. Physical topology

    c. Logical topology

    d. Wired topology

3. Which type of WAN network design is the most fault tolerant?

    a. Dual-homed topology

    b. Fully meshed topology

    c. Hub-and-spoke topology

    d. Partially meshed topology

    e. Point-to-point topology

4. Which is a type of WAN carrier connection that provides redundancy?

    a. Dual-carrier WAN connection

    b. Single-carrier WAN connection

WAN Operations

In this section, you review how WANs operate.

WAN Standards

At which layers of the OSI model do WANs operate?

_____

Which organizations are responsible for WAN standards?

_____

_____

_____

What are some of the Layer 2 WAN technologies?

_____

WAN Terminology and Devices

Match each definition with the appropriate term. This exercise is a one-to-one matching: Each definition has exactly one matching term.

Definitions

a. The boundary between customer equipment and service provider equipment

b. Devices inside the enterprise edge wiring closet that are owned or leased by the organization

c. Provider equipment that resides in the WAN backbone and is capable of supporting routing protocols

d. Digital modem used by DSL or cable Internet service providers

e. Dynamically establishes a dedicated circuit before communication starts

f. Provides an interface to connect subscribers to a WAN link

g. Splits traffic so that it can be routed over the shared network

h. Local service provider facility that connects the CPE to the provider network

i. Physical connection between the CPE to the CO

j. Required by digital leased lines to provide termination of the digital signal and convert it into frames that are ready for transmission on the LAN

k. Consists of the all-digital, long-haul communications lines, switches, routers, and other equipment in the provider network

l. Customer device that provides internetworking and WAN access interface ports

m. Customer device that transmits data over the WAN link

n. Multiport device that sits at the service provider edge to switch traffic

o. Legacy technology device that converts digital signals into analog signals transmitted over telephone lines

p. Legacy technology device that can support hundreds of dial-in and dial-out users

Terms

____ Packet-switched network

____ WAN switch

____ Customer premises equipment (CPE)

____ Central office (CO)

____ Dialup modem

____ Access server

____ Data communications equipment (DCE)

____ Router

____ Data terminal equipment (DTE)

____ Local loop

____ CSU/DSU

____ Circuit-switched network

____ Demarcation point

____ Broadband modem

____ Toll network

____ Core multilayer switch

Check Your Understanding—WAN Operations

Check your understanding of WAN operations by choosing the BEST answer to each of the following questions.

1. Which two statements about the WAN OSI model Layer 1 are true? (Choose two.)

    a. It describes how data will be encapsulated into a frame.

    b. It describes the electrical, mechanical, and operational components needed to transmit bits.

    c. It includes protocols such as PPP, HDLC, and Ethernet.

    d. It includes protocols such as SDH, SONET, and DWDM.

2. Which WAN term defines the point where the subscriber connects to the service provider's network.

    a. Customer premises equipment (CPE)

    b. Data communications equipment (DCE)

    c. Demarcation point

    d. Local loop

    e. Point-of-presence (POP)

3. Which two devices operate in a similar manner to a voiceband modem but use higher broadband frequencies and transmission speeds? (Choose two.)

    a. Cable modem

    b. CSU/DSU

    c. DSL modem

    d. Optical converter

    e. Voiceband modem

4. Which communication method is used in all WAN connections?

    a. Circuit-switched communication

    b. Packet-switched communication

    c. Parallel communication

    d. Serial communication

5. Which two WAN connectivity options are circuit-switched technologies? (Choose two.)

    a. ATM

    b. Ethernet WAN

    c. Frame Relay

    d. ISDN

    e. PSTN

6. Which two WAN connectivity options are packet-switched technologies? (Choose two.)

    a. Ethernet WAN

    b. Frame Relay

    c. ISDN

    d. PSTN

7. Which service provider fiber-optic technology increases the data-carrying capacity by using different wavelengths?

   a. DWDM

   b. SDH

   c. SONET

Traditional WAN Connectivity

In this section, you review traditional WAN connectivity options.

Traditional WAN Connectivity Options

In Figure 7-2, label the traditional WAN connectivity options.

Figure 7-2   Traditional WAN Connectivity Options

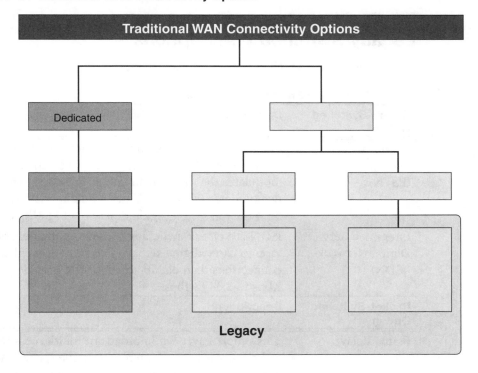

Leased Lines

Review the advantages and disadvantages of leased lines in Table 7-2.

Table 7-2   Advantages and Disadvantages of Leased Lines

Advantage	Description
Simplicity	Point-to-point communication links require minimal expertise to install and maintain.
Quality	Point-to-point communication links usually offer high-quality service, if they have adequate bandwidth. The dedicated capacity removes latency or jitter between the endpoints.

Advantage	Description
Availability	Constant availability is essential for some applications, such as e-commerce. Point-to-point communication links provide permanent, dedicated capacity, which is required for voice over IP (VoIP) or video over IP.

Disadvantage	Description
Cost	Point-to-point links are generally the most expensive type of WAN access. The cost of leased line solutions can become significant when the lines are used to connect many sites over increasing distances. In addition, each endpoint requires an interface on the router, which increases equipment costs.
Limited flexibility	WAN traffic is often variable, and leased lines have a fixed capacity, so that the bandwidth of the line seldom matches the need exactly. Any change to the leased line generally requires a site visit by ISP personnel to adjust capacity.

Legacy Switched WAN Options

Review the legacy switched WAN options in Table 7-3.

Table 7-3   Legacy Switch WAN Options

Circuit-Switched Option	Description
Public switched telephone network (PSTN)a	Traditional local loops can transport binary computer data through the voice telephone network using a voiceband modem. The modem modulates the digital data into an analog signal at the source and demodulates the analog signal to digital data at the destination. PSTNs limit the rate of the signal to less than 56 Kbps.
Integrated Services Digital Network (ISDN)	ISDN is a circuit-switching technology that enables the PSTN local loop to carry digital signals. This provides higher-capacity switched connections than dialup access. ISDN provides for data rates from 45 Kbps to 2.048 Mbps.

Packet-Switched Option	Description
Frame Relay	This simple Layer 2 non-broadcast multiaccess (NBMA) WAN technology is used to interconnect enterprise LANs. A single router interface can be used to connect to multiple sites and can support data rates up to 4 Mbps, with some providers offering even higher rates.
Asynchronous Transfer Mode (ATM)	This technology is capable of transferring voice, video, and data through private and public networks. It is built on a cell-based architecture rather than on a frame-based architecture. ATM cells are always a fixed length of 53 bytes.

Check Your Understanding—Traditional WAN Connectivity

Check your understanding of traditional WAN connectivity options by choosing the BEST answer to each of the following questions.

1. Which traditional WAN connectivity option uses T-carrier or E-carrier lines?

   a. ATM

   b. Frame Relay

   c. ISDN

   d. Leased lines

   e. PSTN

2. Which two traditional WAN connectivity options are circuit switched? (Choose two.)

   a. ATM

   b. Frame Relay

   c. ISDN

   d. Leased lines

   e. PSTN

3. Which two traditional WAN connectivity options are packet switched? (Choose two.)

   a. ATM

   b. Frame Relay

   c. ISDN

   d. Leased lines

   e. PSTN

Modern WAN Connectivity

In this section, you review modern WAN connectivity options.

Modern WANs

Review the local loop connections in Figure 7-3.

Figure 7-3   Modern WAN Local Loop Connections

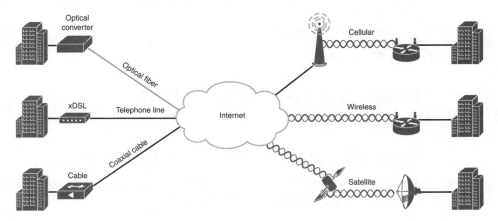

Modern WAN Connectivity Options

In Figure 7-4, label the modern WAN connectivity options.

Figure 7-4   Modern WAN Connectivity Options

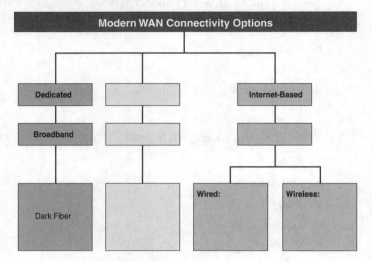

Check Your Understanding—Modern WAN Connectivity

Check your understanding of modern WAN connectivity options by choosing the BEST answer to each of the following questions.

1. Which WAN connectivity option is based on Ethernet LAN technology?

    a. ATM

    b. Cable

    c. DSL

    d. Metro Ethernet

    e. MPLS

2. Which is a service provider WAN solution that uses labels to direct the flow of packets through the provider network?

    a. ATM

    b. Cable

    c. DSL

    d. Metro Ethernet

    e. MPLS

Internet-Based Connectivity

In this section, you review Internet-based connectivity options.

Internet-Based Connectivity Terminology

Match each definition with the appropriate term. This exercise is a one-to-one matching: Each definition has exactly one matching term.

Definitions

a. Situations in which municipalities, cities, and providers install fiber-optic cable runs to the user location

b. Voice-grade telephone service

c. One connection between the client and the ISP

d. One client with four connections— two to each of two different ISPs

e. Networks that often provide high-speed Internet access for free or for substantially less than the price of other broadband services

f. Typically used by rural customers in remote locations where cable and DSL are not available

g. Two connections between one client and one ISP

h. A high-speed, always-on, connection technology that uses existing twisted-pair telephone lines to provide IP services to users

i. Layer 2 protocol that was commonly used by telephone service providers to establish router-to-router and host-to-network connections over dial-up and ISDN access networks

j. A high-speed always-on connection technology that uses a coaxial cable from the cable company to provide IP services to users

k. One client with two connections— one to each of two different ISPs

l. A service provider device that concentrates connections from multiple DSL subscribers

m. A service that allows users with smartphones and tablets to email, surf the web, download apps, and watch videos

n. An encrypted connection between private networks over a public network, such as the Internet

o The cable service provider headend where the fiber media runs are terminated

Terms

____ Cellular

____ CMTS

____ DOCSIS

____ DSL

____ DSLAM

____ Dual-homed

____ Dual-multihomed

____ FTTx

____ Multihomed

____ Municipal Wi-Fi

____ POTS

____ PPP

____ Satellite Internet

____ Single-homed

____ VPN

Labs and Activities

 ### 7.5.11 Lab—Research Broadband Internet Access Technologies

Objectives

Part 1: Investigate Broadband Distribution

Part 2: Research Broadband Access Options for Specific Scenarios

Background / Scenario

Although broadband Internet access options have increased dramatically in recent years, broadband access varies greatly depending on location. In this lab, you will investigate current broadband distribution and research broadband access options for specific scenarios.

Required Resources

Device with Internet access

Part 1: Investigate Broadband Distribution

In Part 1, you will research broadband distribution in a geographical location.

Step 1:   Research broadband distribution.

Use the Internet to research the following questions:

Questions:

a.   For the country in which you reside, what percentage of the population has broadband Internet subscriptions?

_____

b.   What percentage of the population is without broadband Internet options?

_____

Step 2:   Research broadband distribution in the United States.

Search the Internet for the Fixed Broadband Deployment Map. The Fixed Broadband Deployment Map allows users to search and map broadband availability across the United States.

Note: For access options and ISPs for locations outside the United States, perform an Internet search using the keywords **broadband access XYZ**, where XYZ is the name of the country.

   a. Enter your zip code, city and country that you would like to explore and click **Find Broadband**.

   Question:

   List the zip code or city in the space provided.

   _____

   b. Examine the **All Providers Reporting** area of the output. What, if any, wired broadband Internet connections are available at this location? Complete the table below.

ISP	Connection Type	Download Speed

   c. Examine the **All Providers Reporting** area of the output. What, if any, wireless broadband internet connections are available in this location? Complete the table below.

ISP	Connection Type	Download Speed

Part 2: Research Broadband Access Options for Specific Scenarios

In Part 2, you will research and detail broadband options for the following scenarios and select the best last-mile technology to meet the needs of the consumer. You can use the Fixed Broadband Deployment site as a starting point for your research.

Scenario 1: You are moving to Kansas City, Missouri and are exploring home Internet connections. Research and detail two Internet connections from which you can select in this metropolitan area.

ISP	Connection Type	Cost per Month	Download Speed

Choose one from the list of local ISPs that you selected. Give the reasons why you chose that particular ISP.

_____

Scenario 2: You are moving to an area outside of Billings, Montana and are exploring home Internet connections. You will be beyond the reach of cable or DSL connections. Research and detail two Internet connections you can select in this area.

ISP	Connection Type	Cost per Month	Download Speed

Choose one from the list of local ISPs that you selected. Give the reasons why you chose that particular ISP.

Scenario 3: You are moving to New York City and your job requires you to have 24 hours anytime/anywhere access. Research and detail two Internet connections from which you can select in this area.

ISP	Connection Type	Cost per Month	Download Speed

Choose one from the list of local ISPs that you selected. Give the reasons why you chose that particular ISP.

Scenario 4: You are small business owner with 10 employees who telecommute in the Fargo, North Dakota area. The teleworkers live beyond the reach of cable Internet connections. Research and detail two Internet connections you can select in this area.

ISP	Connection Type	Cost per Month	Download Speed

Choose one from the list of local ISPs that you selected. Give the reasons why you chose that particular ISP.

Scenario 5: Your business in Washington, D.C. is expanding to 25 employees and will need to upgrade your broadband access to include equipment colocation and web hosting. Research and detail two Internet connections from which you can select in this area.

ISP	Connection Type	Cost per Month	Download Speed

Choose one from the list of local ISPs that you selected. Give the reasons why you chose that particular ISP.

Reflection Question

How do you think broadband Internet access will change in the future?

7.6.1 Packet Tracer—WAN Concepts

Objectives

In this activity, you will investigate various types of WANs by exploring a topology that uses diverse connectivity technologies.

- Describe different WAN connectivity options.

Background / Scenario

You will explore WAN technologies that are used to connect business and home users to data services.

Note: There is no scoring in this activity.

Instructions

Part 1: Investigate Consumer WAN Technologies for Home and Mobile Devices.

Step 1:   Explore Consumer WAN Technologies.

In this step, you will explore three consumer WAN technologies and home networks.

a.   Look at the two home networks.

Question:

What are the WAN technologies in use?

_____

b.   Examine the connections used in the network topology by selecting the Connections icon (the orange lightning bolt) in the PT devices menu. Hover over the media icons to display their names in the white box at the bottom of the PT window.

Question:

What media is used to connect the two home networks to the ISP? What devices in the home networks are directly connected to the ISP?

_____

c.   Click the DSL modem and open the Physical tab.

Questions:

What ports are available on the device and what is connected to them?

_____

What is the purpose of the DSL modem?

_____

What is the type of connection between the ISP/Telco/Cable Company network and the Home Cable Network? Why is the splitter necessary?

_____

d. Look at the ports on the cable modem.

Questions:

What does the cable modem do? What connections does it have?

_____

Which port does the cable from the cable modem connect to on the home wireless router? Where did the interface IP address come from?

_____

e. Look at the smartphone.

Question:

What is its IP address? Where did the IP address come from?

_____

What data service is the cellphone currently using (cellular data or Wi-Fi)?

_____

Step 2:   Explore the business WAN.

In this step, you will explore the business WAN. The business is a retail tire store. It has a local headquarters where most of the business functions occur and three stores that are connected to the business WAN.

a. Look at the Connections menu.

Question:

What different types of connections do you see in use in the business network?

_____

b. Open the physical view for the StoreNet switch.

Question:

What types of interfaces are present? You may need to zoom and scroll the view to see.

_____

Which interfaces and media are used to connect the store networks to the Business Headquarters network? Why was this done?

_____

What type of WAN service is used to connect the Business Headquarters router to the ISP?

_____

Part 2: Explore Connectivity

Questions:

Ping devices within the Business WAN and the Consumer WAN networks. Also ping between the networks and the between the networks and the web server. Can all hosts ping each other and the web server?

_____

Is this a good situation?

_____

CHAPTER 8

VPN and IPsec Concepts

The "Study Guide" portion of this chapter uses a variety of exercises to test your knowledge of how virtual private networks (VPNs) and IP Security (IPsec) are used to secure site-to-site and remote access connectivity. There are no labs or Packet Tracer activities for this chapter.

As you work through this chapter, use Chapter 8 in *Enterprise Networking, Security, and Automation v7 Companion Guide* or use the corresponding Module 8 in the Enterprise Networking, Security, and Automation online curriculum for assistance.

Study Guide

VPN Technology

In this section, you review benefits of VPN technology.

Virtual Private Networks

Figure 8-1 shows a collection of various types of VPNs managed by an enterprise's main site. The tunnel enables remote sites and users to access the main site's network resources securely.

Figure 8-1   Types of VPNs

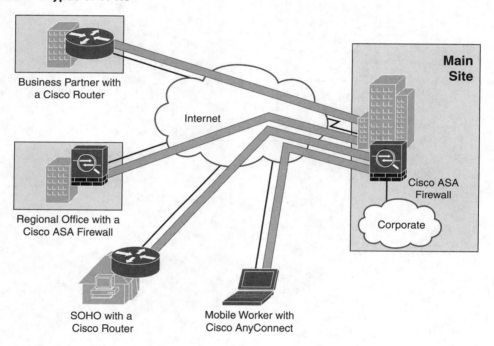

Note the following in Figure 8-1:

- A Cisco Adaptive Security Appliance (ASA) firewall helps organizations provide secure, high-performance connectivity, including VPNs and always-on access, for remote branches and mobile users.

- With a SOHO—stands for small office and home office—a VPN-enabled router can provide VPN connectivity back to the corporate main site.

- Cisco AnyConnect is software that remote workers can use to establish client-based VPN connections with the main site.

VPN Benefits

Briefly describe four benefits of using VPNs.

- _____

  _____

■ _____
  _____
  _____

■ _____
  _____
  _____

■ _____
  _____

Site-to-Site and Remote-Access VPNs

Figures 8-2 and 8-3 show examples of site-to-site and remote-access VPNs.

Figure 8-2   Site-to-Site VPN

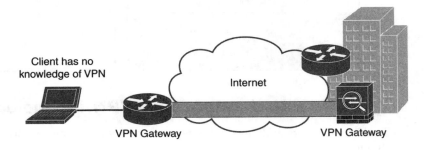

Figure 8-3   Remote-Access VPN

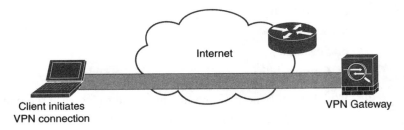

Enterprise and Service Provider VPNs

VPNs can be managed and deployed as

■ **Enterprise VPNs:** Site-to-site and remote-access VPNs are created and managed by the enterprise using both IPsec and SSL VPNs.

■ **Service provider VPNs:** The provider uses Multiprotocol Label Switching (MPLS) at Layer 2 or Layer 3 to create secure channels between an enterprise's sites.

Figure 8-4 lists the different types of enterprise-managed and service provider–managed VPN deployments that are discussed in more detail in this module.

Figure 8-4   Types of Enterprise and Service Provider VPNs

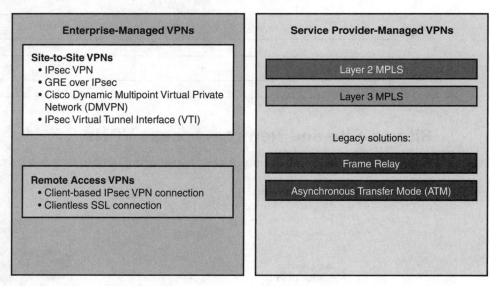

Check Your Understanding—VPN Technology

Check your understanding of VPN technology by choosing the BEST answer to each of the following questions.

1. Which VPN benefit allows an enterprise to easily add more users to the network?

   a. Cost savings

   b. Security

   c. Scalability

   d. Compatibility

2. Which VPN benefit allows an enterprise to increase the bandwidth for remote sites without necessarily adding more equipment or WAN links?

   a. Cost savings

   b. Security

   c. Scalability

   d. Compatibility

3. Which VPN benefit uses advanced encryption and authentication protocols to protect data from unauthorized access?

   a. Cost savings

   b. Security

   c. Scalability

   d. Compatibility

4. Which type of VPN is used to connect a mobile user?

   a. Site-to-site

   b. Remote-access

   c. GRE

   d. IPsec

5. Which VPN solutions are typically used by an enterprise? (Choose three.)

    a. MPLS Layer 2

    b. MPLS Layer 3

    c. IPsec

    d. SSL

    e. Frame Relay

    f. DMVPN

Types of VPNs

In this section, you review different types of VPNs.

Remote-Access VPNs

Figure 8-5 displays two ways that a remote user can initiate a remote-access VPN connection:

Figure 8-5   Two Ways for a Remote User to Connect to a VPN

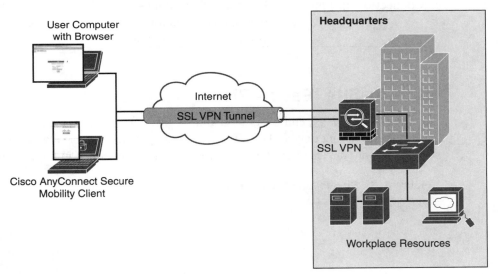

- **Clientless VPN connection:** The connection is secured using a web browser Secure Sockets Layer (SSL) connection, which is called Hypertext Transfer Protocol Secure (HTTPS). The SSL connection is first established, and then HTTP data is exchanged over the connection.

- **Client-based VPN connection:** The connection is secured using VPN client software such as Cisco AnyConnect Secure Mobility Client. Users must initiate the VPN connection using the VPN client and then authenticate to the destination VPN gateway. The VPN client software encrypts the traffic using IPsec or SSL.

SSL and IPsec

SSL uses the public key infrastructure and digital certificates to authenticate peers. Both IPsec and SSL VPN technologies offer access to virtually any network application or resource. However, when security is an issue, IPsec is the superior choice. Review the comparison of IPsec and SSL features in Table 8-1.

Table 8-1   IPsec and SSL Feature Comparison

Feature	IPsec	SSL
Applications supported	Extensive: Supports all IP-based applications.	Limited: Supports only web-based applications and file sharing are supported.
Authentication strength	Strong: Uses two-way authentication with shared keys or digital certificates.	Moderate: Uses one-way or two-way authentication.
Encryption strength	Strong: Uses key lengths from 56 bits to 256 bits.	Moderate to strong: Uses key lengths from 40 bits to 256 bits.
Connection complexity	Medium: Requires a VPN client pre installed on a host.	Low: Requires only a web browser on a host.
Connection options	Limited: Allows only specific devices with specific configurations to connect.	Extensive: Allows any device with a web browser to connect.

Site-to-Site IPsec VPNs

In a site-to-site VPN, end hosts send and receive normal, unencrypted TCP/IP traffic through a VPN terminating device. The VPN terminating device is typically called a VPN gateway. A VPN gateway device could be a router or a firewall, as shown in Figure 8-6.

Figure 8-6   Site-to-Site IPsec VPN

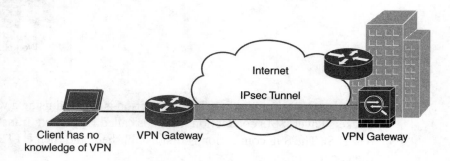

GRE over IPsec

Generic Routing Encapsulation (GRE) is a nonsecure site-to-site VPN tunneling protocol. It can encapsulate various network layer protocols. The terms used to describe the encapsulation of GRE over IPsec tunnel are shown in Figure 8-7.

Figure 8-7   GRE Frame Format

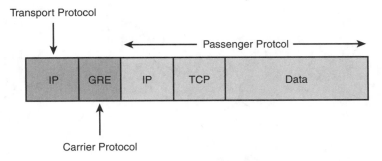

Briefly describe the three protocols in Figure 8-7.

- **Passenger protocol:** _____
  _____

- **Carrier protocol:** _____
  _____

- **Transport protocol:** _____
  _____

Dynamic Multipoint VPNs

Dynamic Multipoint VPN (DMVPN) is a Cisco software solution for building multiple VPNs in an easy, dynamic, and scalable manner. Like other VPN types, DMVPN relies on IPsec to provide secure transport over public networks, such as the Internet.

DMVPN uses a hub-and-spoke configuration to establish a full mesh topology. Spoke sites establish secure VPN tunnels with the hub site, as shown in Figure 8-8.

Figure 8-8   DMVPN Hub-to-Spoke Tunnels

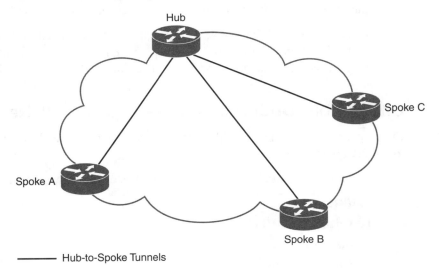

Spoke sites can also obtain information about remote sites from the central site. They can use this information to establish direct VPN tunnels, as shown in Figure 8-9.

Figure 8-9 DMVPN Hub-to-Spoke and Spoke-to-Spoke Tunnels

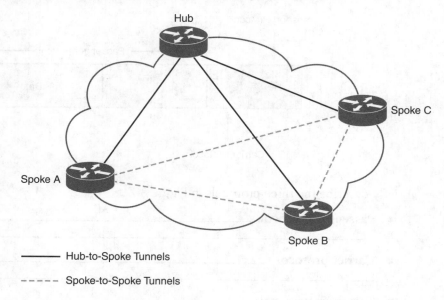

IPsec Virtual Tunnel Interface

Like DMVPN, IPsec virtual tunnel interfaces (VTIs) simplify the configuration process required to support multiple sites and remote access. IPsec VTI configurations are applied to a virtual interface instead of statically mapping the IPsec sessions to a physical interface.

Service Provider MPLS VPNs

Service providers support two types of MPLS VPN solutions:

- **Layer 3 MPLS VPN:** The service provider participates in customer routing by establishing a peering between the customer's routers and the provider's routers.

- **Layer 2 MPLS VPN:** The service provider is not involved in the customer routing. Instead, the provider deploys Virtual Private LAN Service (VPLS) to emulate an Ethernet multiaccess LAN segment over the MPLS network. No routing is involved.

Check Your Understanding—Types of VPNs

Check your understanding of VPN types by choosing the BEST answer to each of the following questions.

1. What type of VPN can be established with a web browser using HTTPS?

   a. IPsec

   b. Client-based VPN

   c. Site-to-site VPN

   d. Clientless VPN

2. Which feature describes SSL VPNs?

   a. All IP-based applications are supported.

   b. They require only a web browser on a host.

    c. Specific devices with specific configurations can connect.

    d. They use two-way authentication with shared keys or digital certificates.

3. What type of protocol is GRE?

    a. Security protocol

    b. Passenger protocol

    c. Carrier protocol

    d. Transport protocol

4. What type of VPN enables an enterprise to rapidly scale secure access across the organization?

    a. DMVPN

    b. Remote-access VPN

    c. Site-to-site VPN

    d. MPLS VPN

5. What type of VPN enables an enterprise to emulate an Ethernet multiaccess LAN with remote sites?

    a. DMVPN

    b. Remote-access VPN

    c. Site-to-site VPN

    d. MPLS VPN

IPsec

In this section, you review how the IPsec framework is used to secure network traffic.

Video—IPsec Concepts

Be sure you review the video in the online curriculum, which covers the following:

- The purpose of IPsec
- IPsec protocols (AH, ESP, SA, IKE)

IPsec Technologies

Using the IPsec framework, IPsec provides these essential security functions:

- **Confidentiality:** IPsec uses encryption algorithms to prevent cybercriminals from reading the packet contents.

- **Integrity:** IPsec uses hashing algorithms to ensure that packets have not been altered between the source and the destination.

- **Origin authentication:** IPsec uses the Internet Key Exchange (IKE) protocol to authenticate the source and the destination. Methods of authentication include using pre-shared keys (passwords), digital certificates, or RSA certificates.

- **Diffie-Hellman:** Secure key exchange can use the DH algorithm.

IPsec is not bound to any specific rules for secure communications. The open slots shown in the IPsec framework in Figure 8-10 can be filled with any of the choices that are available for that IPsec function to create a unique security association (SA).

Figure 8-10   The IPsec Framework

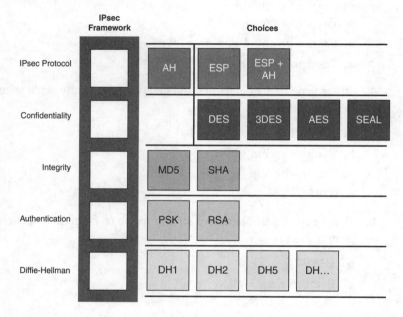

The choices for the IPsec functions in Figure 8-10 are listed in Table 8-2.

Table 8-2   Security Functions

IPsec Function	Description
IPsec protocol	The choices for IPsec protocol include Authentication Header (AH) and Encapsulation Security Protocol (ESP). AH authenticates Layer 3 packets. ESP encrypts Layer 3 packets. (ESP and AH are rarely used as this combination cannot successfully traverse a NAT device.)
Confidentiality	Encryption ensures confidentiality of the Layer 3 packet. Choices include Data Encryption Standard (DES), Triple DES (3DES), Advanced Encryption Standard (AES), and Software-Optimized Encryption Algorithm (SEAL). No encryption is also an option.
Integrity	Integrity involves using a hashing algorithm, such as message-digest 5 (MD5) or Secure Hash Algorithm (SHA), to ensure that data arrives unchanged at the destination.
Authentication	IPsec uses Internet Key Exchange (IKE) to authenticate users and devices that can carry out communication independently. IKE uses several types of authentication, including uername and password, one-time password, biometrics, pre-shared keys (PSKs), and digital certificates using the Rivest, Shamir, and Adleman (RSA) algorithm.
Diffie-Hellman	IPsec uses the DH algorithm to provide a public key exchange method for two peers to establish a shared secret key. There are several different groups to choose from, including DH14, 15, and 16 and DH 19, 20, 21, and 24. DH1, 2, and 5 are no longer recommended.

IPsec Protocol Encapsulation

IPsec encapsulates packets using Authentication Header (AH) or Encapsulation Security Protocol (ESP), as shown in Figure 8-11.

Figure 8-11   Choosing the IPsec Protocol

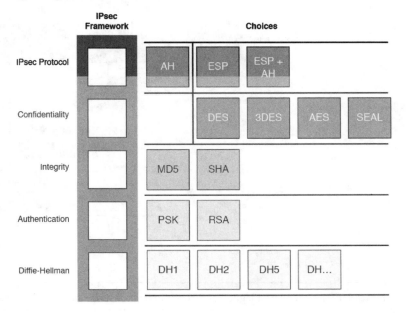

In Figure 8-11, the following choices are available:

- AH is appropriate only when confidentiality is not required or permitted. All text is transported unencrypted.

- ESP provides both confidentiality and authentication. It provides confidentiality by performing encryption on the IP packet. ESP provides authentication for the inner IP packet and ESP header.

Confidentiality

Confidentiality is achieved by encrypting the data. The encryption algorithms highlighted in Figure 8-12 are all symmetric key cryptosystems.

Figure 8-12   Choosing the Confidentiality Encryption Algorithm

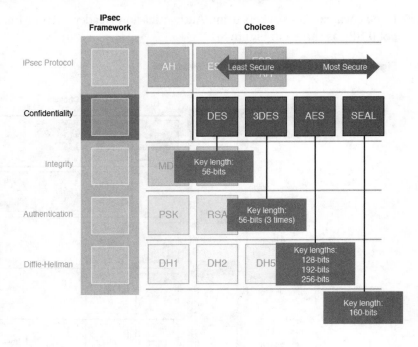

Note: DES is considered legacy and should not be used. 3DES is scheduled to be retired in 2023.

Integrity

Data integrity means that the data that is received is exactly the same data that was sent. A hash message authentication code (HMAC) is a data integrity algorithm that guarantees the integrity of the message by using a hash value. Figure 8-13 highlights the two most common HMAC algorithms.

Figure 8-13   Choosing the HMAC Algorithm

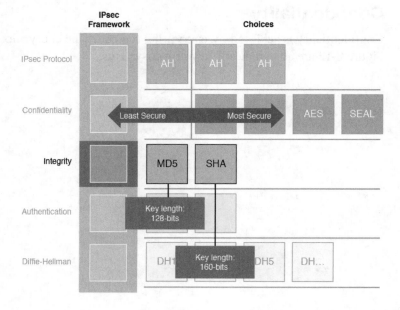

Authentication

The device on the other end of the VPN tunnel must be authenticated before the communication path can be considered secure. Figure 8-14 highlights the two peer authentication methods.

Figure 8-14   Choosing the Authentication Method

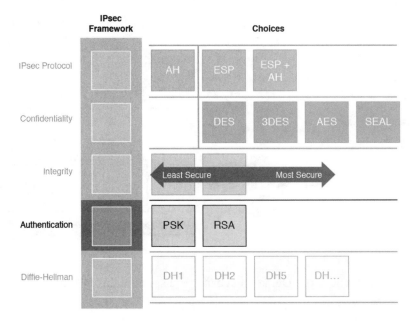

The authentication methods in Figure 8-14 are as follows:

- **Pre-shared key (PSK):** A PSK is easy to configure manually but does not scale well because each IPsec peer must be configured with the PSK of every other peer with which it communicates.

- **Rivest, Shamir, and Adleman (RSA):** RSA authentication uses digital certificates to authenticate the peers. The local device derives a hash and encrypts it with its private key. At the remote end, the encrypted hash is decrypted using the public key of the local end.

Secure Key Exchange with Diffie-Hellman

Encryption algorithms require a symmetric, shared secret key to perform encryption and decryption. The easiest key exchange method is to use a public key exchange method, such as Diffie-Hellman (DH), as shown in Figure 8-15.

Figure 8-15 Choosing the DH Group

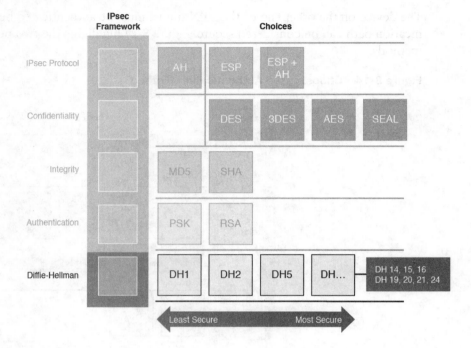

Variations of the DH key exchange are specified as DH groups:

- DH groups 1, 2, and 5 should no longer be used. These groups support key sizes of 768 bits, 1024 bits, and 1536 bits, respectively.

- DH groups 14, 15, and 16 use larger key sizes, with 2048 bits, 3072 bits, and 4096 bits, respectively, and are recommended for use until 2030.

- DH groups 19, 20, 21, and 24, with respective key sizes of 256 bits, 384 bits, 521 bits, and 2048 bits, support elliptic curve cryptography (ECC), which reduces the time needed to generate keys. DH group 24 is the preferred next-generation encryption.

Video—IPsec Transport and Tunnel Mode

Be sure to review the video in the online curriculum. It explains the process of IPv4 packets being sent in transport mode and tunnel mode.

Check Your Understanding—IPsec

Check your understanding of IPsec by choosing the BEST answer to each of the following questions.

1. IPsec can protect traffic in which OSI layers? (Choose four.)

   a. Layer 1

   b. Layer 2

   c. Layer 3

   d. Layer 4

   e. Layer 5

    f. Layer 6

    g. Layer 7

2. Which IPsec function uses pre-shared passwords, digital certificates, or RSA certificates?

    a. IPsec protocol

    b. Confidentiality

    c. Integrity

    d. Authentication

    e. Diffie-Hellman

3. True or false: The IPsec framework must be updated each time a new standard is developed.

    a. True

    b. False

4. Which choices are available for the IPsec protocol function in the IPsec framework? (Choose two.)

    a. AES

    b. AH

    c. DH24

    d. ESP

    e. PSK

    f. RSA

    g. SHA

5. Which choices are available for the confidentiality function in the IPsec framework? (Choose three.)

    a. 3DES

    b. AES

    c. AH

    d. DH24

    e. PSK

    f. SEAL

    g. SHA

6. Which choices are available for the integrity function in the IPsec framework? (Choose two.)

    a. AES

    b. AH

    c. DH24

    d. MD5

    e. PSK

    f. SEAL

    g. SHA

7. Which choices are available for the authentication function in the IPsec framework? (Choose two.)

   a. AES

   b. AH

   c. DH24

   d. PSK

   e. RSA

   f. SEAL

   g. SHA

8. Which Diffie-Hellman group choices are no longer recommended?

   a. DH groups 1, 2, and 5

   b. DH groups 14, 15, and 16

   c. DH groups 19, 20, 21, and 24

Labs and Activities

There are no labs or Packet Tracer activities in this chapter.

CHAPTER 9

QoS Concepts

The "Study Guide" portion of this chapter uses a variety of exercises to test your knowledge of how networking devices implement quality of service (QoS). There are no labs or Packet Tracer activities for this chapter.

As you work through this chapter, use Chapter 9 in *Enterprise Networking, Security, and Automation v7 Companion Guide* or use the corresponding Module 9 in the Enterprise Networking, Security, and Automation online curriculum for assistance.

Study Guide

Network Transmission Quality

In this section, you will review how network transmission characteristics impact quality.

Video Tutorial—The Purpose of QoS

Be sure to review the video in the online course. It explains QoS and why it is needed.

Network Transmission Quality Terminology

Match each definition with the appropriate term. This exercise is a one-to-one matching: Each definition has exactly one matching term.

Definition

a. The number of bits that can be transmitted in a single second.

b. Creates higher expectations for quality delivery.

c. De-jitters a stream of packets out the interface.

d. Happens when congestion occurs.

e. The variable amount of time it takes for the frame to traverse the links between the source and the destination.

f. Caused by variations in delay of received packets.

g. The fixed amount of time it takes to compress data at the source before transmitting to the first internetworking device.

h. Occurs when the demand for bandwidth exceeds the amount available.

i. The time it takes to encapsulate data with all the necessary header information.

j. Holds packets in memory until resources become available to transmit them.

k. Used to classify voice traffic for zero packet loss.

l. Interpolates what the audio should be for a missing packet.

m. The fixed amount of time it takes to transmit a frame from the NIC to the wire.

n. The time it takes to buffer a flow of packets and then send them out in evenly spaced intervals.

Terms

_____ Serialization delay

_____ Queue

_____ Congestion

_____ Packetization delay

_____ Bandwidth

_____ De-jitter delay

_____ Digital signal processor

_____ Packet loss

_____ Propagation delay

_____ QoS mechanisms

_____ Voice and video traffic

_____ Code delay

_____ Jitter

_____ Playout delay buffer

Check Your Understanding—Network Transmission Quality

Check your understanding of network transmission quality by choosing the BEST answer to each of the following questions.

1. What is the variable amount of time it takes for a frame to traverse the links between the source and the destination?

   a. Serialization delay

   b. Propagation delay

   c. Code delay

2. What happens when congestion occurs?

   a. Packet loss

   b. Jitter

   c. Code delay

3. What is the fixed amount of time it takes to transmit a frame from the NIC to the wire?

   a. Serialization delay

   b. Jitter

   c. Code delay

4. What is caused by variation in delay?

   a. Congestion

   b. Packet loss

   c. Jitter

Traffic Characteristics

In this section, you will review the minimum network requirements for voice, video, and data traffic.

Video Tutorial—Traffic Characteristics

Be sure to review the video in the online course. It explains the characteristics of voice, video, and data traffic.

Traffic Characteristics

In Table 9-1, select the type of traffic described by each characteristic.

Table 9-1   Identify Traffic Characteristics

Traffic Characteristic	Voice	Video	Data
Traffic can be predictable and smooth.			
Cisco uses RTP ports 16384–32767 to prioritize this traffic.			
Traffic can be unpredictable, inconsistent, and bursty.			
Traffic is very sensitive to delays and dropped packets.			
Packet size varies every 33 ms.			
If packets are lost in transit, they are re-sent.			
Without QoS and a significant amount of extra bandwidth capacity, this traffic typically degrades.			
Cannot be retransmitted if lost.			
Includes RSTP UDP packets on port 554.			
Must receive a higher UDP priority.			
Does not consume a lot of network resources.			
Requires at least 384 Kbps of bandwidth.			
Traffic can be smooth or bursty.			

Check Your Understanding—Traffic Characteristics

Check your understanding of traffic characteristics by choosing the BEST answer to each of the following questions.

1. Which type of traffic tends to consume a large portion of network capacity?

    a. Voice

    b. Video

    c. Data

2. Which type of traffic requires at least 384 Kbps of bandwidth?

   a. Voice

   b. Video

   c. Data

3. Which type of traffic is unpredictable, inconsistent, and bursty?

   a. Voice

   b. Video

   c. Data

4. Which type of traffic can be predictable and smooth?

   a. Voice

   b. Video

   c. Data

5. Which type of traffic cannot be retransmitted if lost?

   a. Voice

   b. Video

   c. Data

6. Which type of traffic must receive a higher UDP priority?

   a. Voice

   b. Video

   c. Data

Queuing Algorithms

In this section, you will review the queuing algorithms used by networking devices.

Video Tutorial—QoS Algorithms

Be sure to review the video in the online course. It covers the following:

- First-in, first-out (FIFO) queuing (with no QoS)
- Weighted Fair Queuing (WFQ)
- Class-Based Weighted Fair Queuing (CBWFQ)
- Low Latency Queuing (LLQ)

Identify the Queuing Algorithm

What queuing algorithm is illustrated in Figure 9-1?

Figure 9-1   Queuing Algorithm #1

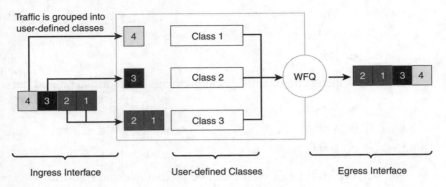

What queuing algorithm is illustrated in Figure 9-2?

Figure 9-2   Queuing Algorithm #2

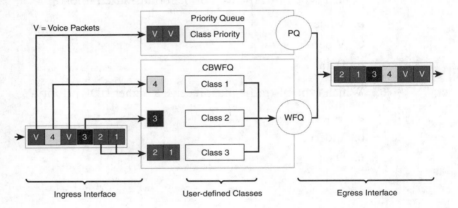

What queuing algorithm is illustrated in Figure 9-3?

Figure 9-3   Queuing Algorithm #3

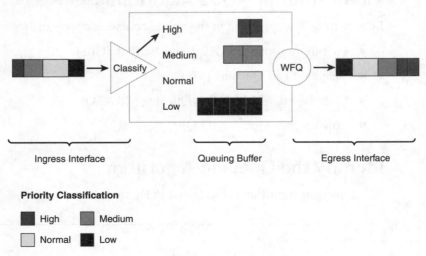

What queuing algorithm is illustrated in Figure 9-4?

Figure 9-4 Queuing Algorithm #4

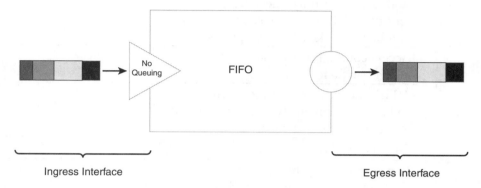

Queuing Algorithm Characteristics

In Table 9-2, select the queuing algorithm described by each characteristic.

Table 9-2 Identify Queuing Algorithm Characteristics

Queuing Algorithm Characteristic	FIFO	WFQ	CBWFQ	LLQ
Important or time-sensitive traffic can be dropped when congestion occurs on the interface.				
Classifies traffic into different flows based on packet header addressing.				
Schedules interactive traffic to the front of a queue to reduce response time.				
Also known as first-come, first-served.				
Poses problems for voice traffic that is largely intolerant of delay, especially variation in delay.				
Cannot support links that use tunneling and encryption.				
The bandwidth assigned to the packets of a class determines the order in which packets are sent.				
Applies priority, or weights, to identify traffic and classify it into conversations or flows.				
Provides support for user-defined traffic classes.				
Effective for large links that have little delay and minimal congestion.				
Allows delay-sensitive data such as voice to be sent before packets in other queues.				

Queuing Algorithm Characteristic	FIFO	WFQ	CBWFQ	LLQ
Used by default in all interfaces except some serial interfaces.				
Adds a strict priority queue for delay-sensitive traffic such as voice traffic to be sent before packets in other queues.				
Access control lists (ACLs) are used to match criteria for each class.				
A FIFO queue is reserved for each class, and traffic belonging to a class is directed to the queue for that class.				
Provides the fastest queuing.				
Packets satisfying the match criteria for a class constitute the traffic for that class.				
This automated scheduling method provides fair bandwidth allocation to all network traffic.				

Check Your Understanding—Queuing Algorithms

Check your understanding of queuing algorithms by choosing the BEST answer to each of the following questions.

1. Which queuing algorithm determines allowed bandwidth while simultaneously scheduling interactive traffic to the front of a queue to reduce response time?

   a. FIFO

   b. WFQ

   c. CBWFQ

   d. LLQ

2. Which queuing algorithm provides support for user-defined traffic classes?

   a. FIFO

   b. WFQ

   c. CBWFQ

   d. LLQ

3. Which queuing algorithm is effective for large links that have little delay and minimal congestion?

   a. FIFO

   b. WFQ

   c. CBWFQ

   d. LLQ

4. Which queuing algorithm classifies traffic into different flows, based on packet header addressing?

   a. FIFO

   b. WFQ

   c. CBWFQ

   d. LLQ

5. Which queuing algorithm allows delay-sensitive data such as voice to be sent before packets in other queues?

   a. FIFO

   b. WFQ

   c. CBWFQ

   d. LLQ

6. Which queuing algorithm applies priority, or weights, to identify traffic and classify it?

   a. FIFO

   b. WFQ

   c. CBWFQ

   d. LLQ

QoS Models

In this section, you will review the different QoS models.

Video Tutorial—QoS Models

Be sure to review the video in the online course. It covers the following:

- Best-effort model

- Integrated Services (IntServ)

- Differentiated Services (DiffServ)

QoS Model Characteristics

In Table 9-3, select the QoS model described by each characteristic.

Table 9-3   Identify the QoS Model Characteristic

QoS Model Characteristic	Best Effort	Integrated Services	Differentiated Services
Provides per-request policy admission control.			
Scalability is only limited by bandwidth limits, in which case all traffic is equally affected.			

QoS Model Characteristic	Best Effort	Integrated Services	Differentiated Services
Uses a "soft QoS" approach in which QoS mechanisms are applied on a hop-by-hop basis.			
Signaling of dynamic port numbers such as H.323.			
No special QoS mechanisms are required.			
Uses RSVP to signal QoS needs to all devices in the end-to-end path.			
Requires a set of complex mechanisms to work in concert throughout the network.			
There are no guarantees of delivery.			
There is no absolute guarantee of service quality.			
Explicit end-to-end resource admission control.			
No packets get preferential treatment.			
Resource intensive due to the stateful architecture requirement for continuous signaling.			
Flow-based approach not scalable to large implementations such as the Internet.			
Provides many different levels of quality.			
Highly scalable.			

Check Your Understanding—QoS Models

Check your understanding of QoS models by choosing the BEST answer to each of the following questions.

1. Which QoS model provides per-request policy admission control?

   a. Best effort

   b. Integrated Services

   c. Differentiated Services

2. Which QoS model requires no special QoS mechanisms?

   a. Best effort

   b. Integrated Services

   c. Differentiated Services

3. Which QoS model provides many different levels of quality?

   a. Best effort

   b. Integrated Services

   c. Differentiated Services

4. Which QoS model uses explicit end-to-end resource admission control?

   a. Best effort

   b. Integrated Services

   c. Differentiated Services

5. Which QoS model is the most scalable?

   a. Best effort

   b. Integrated Services

   c. Differentiated Services

QoS Implementation Techniques

In this section, you will review how QoS mechanisms ensure transmission quality.

Video Tutorial—QoS Implementation Techniques

Be sure to review the video in the online course. It covers the following:

- Implementation tools (classification and marking, congestion avoidance, and congestion management)
- Traffic marking

QoS Implementation Techniques Overview

QoS includes the following categories of QoS tools:

- Classification and marking tools
- Congestion avoidance tools
- Congestion management tools
- Traffic marking tools

As packets enter the interface, they are classified and marked according to the QoS policy established by the network administrator. As the packet queue fills up on an interface, congestion can be avoided by using policing and shaping tools to selectively drop lower-priority traffic.

Traffic Marking Tools

For each QoS tool shown in Table 9-4, fill in the Layer field (2 or 3) that is marked and the number of bits. Because there are two QoS tools for IPv4 and IPv6, the first one is filled in for you.

Table 9-4   QoS Tools for Traffic Marking

QoS Tool	Layer	Marking Field	Bits
Ethernet (802.1Q, 802.1p)			
Wi-Fi (802.11)			
MPLS			
IPv4 and IPv6	3	IP Precedence (IPP)	3
IPv4 and IPv6			

Marking at Layer 2

The 802.1Q standard for VLAN tagging includes a 3-bit field for identifying the Class of Service (CoS). This means that a Layer 2 Ethernet frame can be marked with one of eight levels of priority (values 0 through 7). In Table 9-5, complete the Description column to indicate the meaning of each of the CoS values 0 through 5.

Table 9-5   Description of the CoS Values

CoS Value	CoS Binary Value	Description
0	000	
1	001	
2	010	
3	011	
4	100	
5	101	
6	110	Reserved
7	111	Reserved

Marking at Layer 3

IPv4 and IPv6 specify an 8-bit field in their packet headers to mark packets. Called Type of Service (ToS) in IPv4 and Traffic Class in IPv6, these fields are used to carry the packet marking as assigned by the QoS classification tools. In Figure 9-5, label the fields for each of the RFCs.

Figure 9-5   Type of Service and Traffic Class Fields

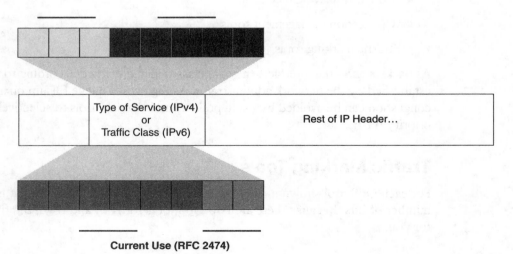

Old Use (RFC 791)

Type of Service (IPv4)
or
Traffic Class (IPv6)

Rest of IP Header...

Current Use (RFC 2474)

The 6-bit DSCP field allows for 64 values, which are organized into three categories:

- **Best Effort (BE):** Uses DSCP value 0

- **Expedited Forwarding (EF):** Uses DSCP value 46

- **Assured Forwarding (AF):** The first three most significant bits define the class (class 1–4); the next two bits define the drop preference (low, medium, or high), and the final bit is set to zero

In Table 9-6, fill in the decimal and binary values, class, and drop preference for each AF value. A few of the rows are already filled in for you.

Table 9-6   Assured Forwarding Values

AF value	Decimal	Binary	Class	Drop Preference
AF41				
AF31	26	011010	3	Low
AF21				
AF11				
AF42				
AF32	28	011100	3	Medium
AF22				
AF12				
AF43				
AF33				
AF23	22	010110	2	High
AF13				

QoS Mechanism Terminology

Match each definition with the appropriate term. This exercise is a one-to-one matching: Each definition has exactly one matching term.

Definition	Term

Definition

a. Used to inform downstream routers that there is congestion in the packet flow.

b. Provides buffer management and allows TCP traffic to throttle back before buffers are exhausted.

c. Queuing and scheduling methods where excess traffic is buffered while it waits to be sent on an egress interface.

d. Adding a value to the packet header.

e. Adds a 3-bit field to identify the Class of Service (CoS) markings.

f. Only QoS option available for switches that are not IP aware.

g. Retains excess packets in a queue and then schedules the excess for later transmission over increments of time.

h. Mechanism for classifying traffic at Layers 4 to 7.

i. Uses the five most significant bits to indicate class and drop preference.

j. When the traffic rate reaches the configured maximum rate, excess traffic is dropped.

k. Carries the QoS information from end to end.

l. An IEEE specification for implementing VLANs in Layer 2 switched networks.

m. Has a DSCP value of 0.

n. The first three bits in this DSCP category map directly to CoS value 5 for voice traffic.

o. Determines what class of traffic packets or frames belong to.

Term

_____ Traffic shaping

_____ Best Effort (BE)

_____ NBAR

_____ 802.1Q

_____ Expedited Forwarding (EF)

_____ ECN bits

_____ Marking

_____ Assured Forwarding (AF)

_____ Congestion avoidance

_____ Layer 2 marking

_____ WRED algorithm

_____ Layer 3 marking

_____ Traffic policing

_____ 802.1p

_____ Classification

Check Your Understanding—QoS Implementation Techniques

Check your understanding of QoS implementation techniques by choosing the BEST answer to each of the following questions.

1. Which of the following detects when traffic rates reach a configured maximum rate and drops excess traffic?

   a. Traffic policing

   b. Traffic shaping

   c. Classification

2. Which of the following determines what class of traffic packets or frames belong to.

   a. Marking

   b. Classification

   c. Traffic shaping

3. Which of the following adds a value to the packet header?

   a. Marking

   b. Classification

   c. 802.1Q

4. Which of the following provides buffer management and allows TCP traffic to throttle back before buffers are exhausted?

   a. Traffic policing

   b. 802.1Q

   c. WRED

5. Which of the following retains excess packets in a queue and then schedules the excess for later transmission over increments of time?

   a. WRED

   b. Traffic policing

   c. Traffic shaping

Labs and Activities

There are no labs or Packet Tracer activities in this chapter.

CHAPTER 10

Network Management

The "Study Guide" portion of this chapter uses a variety of exercises to test your knowledge and skills related to implementing protocols to manage a network. The "Labs and Activities" portion of this chapter includes all the online curriculum labs and Packet Tracer activity instructions.

As you work through this chapter, use Chapter 10 in *Enterprise Networking, Security, and Automation v7 Companion Guide* or use the corresponding Module 10 in the Enterprise Networking, Security, and Automation online curriculum for assistance.

Study Guide

Device Discovery with CDP and LLDP

In this section, you review how to use Cisco Discovery Protocol (CDP) and Link Layer Discovery Protocol (LLDP) to map a network topology.

Configure and Verify CDP

CDP is enabled by default on Cisco devices. However, it may be desirable to disable CDP for security reasons either globally or on the interface. What command, including prompt, disables CDP globally?

_____

_____

_____

What command, including prompt, disables CDP on an interface?

_____

_____

_____

In Example 10-1, fill in the command that displays the CDP global information shown in the output.

Example 10-1   Displaying CDP Global Information

```
Router# _____
Global CDP information:
        Sending CDP packets every 60 seconds
        Sending a holdtime value of 180 seconds
        Sending CDPv2 advertisements is enabled
```

In Example 10-2, fill in the command that displays the CDP interface information shown in the output.

Example 10-2   Displaying CDP Interface Information

```
Router# _____
GigabitEthernet0/0/0 is administratively down, line protocol is down
  Encapsulation ARPA
  Sending CDP packets every 60 seconds
  Holdtime is 180 seconds
GigabitEthernet0/0/1 is up, line protocol is up
  Encapsulation ARPA
  Sending CDP packets every 60 seconds
  Holdtime is 180 seconds
```

```
GigabitEthernet0/0/2 is down, line protocol is down
  Encapsulation ARPA
  Sending CDP packets every 60 seconds
  Holdtime is 180 seconds
Serial0/1/0 is administratively down, line protocol is down
  Encapsulation HDLC
  Sending CDP packets every 60 seconds
  Holdtime is 180 seconds
Serial0/1/1 is administratively down, line protocol is down
  Encapsulation HDLC
  Sending CDP packets every 60 seconds
  Holdtime is 180 seconds
GigabitEthernet0 is down, line protocol is down
  Encapsulation ARPA
  Sending CDP packets every 60 seconds
  Holdtime is 180 seconds
cdp enabled interfaces  : 6
interfaces up           : 1
interfaces down         : 5
```

Configure and Verify LLDP

By default, LLDP is not enabled on Cisco devices. What command, including prompt, enables LLDP globally?

_____

_____

_____

What commands, including prompt, enable LLDP on an interface to send and accept LLDP packets?

_____

_____

_____

_____

_____

In Example 10-3, fill in the command that displays the LLDP global information in the output.

Example 10-3   Displaying LLDP Global Information

```
Router# _____
Global LLDP Information:
    Status: ACTIVE
    LLDP advertisements are sent every 30 seconds
    LLDP hold time advertised is 120 seconds
    LLDP interface reinitialisation delay is 2 seconds
```

In Example 10-4, fill in the command that displays the LLDP neighbor information in the output.

Example 10-4   Displaying LLDP Neighbor Information

```
S1# _____

Capability codes:

    (R) Router, (B) Bridge, (T) Telephone, (C) DOCSIS Cable Device

    (W) WLAN Access Point, (P) Repeater, (S) Station, (O) Other

Device ID          Local Intf     Hold-time  Capability    Port ID

R1                 Fa0/5          117        R             Gi0/0/1

S2                 Fa0/1          112        B             Fa0/1

Total entries displayed: 2
```

Draw and Label the Network Topology

Note: This activity uses CDP as the example. However, LLDP would provide equivalent information to complete the same topology.

Use the command output in Example 10-5 to answer the following questions.

What command was used to generate the output? _____

How many devices are in the network? _____

What devices (type and platform) are included in the network?

_____

What CDP command allows you to record the IP addresses of connected devices?

_____

Based on the command output in Example 10-5, use the space provided in Figure 10-1 to draw and label the topology. Include all the devices, the links between the devices, device names, and interface labels.

Example 10-5   CDP Command Output

```
London# _____

Capability Codes: R - Router, T - Trans Bridge, B - Source Route Bridge

                  S - Switch, H - Host, I - IGMP, r - Repeater, P - Phone

Device ID     Local Intrfce    Holdtme     Capability    Platform     Port ID

LdSw          Gig 0/0          154         S             2960         Gig 0/1

HK1           Ser 0/0/0        124         R             C1900        Ser 0/0/0

HK2           Ser 0/0/1        179         R             C1900        Ser 0/0/1

HK1# _____

Capability Codes: R - Router, T - Trans Bridge, B - Source Route Bridge

                  S - Switch, H - Host, I - IGMP, r - Repeater, P - Phone

Device ID     Local Intrfce    Holdtme     Capability    Platform     Port ID

London        Ser 0/0/0        145         R             C1900        Ser 0/0/0

Sw1           Gig 0/0          148         S             2960         Gig 0/1
```

```
HK2#
Capability Codes: R - Router, T - Trans Bridge, B - Source Route Bridge
                  S - Switch, H - Host, I - IGMP, r - Repeater, P - Phone
Device ID      Local Intrfce    Holdtme     Capability    Platform     Port ID
Sw1            Gig 0/1          128             S         2960         Gig 0/2
London         Ser 0/0/1        125             R         C1900        Ser 0/0/1
```

Figure 10-1   Network Topology

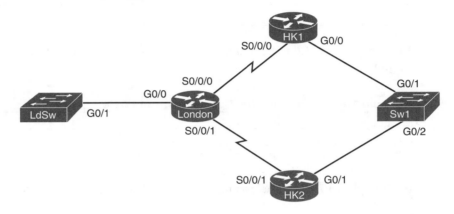

Compare CDP and LLDP

In Table 10-1, indicate the protocol for each characteristic listed.

Table 10-1   CDP and LLDP Characteristics

Field	CDP	LLDP
Requires two commands on the interface to transmit and receive packets.		
Used to gather information about Cisco devices that share the same data link.		
Works with network devices, such as routers, switches, and wireless LAN access points across multiple manufacturers' devices.		
A vendor-neutral neighbor discovery protocol that runs on LANs.		
A media- and protocol-independent protocol that runs on all Cisco devices.		
A protocol that advertises its identity and capabilities to other devices and receives the information from physically connected Layer 2 devices from multiple manufacturers.		
Advertisements share information about the type of device that is discovered, the names of the devices, and the number and type of interfaces.		

NTP

In this section, you review how to implement Network Time Protocol (NTP) between an NTP client and NTP server.

Set the Clock

What are the two methods for setting the date and time on a router or a switch?

- ■ _____

- ■ _____

What is the command to manually set the time and date to December 1, 2020, 3:00 p.m.?

_____

_____

_____

In Example 10-6, fill in the command that displays the current time and date shown in the output.

Example 10-6   Displaying the Current Time and Date

```
Router# _____
*15:0:19.942 UTC Fri Dec 1 2017
```

In Example 10-7, fill in the command used to determine that the clock was manually set.

Example 10-7   Determining How the Clock was Configured

```
Router# _____
*15:10:32.713 UTC Fri Dec 1 2017
Time source is user configuration
```

NTP Operation

In the following paragraph, fill in the number for each stratum level.

NTP networks use a hierarchical system of time sources. Each level in this hierarchical system is called a stratum. Stratum ___ devices are high-precision timekeeping devices. Stratum ___ devices are directly connected to one or more of these high-precision timekeeping devices. Stratum ___ devices, such as NTP clients, synchronize their time using NTP packets from stratum ___ NTP servers.

Configure and Verify NTP

The NTP server is at 10.10.10.10. Record the command, including router prompt, that would configure R1 to synchronize with the NTP server.

_____

In Example 10-8, record the commands to verify the NTP configuration on R1.

Example 10-8   NTP Verification Commands

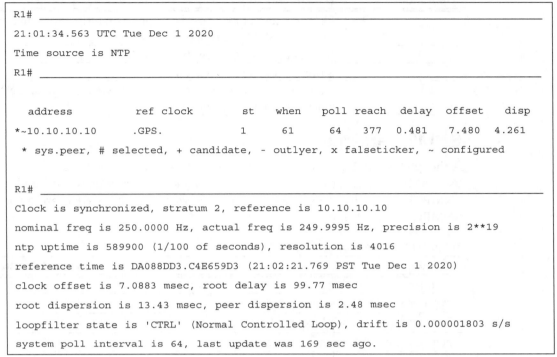

```
R1# _____
21:01:34.563 UTC Tue Dec 1 2020
Time source is NTP
R1# _____

   address          ref clock       st    when    poll reach  delay  offset   disp
*~10.10.10.10       .GPS.            1     61      64   377   0.481   7.480  4.261
 * sys.peer, # selected, + candidate, - outlyer, x falseticker, ~ configured


R1# _____
Clock is synchronized, stratum 2, reference is 10.10.10.10
nominal freq is 250.0000 Hz, actual freq is 249.9995 Hz, precision is 2**19
ntp uptime is 589900 (1/100 of seconds), resolution is 4016
reference time is DA088DD3.C4E659D3 (21:02:21.769 PST Tue Dec 1 2020)
clock offset is 7.0883 msec, root delay is 99.77 msec
root dispersion is 13.43 msec, peer dispersion is 2.48 msec
loopfilter state is 'CTRL' (Normal Controlled Loop), drift is 0.000001803 s/s
system poll interval is 64, last update was 169 sec ago.
```

SNMP

In this section, you review how Simple Network Management Protocol (SNMP) operates.

SNMP Operation

Fill in the missing words and phrases in the following paragraph.

SNMP is a(n) _____ layer protocol that provides a standardized way of communicating information between SNMP agents and SNMP managers using UDP port _____. The SNMP manager is part of a network management system (NMS). The SNMP manager can collect information from agents using _____ messages. Each agent stores data about the device in the _____ (_____) locally so that it is ready to respond to these messages from the NMS. Agents can also be configured to forward directly to the NMS by using _____ messages.

In Table 10-2, indicate the SNMP message type for each of the descriptions provided.

Table 10-2   SNMP Message Type

Operation	Description
	Retrieves a value from a specific variable.
	Retrieves a value from a variable within a table. The SNMP manager does not need to know the exact variable name; a sequential search is performed to find the needed variable from within a table.

Operation	Description
	Retrieves large blocks of data, such as multiple rows in a table; works only with SNMPv2 or later.
	Replies to messages sent by an NMS.
	Stores a value in a specific variable.
	An unsolicited message sent by an SNMP agent to an SNMP manager when some event has occurred.

SNMP Versions

Although SNMPv1 is legacy, Cisco IOS supports all three versions. All versions of SNMP use SNMP managers, agents, and MIBs. In today's networks, you will most likely encounter SNMPv3 or SNMPv2c. In Table 10-3, indicate whether each SNMP characteristic applies to SNMPv2c, SNMPv3, or both.

Table 10-3 Comparing SNMPv2c and SNMPv3

Characteristic	SNMPv2c	SNMPv3	Both
Used for interoperability and includes message integrity			
Provides services for security models			
Uses community-based forms of security			
Includes expanded error codes with types			
Provides services for both security models and security levels			
Authenticates the source of management messages			
Cannot provide encrypted management messages			
Supported by Cisco IOS software			

Community Strings

In SNMPv1 and SNMPv2c, access to the MIB is controlled through the use of two types of

_____

- _____
- _____

Why is this type of access no longer considered best practice?

_____
_____

MIB Object ID

The MIB defines a variable using an MIB object ID. These IDs are derived hierarchically using the scheme shown in Figure 10-2. Label Figure 10-2 with the most common public variables.

Figure 10-2   Management Information Base Object ID Scheme

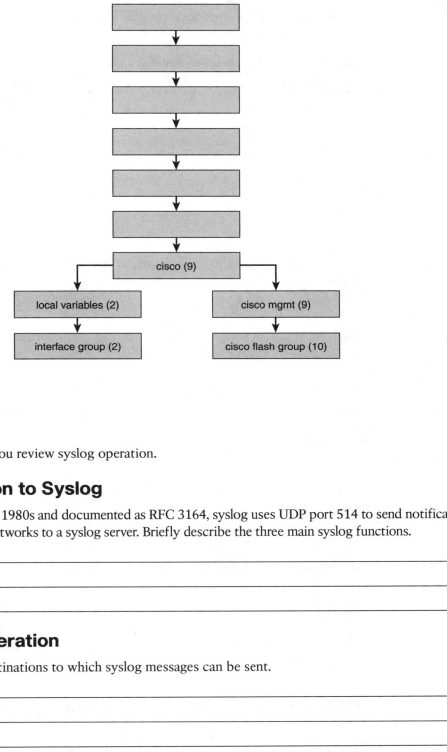

Syslog

In this section, you review syslog operation.

Introduction to Syslog

Developed in the 1980s and documented as RFC 3164, syslog uses UDP port 514 to send notifications across IP networks to a syslog server. Briefly describe the three main syslog functions.

- _____
- _____
- _____

Syslog Operation

List the four destinations to which syslog messages can be sent.

- _____
- _____
- _____
- _____

Syslog Message Format

Every syslog message contains a severity level and a facility. In Table 10-4, fill in the missing information for severity name and level.

Table 10-4 Syslog Message Severity Levels

Severity Name	Severity Level	Explanation
		System unusable
		Immediate action needed
		Critical condition
		Error condition
		Warning condition
		Normal but significant condition
		Informational message
		Debugging message

What command, including router prompt, configures a Cisco device to add a timestamp to syslog messages?

When configuring routers, one of the messages you most commonly see is the interface up/up message, as shown in Example 10-9.

Example 10-9 Interface up/up Syslog Message

```
*Mar  1 11:52:45: %LINK-3-UPDOWN: Interface GigabitEthernet0/0/0, changed state to up

*Mar  1 11:52:46: %LINEPROTO-5-UPDOWN: Line protocol on Interface
GigabitEthernet0/0/0, changed state to up
```

In Table 10-5, use the second part of the output from Example 10-9 to provide an example of each field in the syslog message format.

Table 10-5 Syslog Message Format

Field	Example
Timestamp	
Facility	
Severity	
Mnemonic	
Description	

Check Your Understanding—Syslog Operation

Check your understanding of syslog operation by choosing the BEST answer to each of the following questions, based on the following syslog output:

```
*Jun 12 17:46:01.619: %IFMGR-7-NO_IFINDEX_FILE: Unable to open nvram:/ifIndex-table
No such file or directory
```

1. What is the severity level of this syslog message?

   a. Error

   b. Informational

   c. Warning

   d. Debugging

2. Refer to the syslog output. What is the mnemonic for this syslog message?

   a. IFMGR

   b. Unable to open nvram

   c. NO_IFINDEX_FILE

   d. ifIndex-table

3. Refer to the syslog output. What is the syslog reporting facility?

   a. IFMGR

   b. Unable to open nvram

   c. NO_IFINDEX_FILE

   d. ifIndex-table

Router and Switch File Maintenance

In this section, you review how to use commands to back up and restore an IOS configuration file.

Router File Systems

Managing configuration files is important for purposes of backup and retrieval in the event of a device failure. Indicate the commands used to generate the output in Example 10-10.

Example 10-10   Cisco IOS File System Commands

```
Router# _____
File Systems:


         Size(b)       Free(b)       Type   Flags   Prefixes
              -             -        opaque    rw    archive:
              -             -        opaque    rw    system:
              -             -        opaque    rw    tmpsys:
              -             -        opaque    rw    null:
              -             -        network   rw    tftp:
*     256610304     112222208        disk      rw    flash0: flash:#
              -             -        disk      rw    flash1:
         262136        249536        nvram     rw    nvram:
              -             -        opaque    wo    syslog:
              -             -        opaque    rw    xmodem:
```

```
                  -              -    opaque    rw   ymodem:
                  -              -    network   rw   rcp:
                  -              -    network   rw   http:
                  -              -    network   rw   ftp:
                  -              -    network   rw   scp:
                  -              -    opaque    ro   tar:
                  -              -    network   rw   https:
                  -              -    opaque    ro   cns:
          127090688       59346944   usbflash  rw   usbflash0:


Router# _____
Directory of flash0:/


  1  -rw-   68831808   Apr 3 2013 21:53:06 +00:00   c1900-universalk9-mz.SPA.152-4.
                                                    M3.bin
  2  -rw-       2903   Aug 9 2012 16:12:34 +00:00   cpconfig-19xx.cfg
  3  -rw-    3000320   Aug 9 2012 16:12:46 +00:00   cpexpress.tar
  4  -rw-       1038   Aug 9 2012 16:12:56 +00:00   home.shtml
  5  -rw-     122880   Aug 9 2012 16:13:04 +00:00   home.tar
  6  -rw-    1697952   Aug 9 2012 16:13:18 +00:00   securedesktop-ios-3.1.1.45-k9.pkg
  7  -rw-     415956   Aug 9 2012 16:13:30 +00:00   sslclient-win-1.1.4.176.pkg
  8  -rw-       1389   Feb 6 2013 17:40:08 +00:00   my-running-config


256487424 bytes total (182394880 bytes free)


Router# _____
Router: _____
nvram:/
Router# _____
Directory of nvram:/


  253  -rw-        1279                      <no date>   startup-config
  254  ----           5                      <no date>   private-config
  255  -rw-        1279                      <no date>   underlying-config
    1  -rw-        2945                      <no date>   cwmp_inventory
    4  ----           0                      <no date>   rf_cold_starts
    5  ----          92                      <no date>   persistent-data
    6  -rw-          17                      <no date>   ecfm_ieee_mib
    7  -rw-         559                      <no date>   IOS-Self-Sig#1.cer
    8  -rw-         559                      <no date>   IOS-Self-Sig#2.cer
    9  -rw-         559                      <no date>   IOS-Self-Sig#3.cer
```

```
10  -rw-          559              <no date>   IOS-Self-Sig#4.cer
11  -rw-          559              <no date>   IOS-Self-Sig#5.cer
12  -rw-          559              <no date>   IOS-Self-Sig#6.cer
13  -rw-          559              <no date>   IOS-Self-Sig#7.cer
14  -rw-          559              <no date>   IOS-Self-Sig#8.cer

15  -rw-            0              <no date>   ifIndex-table
```

Use a Text File to Back Up a Configuration

Configuration files can be saved to a text file by using Tera Term, as shown in Figure 10-3.

Figure 10-3   Backup Configuration with Tera Term

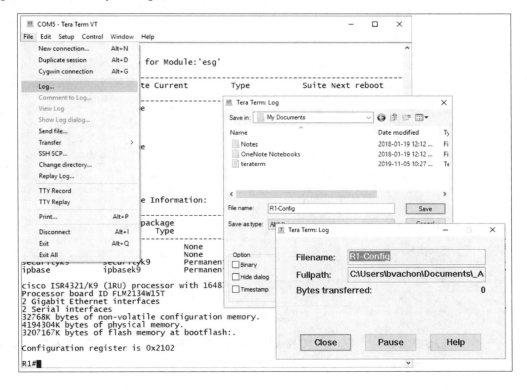

List the five steps to back up a configuration using Tera Term.

Step 1. _____

Step 2. _____

Step 3. _____

_____

_____

Step 4. _____

Step 5. _____

Use a Text File to Restore a Configuration

You can use Tera Term to restore a configuration, as shown in Figure 10-4.

Figure 10-4   Restoration Configuration with Tera Term

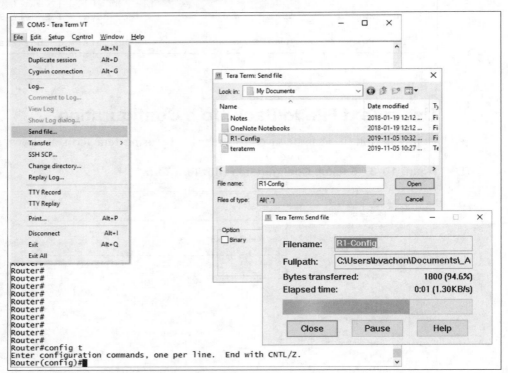

List the two steps to restore a configuration using Tera Term.

Step 1. _____

Step 2. _____

_____

Use TFTP to Back Up and Restore a Configuration

List the three steps required to back up a configuration to a TFTP server.

Step 1.   Enter the **copy running-config tftp** command and press **Enter**.

Step 2.   Enter the IP address of the host where the configuration file will be stored and press **Enter**.

Step 3.   Enter the name to assign to the configuration file and press **Enter**.

List the three steps required to restore a configuration from a TFTP server.

Step 1.   Enter the **copy tftp running-config** command and press **Enter**.

Step 2.   Enter the IP address of the host where the configuration file is stored and press **Enter**.

Step 3.   Enter the name to assign to the configuration file and press **Enter**.

Use USB to Back Up and Restore a Configuration

The Universal Serial Bus (USB) storage feature enables certain models of Cisco routers to support USB flash drives. The USB flash feature provides an optional secondary storage capability and an additional boot device. Images, configurations, and other files can be copied to or from the Cisco USB flash memory with the same reliability available when storing and retrieving files using a Compact Flash card.

What command, including router prompt, displays the contents of an attached USB drive?

_____

What command, including router prompt, copies the configuration in RAM to a USB drive?

_____

Password Recovery Procedures

The detailed procedure for password recovery varies depending on the device. However, all the password recovery procedures follow the same basics process. List the six steps common to password recovery on Cisco devices.

Step 1. _____

Step 2. _____

Step 3. _____

Step 4. _____

Step 5. _____

Step 6. _____

Console access to the device through a terminal or terminal emulator software on a PC is required for password recovery. What are the five required terminal settings to access the device?

- _____
- _____
- _____
- _____
- _____

Labs and Packet Tracers

Be sure to review the three labs and one Packet Tracer activity for this section.

IOS Image Management

In this section, you review how to implement protocols to manage a network.

Video—Managing Cisco IOS Images

Be sure to review the video in the online course. It demonstrates the process of upgrading IOS on a Cisco router.

Back Up an IOS Image to a TFTP Server

To back up an IOS image to a TFTP server, complete the following steps:

Step 1. Verify connectivity to the TFTP server.

Step 2. Verify that the TFTP server has enough memory to accept the image file.

Step 3. Copy the image to the TFTP server.

Figure 10-5 shows the image isr4200-universalk9_ias.16.09.04.SPA.bin being copied from R1 to the TFTP server at 172.16.1.100. In Example 10-11, record the commands required to complete this task.

Figure 10-5 Backing Up IOS to a TFTP Server

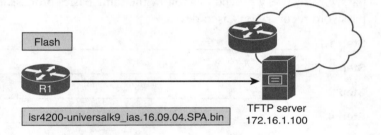

TFTP server
172.16.1.100

Example 10-11 Backing Up IOS to a TFTP Server

```
R1# _____
Type escape sequence to abort.
Sending 5, 100-byte ICMP Echos to 172.16.1.100, timeout is 2 seconds:
!!!!!
Success rate is 100 percent (5/5),
round-trip min/avg/max = 56/56/56 ms
R1# _____
-# - --length-- -----date/time------ path
8    517153193    Apr 2 2019 21:29:58   +00:00
                          isr4200-universalk9_ias.16.09.04.SPA.bin
(output omitted)
R1# _____
Source filename []? _____
Address or name of remote host []? _____
Destination filename [isr4200-universalk9_ias.16.09.04.SPA.bin]?
Writing isr4200-universalk9_ias.16.09.04.SPA.bin...
!!!!!!!!!!!!!!!!!!!!!!!!!!!!!!!!!!!!!!!!
(output omitted)
517153193 bytes copied in 863.468 secs (269058 bytes/sec)
```

The boot system Command

In Example 10-12, record the missing commands that you would use to configure the router to load the new IOS image during bootup.

Example 10-12   Setting the Router to Load the New IOS Image During Bootup

```
R1# _____

R1(config)# _____

R1(config)# exit

R1# _____

R1# reload
```

Labs and Activities

Command Reference

In Table 10-6, record the command, including the correct router or switch prompt, that fits each description.

Table 10-6　Commands for Module 10, "Network Management"

Command	Description
	Configure a router to enable CDP globally
	Enable CDP on an interface
	Verify the CDP status on the router
	View abbreviated output of CDP neighbors
	View CDP neighbor information, including the IP address and IOS image
	Configure a router to enable LLDP globally
	Enable an interface to send LLDP packets
	Enable an interface to process LLDP packets
	View abbreviated output of LLDP neighbors
	View LLDP neighbor information, including the IP address and IOS image
	Manually set the clock to 8:00 p.m., December 15, 2020
	Verify the NTP synchronization (two possible commands)
	Configure syslog messages to display a timestamp

10.1.5 Packet Tracer—Use CDP to Map a Network

Addressing Table

Device	Interface	IP Address	Subnet Mask	Local Interface and Connected Neighbor
Edge1	G0/0	192.168.1.1	255.255.255.0	G0/1 - S1
	S0/0/0			S0/0/0 - ISP
	S0/0/1	209.165.200.10	255.255.255.252	S0/0/1 - ISP

Objectives

Map a network using CDP and SSH remote access.

Background / Scenario

A senior network administrator requires you to map the Remote Branch Office network and discover the name of a recently installed switch that still needs an IP address to be configured. Your task is to create a map of the branch office network. You must record all of the network device names, IP addresses and subnet masks, and physical interfaces interconnecting the network devices, as well as the name of the switch that does not have an IP address.

To map the network, you will use SSH for remote access and the Cisco Discovery Protocol (CDP) to discover information about neighboring network devices. Because CDP is a Layer 2 protocol, it can be used to discover information about devices that do not have IP addresses. You will record the gathered information to complete the Addressing Table and provide a topology diagram of the Remote Branch Office network.

The local and remote administrative usernames and passwords are

Local Network

Username: **admin01**

Password: **S3cre7P@55**

Branch Office Network

Username: **branchadmin**

Password: **S3cre7P@55**

Instructions

Part 1: Use SSH to Remotely Access Network Devices

In Part 1, use the Admin-PC to remotely access the Edge1 gateway router. Next, from the Edge1 router you will SSH into the Remote Branch Office.

a. On the Admin-PC, open a command prompt.

b. SSH into the gateway router at 192.168.1.1 using the username **admin01** and the password **S3cre7P@55**.

```
PC> ssh -l admin01 192.168.1.1
Open
Password:


Edge1#
```

Note: Notice that you are placed directly into privileged EXEC mode. This is because the admin01 user account is set to privilege level 15.

c. Use the **show ip interface brief** and **show interfaces** commands to document the Edge1 router's physical interfaces, IP addresses, and subnet masks in the Addressing Table.

d. From Edge1, use SSH to access the Remote Branch Office at 209.165.200.10 with the username **branchadmin** and the same password as above:

```
Edge1# ssh -l branchadmin 209.165.200.10
Open
Password:


Branch-Edge#
```

Question:

After connecting to the Remote Branch Office, what piece of previously missing information can now be added to the Addressing Table above?

Part 2: Use CDP to Discover Neighboring Devices

You are now remotely connected to the Branch-Edge router. Using CDP, begin looking for connected network devices.

a. Issue the **show ip interface brief** and **show interfaces** commands to document the Branch-Edge router's network interfaces, IP addresses, and subnet masks. Add the missing information to the Addressing Table to map the network:

```
Branch-Edge# show ip interface brief
Branch-Edge# show interfaces
```

b. Security best practice recommends only running CDP when needed, so CDP may need to be turned on. Use the **show cdp** command to display its status.

```
Branch-Edge# show cdp
% CDP is not enabled
```

c. You need to turn on CDP, but it is a good idea to broadcast only CDP information to internal network devices and not to external networks. To do this, turn on the CDP protocol and then disable CDP on the S0/0/1 interface.

```
Branch-Edge# configure terminal
Branch-Edge(config)# cdp run
Branch-Edge(config)# interface s0/0/1
Branch-Edge(config-if)# no cdp enable
Branch-Edge(config-if)# exit
```

d. Issue a **show cdp neighbors** command to find any neighboring network devices.

Note: CDP will only show connected Cisco devices that are also running CDP.

```
Branch-Edge# show cdp neighbors
```

Question:

Is there a neighboring network device? What type of device is it? What is its name? On what interface is it connected? Is the device's IP address listed? Record the information in the Addressing Table.

Note: It may take some time for CDP updates to be received. If you see no output from the command, press the Fast Forward Time button several times.

---

e. To find the IP address of the neighboring device, use the **show cdp neighbors detail** command and record the ip address:

```
Branch-Edge# show cdp neighbors detail
```

Question:

Aside from the neighboring device's IP address, what other piece of potentially sensitive information is listed?

---

f. Now that you know the IP address of the neighbor device, connect to it with SSH to discover other devices that may be its neighbors.

Note: To connect with SSH use the same Remote Branch Office username and password.

```
Branch-Edge# ssh -l branchadmin <the ip address of the neighbor device>
```

Question:

After successfully connecting with SSH, what does the command prompt show?

---

g. You are remotely connected to the next neighbor. Use the **show cdp neighbors** command, and the **show cdp neighbors detail** command, to discover other connected neighbor devices.

Question:

What types of network devices neighbor this device? Record any newly discovered devices in the Addressing Table. Include their hostname, interfaces, and IP addresses.

---

h. Continue discovering new network devices using SSH and the show CDP commands. Eventually, you will reach the end of the network, and there will be no more devices to discover.

Question:

What is the name of the switch that does not have an IP address on the network?

---

i. Draw a topology of the Remote Branch Office network using the information you have gathered using CDP.

10.2.6 Packet Tracer—Use LLDP to Map a Network

Addressing Table

Device	Interface	IP Address	Subnet Mask	Local Interface and Connected Neighbor
Edge	G0/0	192.168.1.1	255.255.255.0	
	S0/0/0			S0/0/0 - ISP
	SVI	192.168.1.2		
	G0/0	209.165.200.10		G0/0 - ISP

Objectives

Map a network using LLDP and SSH remote access.

Background / Scenario

A senior network administrator requires you to map the Remote Branch Office network and discover information about all of the devices in the network. You must record all of the network device names, IP addresses and subnet masks, and physical interfaces interconnecting the network devices.

To map the network, you will use SSH for remote access and the Link Layer Discovery Protocol (LLDP) to discover information about neighboring network devices. Because LLDP is a Layer 2 protocol, it can be used to discover information about devices that do not have Layer 3 connectivity. You will record the information that you gather to complete the Addressing Table and provide a topology diagram of the Remote Branch Office network.

You will need the IP address for the remote branch office, which is 209.165.200.10. The local and remote administrative usernames and passwords are:

Local Network

Username: **admin01**

Password: **S3cre7P@55**

Remote Branch Office Network

Username: **RBOadmin**

Password: **S3cre7P@55**

Instructions

Part 1: Use SSH to Remotely Access Network Devices

In Part 1, you will use the Admin-PC to remotely access the Edge gateway router. Next, from the Edge router you will SSH into the Remote RBO Office.

- **a.** On the Admin-PC, open a command prompt.

- **b.** SSH into the gateway router at 192.168.1.1 using the username **admin01** and the password **S3cre7P@55**.

```
PC> ssh -l admin01 192.168.1.1
Open
Password:

Edge#
```

Note: Notice that you are placed directly into privileged EXEC mode. This is because the admin01 user account is set to privilege level 15.

- **c.** The **Edge** router was previously configured to use CDP. Switch **S1** has already been configured to use LLDP. Issue the **show cdp** command to verify CDP is currently active. Disable CDP by issuing the following command:

```
Edge(config)# no cdp run
```

- **d.** **LLDP** can be configured to both transmit and receive on a specific interface. Configure **Edge** so that it receives LLDP messages from **S1** but does not send messages to **S1** for security purposes. Enable **LLDP**.

```
Edge(config)# lldp run
Edge(config)# int g0/0
Edge(config-if)# no lldp transmit
Edge(config-if)# exit
```

- **e.** Use the **show lldp neighbors** command to verify that **Edge** is receiving messages from **S1**.

- **f.** Connect to **S1** with SSH from **Edge** router using the **admin01** credentials. Issue the **show lldp neighbors** command. Notice that **S1** did not receive information from **Edge**.

```
Edge# ssh -l admin01 192.168.1.2
Password:

S1> show lldp neighbors
S1> exit
```

g. Exit from the connection with S1 to return to the Edge router CLI. Use the **show ip interface brief** and **show interfaces** commands to document the Edge router's physical interfaces, IP addresses, and subnet masks in the Addressing Table.

```
Edge# show ip interface brief

Edge# show interfaces
```

h. From your session with Edge router, connect with SSH to the Remote RBO Office at 209.165.200.10 with the username **RBOadmin** and the same password used for admin01.

```
Edge# ssh -1 RBOadmin 209.165.200.10

Password:


RBO-Edge#
```

Question:

After connecting to the Remote RBO Office at 209.165.200.10, what piece of previously missing information can now be added to the Addressing Table above?

Part 2: Use LLDP to Discover Neighboring Devices

You are now remotely connected to the RBO-Edge router. Using LLDP, begin looking for connected network devices.

a. Issue the **show ip interface brief** and **show interfaces** commands to document the RBO-Edge router's network interfaces, IP addresses, and subnet masks. Add the missing information to the Addressing Table.

b. Security best practice recommends only running LLDP when needed, so LLDP may need to be turned on. Use a **show lldp** command to test its status.

```
RBO-Edge# show lldp

% LLDP is not enabled
```

c. You need to turn on LLDP, but it is a good idea to only send LLDP information to internal network devices and not to external networks. Discover which interface is connected to the Internet by issuing the command **show ip interface brief**. Enable the LLDP protocol and completely disable LLDP on the interface that is connected to the Internet.

```
RBO-Edge# configure terminal
RBO-Edge(config)# lldp run
RBO-Edge(config)# interface g0/0
RBO-Edge(config-if)# no lldp transmit
RBO-Edge(config-if)# no lldp receive
RBO-Edge(config-if)# exit
```

d. Issue a **show lldp neighbors** command to find any neighboring network devices.

Note: LLDP will only show connected devices that are also running LLDP.

```
RBO-Edge# show lldp neighbors
```

Question:

Is there a neighboring network device? What type of device is it? What is its name? On what interface is it connected? Is the device's IP address listed? Record the information in the Addressing Table.

_____

e. Use the **show ip route** command to determine the address of the device that you found with the **show lldp neighbors** command. Based on the information provided about the local address in the routing table and the prefix length of the network, use that information to determine the neighbor address.

f. To find additional information from the neighboring device, use the **show lldp neighbors detail** command:

```
RBO-Edge# show lldp neighbors detail
```

Question:

What other piece of potentially sensitive information is listed?

_____

Note: The current version of Packet Tracer does not provide the Management Address of the neighbor device. In this activity, several neighbor device addresses have been provided in the Addressing Table.

g. Connect to the neighbor device with SSH to discover other devices that may be its neighbors.

Note: To connect with SSH use the same Remote RBO Office username and password.

```
RBO-Edge# ssh -l RBOadmin <the ip address of the neighbor device>
```

Question:

After successfully connecting with SSH, what does the command prompt show?

_____

h. You are remotely connected to the next neighbor. Use the **show lldp neighbors** command and the **show lldp neighbors detail** command to discover other connected neighbor devices.

Question:

What types of network devices neighbor this device? Record any newly discovered devices in the Addressing Table. Include their hostname, interfaces, and IP addresses.

_____

Add the newly discovered device name next to the SVI entry for address 192.168.4.131.

i. Connect to the SVI for address 192.168.4.131 using SSH and credentials used previously. If prompted for an enable secret password, use the same password as used for **RBOAdmin**. Use the **show lldp neighbors** command and the **show lldp neighbors detail** command to discover other connected neighbor devices.

Question:

What types of network devices neighbor this device? Record any newly discovered devices in the Addressing Table. Include their hostname, interfaces, and IP addresses.

Place the newly discovered device name next to the SVI entry for address 192.168.4.132.

j. Connect to the SVI for address 192.168.4.133 using SSH and credentials used previously. Issue the command **show lldp**; you should receive a message:

```
% LLDP is not enabled
```

Enable **lldp** globally as in Step C. There is no need to configure **transmit** or **receive** options because they are on by default. Use the **show lldp neighbors** command and the **show lldp neighbors detail** command to discover other connected neighbor devices.

Question:

What types of network devices neighbor this device? Record any newly discovered devices in the Addressing Table. Include their hostname, interfaces, and IP addresses. It may be beneficial to reconnect to the previously discovered devices to display neighbors one more time to complete the entire addressing table now that all devices are configured for LLDP.

---

k. Draw a topology of the Remote RBO Office network using the information that you have gathered with LLDP.

10.3.4 Packet Tracer—Configure and Verify NTP

Addressing Table

Device	Interface	IP Address	Subnet Mask
N1	NIC	209.165.200.225	255.255.255.0
R1	G0/0	209.165.200.226	255.255.255.0
R2	G0/0	209.165.200.227	255.255.255.0

Objectives

In this activity, you will configure NTP on R1 and R2 to allow time synchronization.

Background / Scenario

Network Time Protocol (NTP) synchronizes the time of day among a set of distributed time servers and clients. While there are a number of applications that require synchronized time, this lab will focus on correlating events that are listed in the system log and other time-specific events from multiple network devices. NTP uses the User Datagram Protocol (UDP) as its transport protocol. All NTP communications use Coordinated Universal Time (UTC).

An NTP server usually receives its time from an authoritative time source, such as an atomic clock attached to a time server. The NTP server then distributes this time across the network. NTP is extremely efficient. No more than one packet per minute is necessary to synchronize two devices to within a millisecond of each other.

Instructions

Step 1:   NTP Server

   a.   Server N1 is already configured as the NTP Server for this topology. Verify its configuration under **Services > NTP**.

   b.   From R1, ping N1 (209.165.200.225) to verify connectivity. The ping should be successful.

   c.   Repeat the ping to N1 from R2 to verify connectivity to N1.

Step2:   Configure the NTP Clients

   Cisco devices can be configured to refer to an NTP server to use to synchronize their clocks. It is important to keep time consistent among all devices. Configure R1 and R2 as NTP clients so their clocks are synchronized. Both R1 and R2 will use N1 server as their NTP server.

   a.   Check the current NTP and clock settings as shown below:

```
R1# show ntp status
%NTP is not enabled.
R1# show clock detail
*0:1:53.745 UTC Mon Mar 1 1993
Time source is hardware calendar
```

b. Configure R1 and R2 as NTP Clients. Use the **ntp server** command to specify an NTP server, as shown below:

```
R1# conf t
R1(config)# ntp server 209.165.200.225
```

c. Repeat this configuration on **R2**.

Step 3: Verify NTP settings

a. Check the clocks on R1 and R2 again to verify that they are synchronized:

```
R1# show clock detail
12:7:18.451 UTC Sat Oct 12 2019
Time source is NTP
```

Note: When working on physical routers, allow a few minutes before R1 and R2 clocks are synchronized. With Packet Tracer you can use the Fast Forward Time button to speed up synchronization.

Execute the same command on **R2**.

Question:

Are the clocks synchronized?

_____

b. Check the NTP status and NTP associations by using the following commands to verify NTP operation and configuration.

```
R1# show ntp status
Clock is synchronized, stratum 2, reference is 209.165.200.225
<Output omitted>


R1# show ntp associations

address     ref  clock         st  when  poll  reach  delay  offset  disp
*~209.165.200.225127.127.1.1  1    11    32    377    9.00   4.00    0.24
 * sys.peer, # selected, + candidate, - outlyer, x falseticker, ~
configured
```

10.4.10 Lab—Research Network Monitoring Software

Objectives

Part 1: Survey Your Understanding of Network Monitoring

Part 2: Research Network Monitoring Tools

Part 3: Select a Network Monitoring Tool

Background / Scenario

Network monitoring is needed for any sized network. Proactively monitoring the network infrastructure can assist network administrators with their day-to-day duties. The wide variety of available networking tools vary in cost, depending on the features, number of network locations, and number of nodes supported.

In this lab, you will conduct research on available network monitoring software. You will gather information on software products and features of those products. You will investigate one product in greater detail and list some of the key features available.

Required Resources

- PC with Internet access

Instructions

Part 1: Survey Your Understanding of Network Monitoring

Describe network monitoring as you understand it. Give an example of how it might be used in a production network.

Part 2: Research Network Monitoring Tools

Step 1:   Research and find three network monitoring tools.

List the three tools that you found.

Step 2:   Complete the following form for the network monitoring tools selected.

Vendor	Product Name	Features

Part 3: Select a Network Monitoring Tool

Step 1:   Select one or more monitoring tools from your research.

From your research, identify one or more tools you would choose for monitoring your network. List the tools and explain your reasons for choosing them, including specific features that you consider important.

Step 2:   Investigate the PRTG network monitoring tool.

Search the Internet for the terms Paessler and PRTG, and look for a feature list. Give examples of some of the features that you found for PRTG in the space provided below.

_____

Reflection Question

Based on your research, what conclusions have you reached regarding network monitoring software?

_____

Packet Tracer
☐ Activity

10.6.10 Packet Tracer—Back Up Configuration Files

Objectives

Part 1: Establish Connectivity to TFTP Server

Part 2: Transfer the Configuration File from TFTP Server

Part 3: Backup Configuration and IOS to TFTP Server

Background / Scenario

In this activity, you will restore a configuration from a backup and then perform a new backup. Due to an equipment failure, a new router has been put in place. Fortunately, backup configuration files have been saved to a Trivial File Transfer Protocol (TFTP) Server. You are required to restore the files from the TFTP Server to get the router back online as quickly as possible.

Instructions

Part 1: Establish Connectivity to the TFTP Server

Note: Because this is a new router, the initial configuration will be performed using a console connection to the router.

    a. Click **PCA**, then the **Desktop** tab, followed by **Terminal** to access the **RTA** command line.

    b. Configure and activate the **Gigabit Ethernet 0/0** interface. The IP address should match the default gateway for the **TFTP Server.**

    c. Test connectivity to **TFTP Server.** Troubleshoot, if necessary.

Part 2: Transfer the Configuration File from the TFTP Server

    a. From privileged EXEC mode, issue the following command:

```
Router# copy tftp running-config
Address or name of remote host []? 172.16.1.2
Source filename []? RTA-confg
Destination filename [running-config]? <cr>
```

The router should return the following:

```
Accessing tftp://172.16.1.2/RTA-confg...
Loading RTA-confg from 172.16.1.2: !
[OK - 785 bytes]
785 bytes copied in 0.001 secs
RTA#
%SYS-5-CONFIG_I: Configured from console by console
RTA#
```

b. Issue the command to display the current configuration.

Question:

What changes were made?

_____

c. Issue the appropriate **show** command to display the interface status.

Question:

Are all interfaces active?

_____

d. Correct any issues related to interface problems and test connectivity between PCA and the TFTP server.

Part 3: Back Up Configuration and IOS to TFTP Server

a. Change the hostname of RTA to RTA-1.

b. Save the configuration to NVRAM.

c. Copy the configuration to the **TFTP Server** using the **copy** command:

```
RTA-1# copy running-config tftp:
Address or name of remote host []? 172.16.1.2
Destination filename [RTA-1-confg]? <cr>
```

d. Issue the command to display the files in flash.

e. Backup the IOS in flash to the **TFTP Server** using the following command:

```
RTA-1# copy flash tftp:
Source filename []? c1900-universalk9-mz.SPA.151-4.M4.bin
Address or name of remote host []? 172.16.1.2
Destination filename [c1900-universalk9-mz.SPA.151-4.M4.bin]? <cr>
```

Question:

What special character repeatedly displays indicating that the IOS file is being copied to the TFTP server successfully?

_____

f. Open the TFTP Server and click the Services tab, select TFTP, and scroll through the list of IOS files.

Question:

Has the IOS file **c1900-universalk9-mz.SPA.151-4.M4.bin** been copied to the TFTP Server?

_____

10.6.11 Lab—Use Tera Term to Manage Router Configuration Files

Topology

Addressing Table

Device	Interface	IP Address	Subnet Mask	Default Gateway
R1	G0/0/1	192.168.1.1	255.255.255.0	N/A
S1	VLAN 1	192.168.1.11	255.255.255.0	192.168.1.1
PC-A	NIC	192.168.1.3	255.255.255.0	192.168.1.1

Objectives

Part 1: Configure Basic Device Settings

Part 2: Use Terminal Emulation Software to Create a Backup Configuration File

Part 3: Use a Backup Configuration File to Restore a Router and Switch Configuration

Background / Scenario

It is a recommended best practice to maintain backup configuration files for routers and switches in the event that they need to be restored to a previous configuration. Terminal emulation software can be used to easily back up or restore a router or switch configuration file.

In this lab, you will

- Use Tera Term to back up a router running-configuration file.

- Erase the router startup configuration file.

- Reload the router.

- Restore the missing router configuration from the backup configuration file.

Note: The routers used with CCNA hands-on labs are Cisco 4221 with Cisco IOS XE Release 16.9.4 (universalk9 image). The switches used in the labs are Cisco Catalyst 2960s with Cisco IOS Release 15.2(2) (lanbasek9 image). Other routers, switches, and Cisco IOS versions can be used. Depending on the model and Cisco IOS version, the commands available and the output produced might vary from what is shown in the labs. Refer to the Router Interface Summary Table at the end of the lab for the correct interface identifiers.

Note: Ensure that the routers and switches have been erased and have no startup configurations. If you are unsure contact your instructor.

Required Resources

- One router (Cisco 4221 with Cisco IOS XE Release 16.9.4 universal image or comparable)
- One switch (Cisco 2960 with Cisco IOS Release 15.2(2) lanbasek9 image or comparable)
- One PC (Windows with a terminal emulation program, such as Tera Term)
- Console cables to configure the Cisco IOS devices via the console ports
- Ethernet cables as shown in the topology

Part 1: Configure Basic Device Settings

In Part 1, you will set up the network topology and configure basic settings, such as the interface IP addresses, device access, and passwords on the router.

Step 1:   Cable the network as shown in the topology.

Attach the devices as shown in the topology and cable as necessary.

Step 2:   Configure the PC-A network settings according to the Addressing Table.

Step 3:   Configure basic settings for the router.

    a.   Assign a device name to the router.

    b.   Disable DNS lookup to prevent the router from attempting to translate incorrectly entered commands as though they were host names.

    c.   Assign **class** as the privileged EXEC encrypted password.

    d.   Assign **cisco** as the console password and enable login.

    e.   Assign **cisco** as the VTY password and enable login.

    f.   Encrypt the plaintext passwords.

    g.   Create a banner that warns anyone accessing the device that unauthorized access is prohibited.

    h.   Configure interfaces as listed in the earlier table.

    i.   Save the running configuration to the startup configuration file.

Step 4:   Configure basic settings for the switch.

    a.   Assign a device name to the switch.

    b.   Disable DNS lookup to prevent the router from attempting to translate incorrectly entered commands as though they were host names.

    c.   Assign **class** as the privileged EXEC encrypted password.

    d.   Assign **cisco** as the console password and enable login.

    e.   Assign **cisco** as the VTY password and enable login.

    f.   Encrypt the plaintext passwords.

    g.   Create a banner that warns anyone accessing the device that unauthorized access is prohibited.

    h.   Shut down all unused interfaces.

    i.   Configure interface VLAN 1 as specified in the earlier table.

    j.   Save the running configuration to the startup configuration file.

Part 2: Create a Backup Configuration File

In Tera Term or other terminal emulation program, you can create a log of your commands and output to a device via a connection. In this part, you will record your interaction with a device using the logging feature of Tera Term.

Note: If Tera Term is not installed, you can download the latest version from a number of Internet sites. Simply search for a Tera Term download.

Step 1:   Create a log file.

    a.   Connect to the router via Serial connection in Tera Term as necessary. In the New Connection window, select the **Serial** radio button and the appropriate communications port for your PC (i.e., COM1).

    b.   From the **File** menu, choose **Log…**, and save the **teraterm.log** file to the Desktop. Ensure that the **Append** and **Plain text** check boxes are enabled (checked).

    c.   The Tera Term log file will create a record of every command issued and every output displayed.

> **Note:** You can use this feature to capture the output from several commands in sequence and use it for network documentation purposes. For example, you could issue the **show version**, **show ip interface brief**, and **show running-config** commands to capture information about the router.

Step 2:   Display the router running-configuration.

    a.   Use the console password to log in to the router.

    b.   Enter privileged EXEC mode.

    c.   From privileged EXEC mode enter the **show running-config** command.

    d.   Continue pressing the space bar when **--More--** is displayed until you see the router R1# prompt return.

    e.   From the **File** menu, choose **Show Log Dialog**. Click **Close** to end the log session.

> **Note:** You can also copy and paste the text from the Tera Term window directly into a text editor.

Part 3: Use a Backup Configuration File to Restore a Router and Switch Configuration

Step 1:   Erase the router startup-configuration and reload it.

    a.   From privileged EXEC mode erase the startup configuration.

```
R1# erase startup-config
Erasing the nvram filesystem will remove all configuration files!
Continue? [confirm]
[OK]
Erase of nvram: complete
```

b. Reload the router.

```
R1# reload
Proceed with reload? [confirm]
```

c. At the System Configuration Dialog prompt, type **no**; a router prompt displays, indicating an unconfigured router.

```
        --- System Configuration Dialog ---

Would you like to enter the initial configuration dialog? [yes/no]:

Press RETURN to get started!
<output omitted>
Router>
```

d. Enter privileged EXEC mode and enter a **show running-config** command to verify that all of the previous configurations were erased.

Step 2: Edit the saved configuration backup file to prepare it for restoring the router configuration.

To restore the router configuration from a saved running configuration backup file, you must edit the text.

a. Open the **teraterm.log** text file.

b. Remove each instance of **--More--** in the text file.

Note: The --More-- was generated by pressing the Spacebar when displaying the running configuration.

---

c. Delete the initial lines of the backup configuration file, so that the first line starts with the first configuration command as shown below.

```
service timestamps debug datetime msec
service timestamps log datetime msec
service password-encryption
```

d. In the lines for interface GigabitEthernet0/0/1, insert a new line to enable the interface.

```
interface GigabitEthernet0/0/1
 ip address 192.168.1.1 255.255.255.0
 duplex auto
 speed auto
```

Change to:

```
interface GigabitEthernet0/0/1
 ip address 192.168.1.1 255.255.255.0
 duplex auto
 speed auto
 no shutdown
```

e. After you have made all of the edits to the backup configuration file, save your changes to filename **R1-config-backup**.

> **Note**: When saving the file, an extension such as **.txt** may be added to the filename automatically.

Step 3: Restore the router configuration.

You can restore the edited running configuration directly to the console terminal in router global configuration mode, and the configurations are entered as if they were commands entered individually at the command prompt.

a. From the Tera Term console connection to the router, enter global configuration mode.

b. From the **File** menu, select **Send file**.

c. Locate **R1-config-backup** and select **Open**.

d. Save the running configuration to the startup configuration file.

```
R1# copy running-config startup-config
```

e. Verify the new running configuration.

Step 4: Backup and restore the switch.

Go back to the beginning of Part 2 and follow the same steps to back up and restore the switch configuration.

Reflection Question

Why do you think it is important to use a text editor instead of a word processor to copy and save your command configurations?

Router Interface Summary Table

Router Model	Ethernet Interface #1	Ethernet Interface #2	Serial Interface #1	Serial Interface #2
1800	Fast Ethernet 0/0 (F0/0)	Fast Ethernet 0/1 (F0/1)	Serial 0/0/0 (S0/0/0)	Serial 0/0/1 (S0/0/1)
1900	Gigabit Ethernet 0/0 (G0/0)	Gigabit Ethernet 0/1 (G0/1)	Serial 0/0/0 (S0/0/0)	Serial 0/0/1 (S0/0/1)
2801	Fast Ethernet 0/0 (F0/0)	Fast Ethernet 0/1 (F0/1)	Serial 0/1/0 (S0/1/0)	Serial 0/1/1 (S0/1/1)
2811	Fast Ethernet 0/0 (F0/0)	Fast Ethernet 0/1 (F0/1)	Serial 0/0/0 (S0/0/0)	Serial 0/0/1 (S0/0/1)
2900	Gigabit Ethernet 0/0 (G0/0)	Gigabit Ethernet 0/1 (G0/1)	Serial 0/0/0 (S0/0/0)	Serial 0/0/1 (S0/0/1)
4221	Gigabit Ethernet 0/0/0 (G0/0/0)	Gigabit Ethernet 0/0/1 (G0/0/1)	Serial 0/1/0 (S0/1/0)	Serial 0/1/1 (S0/1/1)
4300	Gigabit Ethernet 0/0/0 (G0/0/0)	Gigabit Ethernet 0/0/1 (G0/0/1)	Serial 0/1/0 (S0/1/0)	Serial 0/1/1 (S0/1/1)

Note: To find out how the router is configured, look at the interfaces to identify the type of router and how many interfaces the router has. There is no way to effectively list all the combinations of configurations for each router class. This table includes identifiers for the possible combinations of Ethernet and Serial interfaces in the device. The table does not include any other type of interface, even though a specific router may contain one. An example of this might be an ISDN BRI interface. The string in parentheses is the legal abbreviation that can be used in Cisco IOS commands to represent the interface.

10.6.12 Lab—Use TFTP, Flash, and USB to Manage Configuration Files

Topology

Addressing Table

Device	Interface	IP Address	Subnet Mask	Default Gateway
R1	G0/0/1	192.168.1.1	255.255.255.0	N/A
S1	VLAN 1	192.168.1.11	255.255.255.0	192.168.1.1
PC-A	NIC	192.168.1.3	255.255.255.0	192.168.1.1

Objectives

Part 1: Build the Network and Configure Basic Device Settings

Part 2: Use TFTP to Back Up and Restore the Switch Running Configuration

Part 3 Use TFTP to Back Up and Restore the Router Running Configuration

Part 4: Back Up and Restore Running Configurations Using Router Flash Memory

Part 5: (Optional) Use a USB Drive to Back Up and Restore the Running Configuration

Background / Scenario

Cisco networking devices are often upgraded or swapped out for a number of reasons. It is important to maintain backups of the latest device configurations, as well as a history of configuration changes. A TFTP server is often used to back up configuration files and IOS images in production networks. A TFTP server is a centralized and secure method used to store the backup copies of the files and restore them as necessary. Using a centralized TFTP server, you can back up files from many different Cisco devices.

In addition to a TFTP server, most of the current Cisco routers can back up and restore files locally from CompactFlash (CF) memory or a USB flash drive. The CF is a removable memory module that has replaced the limited internal flash memory of earlier router models. The IOS image for the router resides in the CF memory, and the router uses this IOS Image for the boot process. With the larger size of the CF memory, additional files can be stored for backup purposes. A removable USB flash drive can also be used for backup purposes.

In this lab, you will use TFTP server software to back up the Cisco device running configuration to the TFTP server. You can edit the file using a text editor and copy the new configuration back to a Cisco device. The instructions here for the TFTP server configuration and operation are generic, and there may be some differences in terminology with your TFTP server software.

Note: The routers used with CCNA hands-on labs are Cisco 4221 with Cisco IOS XE Release 16.9.4 (universalk9 image). The switches used in the labs are Cisco Catalyst 2960s with Cisco IOS Release 15.2(2) (lanbasek9 image). Other routers, switches, and Cisco IOS versions can be used. Depending on the model and Cisco IOS version, the commands available and the output produced might vary from what is shown in the labs. Refer to the Router Interface Summary Table at the end of the lab for the correct interface identifiers.

Note: Ensure that the routers and switches have been erased and have no startup configurations. If you are unsure contact your instructor.

Required Resources

- One router (Cisco 4221 with Cisco IOS XE Release 16.9.3 universal image or comparable)
- One switch (Cisco 2960 with Cisco IOS Release 15.2(2) lanbasek9 image or comparable)
- One PC (Windows with a terminal emulation program, such as Tera Term)
- Console cables to configure the Cisco IOS devices via the console ports
- Ethernet cables as shown in the topology
- USB flash drive (Optional)

Instructions

Part 1: Build the Network and Configure Basic Device Settings

In Part 1, you will set up the network topology and configure basic settings, such as the interface IP addresses for router R1, switch S1, and PC-A.

Step 1:   Cable the network as shown in the topology.

Attach the devices as shown in the topology diagram, and cable as necessary.

Step 2:   Configure basic settings for the router.

    a.   Assign a device name to the router.

    b.   Disable DNS lookup to prevent the router from attempting to translate incorrectly entered commands as though they were host names.

    c.   Assign **class** as the privileged EXEC encrypted password.

    d.   Assign **cisco** as the console password and enable login.

    e.   Assign **cisco** as the VTY password and enable login.

    f.   Encrypt the plaintext passwords.

    g.   Create a banner that warns anyone accessing the device that unauthorized access is prohibited.

    h.   Configure interfaces as listed in the earlier table.

    i.   Save the running configuration to the startup configuration file.

Note: Use the question mark (?) to help with the correct sequence of parameters needed to execute this command.

Step 3: Configure basic settings for the switch.

    a. Assign a device name to the switch.

    b. Disable DNS lookup to prevent the router from attempting to translate incorrectly entered commands as though they were host names.

    c. Assign **class** as the privileged EXEC encrypted password.

    d. Assign **cisco** as the console password and enable login.

    e. Assign **cisco** as the VTY password and enable login.

    f. Encrypt the plaintext passwords.

    g. Create a banner that warns anyone accessing the device that unauthorized access is prohibited.

    h. Shut down all unused interfaces.

    i. Configure interface VLAN 1 as specified in the earlier table.

    j. Save the running configuration to the startup configuration file.

Note: Use the question mark (?) to help with the correct sequence of parameters needed to execute this command.

Step 4: Verify connectivity from PC-A.

    a. Ping from PC-A to S1.

    b. Ping from PC-A to R1.

    If the pings are not successful, troubleshoot the basic device configurations before continuing.

Part 2: Use TFTP to Back Up and Restore the Switch Running Configuration

Step 1: Verify connectivity to switch S1 from PC-A.

The TFTP application uses the UDP Layer 4 transport protocol, which is encapsulated in an IP packet. For TFTP file transfers to function, there must be Layer 1 and 2 (Ethernet, in this case) and Layer 3 (IP) connectivity between the TFTP client and the TFTP server. The LAN topology in this lab uses only Ethernet at Layers 1 and 2. However, TFTP transfers can also be accomplished over WAN links that use other Layer 1 physical links and Layer 2 protocols. As long as there is IP connectivity between the client and server, as demonstrated by ping, the TFTP transfer can take place. If the pings are not successful, troubleshoot the basic device configurations before continuing.

Note: A common misconception is that you can TFTP a file over the console connection. This is not the case because the console connection does not use IP. The TFTP transfer can be initiated from the client device (router or switch) using the console connection, but there must be IP connectivity between the client and server for the file transfer to take place.

Step 2: Start the TFTP server.

Start the TFTP program on PC-A. Ensure that the TFTP program is using a directory that you have WRITE permission for, such as a folder on your desktop.

Step 3: Explore the copy command on a Cisco device.

a. Console into switch S1 and, from the privileged EXEC mode prompt, enter **copy ?** to display the options for source or "from" location and other available copy options. You can specify **flash:** or **flash0:** as the source. However, if you simply provide a filename as the source, **flash0:** is assumed and is the default. Note that **running-config** is also an option for the source location.

```
S1# copy ?
  /erase          Erase destination file system.
  /error          Allow to copy error file.
  /noverify       Don't verify image signature before reload.
  /verify         Verify image signature before reload.
  bs:             Copy from bs: file system
  cns:            Copy from cns: file system
  flash:          Copy from flash: file system
  ftp:            Copy from ftp: file system
  http:           Copy from http: file system
  https:          Copy from https: file system
  logging         Copy logging messages
  null:           Copy from null: file system
  nvram:          Copy from nvram: file system
  rcp:            Copy from rcp: file system
  running-config  Copy from current system configuration
  scp:            Copy from scp: file system
  startup-config  Copy from startup configuration
  system:         Copy from system: file system
  tar:            Copy from tar: file system
  tftp:           Copy from tftp: file system
  tmpsys:         Copy from tmpsys: file system
  vb:             Copy from vb: file system
  xmodem:         Copy from xmodem: file system
  ymodem:         Copy from ymodem: file system
```

b. Use the **?** to display the destination options after a source file location is chosen. The **flash:** file system for S1 is the source file system in this example.

```
S1# copy flash: ?
  flash:          Copy to flash: file system
  ftp:            Copy to ftp: file system
  http:           Copy to http: file system
  https:          Copy to https: file system
  null:           Copy to null: file system
  nvram:          Copy to nvram: file system
  rcp:            Copy to rcp: file system
  running-config  Update (merge with) current system configuration
  scp:            Copy to scp: file system
  startup-config  Copy to startup configuration
```

```
system:          Copy to system: file system
tftp:            Copy to tftp: file system
tmpsys:          Copy to tmpsys: file system
vb:              Copy to vb: file systesystem
```

Step 4: Transfer the running-config file from switch S1 to TFTP server on PC-A.

a. From the privileged EXEC mode on the switch, enter the **copy running-config tftp:** command. Provide the remote host address of the TFTP server (PC-A), 192.168.1.3. Press Enter to accept default destination filename (**s1-confg**) or provide your own filename. The exclamation marks (**!!**) indicate the transfer process is in progress and is successful.

```
S1# copy running-config tftp:
Address or name of remote host []? 192.168.1.3
Destination filename [s1-confg]?
!!
1465 bytes copied in 0.663 secs (2210 bytes/sec)
S1#
```

The TFTP server may also display transfer progress.

Note: If you do not have permission to write to the current directory that is used by the TFTP server, the following error message displays:

```
S1# copy running-config tftp:
Address or name of remote host []? 192.168.1.3
Destination filename [s1-confg]?
%Error opening tftp://192.168.1.3/s1-confg (Permission denied)
```

Note: Other issues, such as a firewall blocking TFTP traffic, can prevent the TFTP transfer. Please check with your instructor for further assistance.

b. Check the directory on the TFTP server (usually the default directory for the TFTP server software) to verify that the file was transferred successfully. Your TFTP server may have a dialog for this, or you can simply use the File Explorer provided by your Operating System.

Step 5: Create a modified switch running configuration file.

The saved running configuration file, **s1-confg**, can also be restored to the switch by using the **copy** command from the switch. The original or a modified version of the file can be copied to the flash file system of the switch.

a. Navigate to the TFTP directory on PC-A by using the file system of PC-A, and then locate the **s1-confg** file. Open this file using a text editor program, such as WordPad.

b. With the file open, locate the **hostname S1** line. Replace **S1** with **Switch1**. Delete all the self-generated crypto keys, as necessary. A sample of the keys is displayed below. These keys are not exportable and can cause errors while updating the running configuration.

```
crypto pki trustpoint TP-self-signed-1566151040
 enrollment selfsigned
 subject-name cn=IOS-Self-Signed-Certificate-1566151040
 revocation-check none
```

```
    rsakeypair TP-self-signed-1566151040
 !
 !
 crypto pki certificate chain TP-self-signed-1566151040
  certificate self-signed 01
    3082022B 30820194 A0030201 02020101 300D0609 2A864886 F70D0101
 05050030
    31312F30 2D060355 04031326 494F532D 53656C66 2D536967 6E65642D
 43657274
 <output omitted>
    E99574A6 D945014F B6FE22F3 642EE29A 767EABF7 403930CA D2C59E23
 102EC12E
    02F9C933 B3296D9E 095EBDAF 343D17F6 AF2831C7 6DA6DFE3 35B38D90
 E6F07CD4
    40D96970 A0D12080 07A1C169 30B9D889 A6E2189C 75B988B9 0AF27EDC
 6D6FA0E5
    CCFA6B29 729C1E0B 9DADACD0 3D7381
         quit
```

c. Save this file as a plain text file with a new filename, **Switch1-confg.txt**, in this example.

Note: When saving the file, an extension, such as **.txt**, may be added to the filename automatically.

---

d. If your TFTP software has the option, use it to show the contents of its directory to verify that the file is present.

Step 6: Copy the modified running configuration file from the TFTP server to switch S1.

a. From the privileged EXEC mode on the switch, enter the **copy tftp running-config** command. Provide the remote host address of the TFTP server, 192.168.1.3. Enter the new filename, **Switch1-confg.txt**. The exclamation mark (!) indicates the transfer process is in progress and is successful.

```
S1# copy tftp: running-config
Address or name of remote host []? 192.168.1.3
Source filename []? Switch1-confg.txt
Destination filename [running-config]?
Accessing tftp://192.168.1.3/Switch1-confg.txt...
Loading Switch1-confg.txt from 192.168.1.3 (via Vlan1): !
[OK - 1580 bytes]
[OK]
1580 bytes copied in 9.118 secs (173 bytes/sec)
*Mar  1 00:21:16.242: %PKI-4-NOAUTOSAVE: Configuration was modified.
Issue "write memory" to save new certificate
*Mar  1 00:21:16.251: %SYS-5-CONFIG_I: Configured from
tftp://192.168.1.3/Switch1-confg.txt by console
Switch1#
```

After the transfer has completed, the prompt has changed from S1 to Switch1, because the running configuration is updated with the **hostname Switch1** command in the modified running configuration.

b. Enter the **show running-config** command to examine running configuration file.

```
Switch1# show running-config
Building configuration...

Current configuration : 3062 bytes
!
! Last configuration change at 00:09:34 UTC Mon Mar 1 1993
!
version 15.0
no service pad
service timestamps debug datetime msec
service timestamps log datetime msec
no service password-encryption
!
hostname Switch1
!
boot-start-marker
boot-end-marker
<output omitted>
```

Note: This procedure merges the running-config from the TFTP server with the current running-config in the switch or router. If changes were made to the current running-config, the commands in the TFTP copy are added. Alternatively, if the same command is issued, it updates the corresponding command in the switch or router current running-config.

If you want to completely replace the current running-config with the one from the TFTP server, you must erase the switch startup-config and reload the device. You will then need to configure the VLAN 1 management address, so there is IP connectivity between the TFTP server and the switch.

Part 3: Use TFTP to Back Up and Restore the Router Running Configuration

The backup and restore procedure from Part 3 can also be performed with a router. In Part 4, the running configuration file will be backed up and restored using a TFTP server.

Step 1:   Verify connectivity to router R1 from PC-A.

If the pings are not successful, troubleshoot the basic device configurations before continuing.

Step 2:   Transfer the running configuration from router R1 to TFTP server on PC-A.

a. From the privileged EXEC mode on R1, enter the **copy running-config tftp** command. Provide the remote host address of the TFTP server, 192.168.1.3, and accept the default filename.

b. Verify that the file has been transferred to the TFTP server.

Step 3:   Restore the running configuration file to the router.

a. Erase the startup-config file on the router.

b. Reload the router.

c. Configure the G0/0/1 interface on the router with an IP address 192.168.1.1.

d. Verify connectivity between the router and PC-A.

e. Use the **copy** command to transfer the running-config file from the TFTP server to the router. Use **running-config** as the destination.

f. Verify the router has updated the running-config.

Part 4: Back Up and Restore Configurations Using Router Flash Memory

Current generation Cisco routers do not have internal flash memory. The flash memory for these routers uses CompactFlash (CF) memory. The use of CF memory allows for more available flash memory and easier upgrades without the need to open the router case. Besides storing the necessary files, such as IOS images, the CF memory can store other files, such as a copy of the running configuration. In Part 5, you will create a backup copy of the running configuration file and save it on the USB memory on the router.

Note: If the router does not use CF, the router may not have enough flash memory for storing the backup copy of the running configuration file. You should still read through the instructions and become familiar with the commands.

Step 1: Display the router file systems.

The **show file systems** command displays the available file systems on the router. The **flash0:** file system is the default file system on this router as indicated by the asterisk (*) symbol (at the beginning of the line). The **flash0:** file system can also be referenced using the name **flash:**. The total size of the **flash0:** is approximately 7 GB with about 6 GB available. Currently **flash0:** and **nvram:** are the only available file systems.

```
R1# show file systems
File Systems:

       Size(b)       Free(b)      Type    Flags    Prefixes
             -             -      opaque     rw     system:
             -             -      opaque     rw     tmpsys:
*   7194652672    6299918336      disk       rw     bootflash: flash:
    1804468224    1723789312      disk       ro     webui:
             -             -      opaque     rw     null:
             -             -      opaque     ro     tar:
             -             -      network    rw     tftp:
             -             -      opaque     wo     syslog:
      33554432      33543116      nvram      rw     nvram:
             -             -      network    rw     rcp:
             -             -      network    rw     ftp:
             -             -      network    rw     http:
             -             -      network    rw     scp:
             -             -      network    rw     sftp:
             -             -      network    rw     https:
             -             -      opaque     ro     cns:
```

Question:

Where is the startup-config file located?

Note: Verify there is at least 1 MB (1,048,576 bytes) of free space. If there is not enough space in the flash memory, please contact your instructor for further instructions. You can determine the size of flash memory and space available using the **show flash** or **dir flash:** command at the privileged EXEC prompt.

Step 2:   Copy the router running configuration to flash.

A file can be copied to flash by using the **copy** command at the privileged EXEC prompt. In this example, the file is copied into **flash0:** because there is only one flash drive available as displayed in the previous step, and it is also the default file system. The **R1-running-config-backup** file is used as the filename for the backup running configuration file.

Note: Remember that filenames are case-sensitive in the IOS file system.

a.   Copy the running configuration to flash memory.

```
R1# copy running-config flash:
Destination filename [running-config]? R1-running-config-backup
2169 bytes copied in 0.968 secs (2241 bytes/sec)
```

b.   Use **dir** command to verify the running-config has been copied to flash.

```
R1# dir flash:
Directory of bootflash:/

    11  drwx   16384  Aug  2  2019 04:15:13 +00:00  lost+found
370945  drwx    4096  Sep 25 2019 20:17:11 +00:00  .installer
338689  drwx    4096  Aug  2  2019 04:15:55 +00:00  .ssh
217729  drwx    4096  Aug  2  2019 04:17:59 +00:00  core
379009  drwx    4096  Sep 25 2019 20:19:13 +00:00  .prst_sync
 80641  drwx    4096  Aug  2  2019 04:16:09 +00:00  .rollback_timer
161281  drwx    4096  Aug  2  2019 04:16:11 +00:00  gs_script
112897  drwx   77824  Sep 25 2019 20:23:03 +00:00  tracelogs
362881  drwx    4096  Aug 23 2019 17:19:54 +00:00  .dbpersist
298369  drwx    4096  Aug  2  2019 04:16:41 +00:00  virtual-instance
    12  -rw-      30  Sep 25 2019 20:19:13 +00:00  throughput_monitor_
                                                   params
  8065  drwx    4096  Aug  2  2019 04:17:55 +00:00  onep
    13  -rw-      35  Sep 25 2019 20:20:19 +00:00  pnp-tech-time
249985  drwx    4096  Aug 20 2019 17:40:11 +00:00  Archives
    14  -rw-   64414  Sep 25 2019 20:20:28 +00:00  pnp-tech-discovery-
                                                   summary
    15  -rw-     509  Sep 25 2019 20:24:32 +00:00  R1-running-config-
                                                   backup
    17  -rw- 5032908  Sep 19 2019 14:16:23 +00:00  isr4200_4300_
                                                   rommon_1612_1r_SPA.
                                                   pkg
    18  -rw- 517153193  Sep 21 2019 04:24:04 +00:00  isr4200-
                                                   universalk9_
                                                   ias.16.09.04.SPA.
                                                   bin

7194652672 bytes total (6299643904 bytes free)
```

c.   Use the **more** command to view the running-config file in flash memory. Examine the file output and scroll to the Interface section. Notice the **no shutdown**

command is not included with the GigabitEthernet0/1. The interface is shut down when this file is used to update the running configuration on the router.

```
R1# more flash:R1-running-config-backup
<output omitted>
interface GigabitEthernet0/1
 ip address 192.168.1.1 255.255.255.0
 duplex auto
 speed auto
<output omitted>
```

Step 3:   Erase the startup configuration and reload the router.

Step 4:   Restore the running configuration from flash.

  a.   Verify the router has the default initial configuration.

  b.   Copy the saved running-config file from flash to update the running-config.

```
Router# copy flash:R1-running-config-backup running-config
```

  c.   Use the **show ip interface brief** command to view the status of the interfaces. The interface GigabitEthernet0/1 was not enabled when the running configuration was updated, because it is administratively down.

```
R1# show ip interface brief
Interface              IP-Address      OK? Method Status                Protocol
GigabitEthernet0/0/0   unassigned      YES unset  administratively down down
GigabitEthernet0/0/1   192.168.1.1     YES TFTP   administratively down down
Serial0/1/0            unassigned      YES unset  administratively down down
Serial0/1/1            unassigned      YES unset  administratively down down
```

The interface can be enabled using the **no shutdown** command in the interface configuration mode on the router.

Another option is to add the **no shutdown** command for the GigabitEthernet0/0/1 interface to the saved file before updating the router running configuration file. This will be done in Part 5 using a saved file on a USB flash drive.

Note: Because the IP address was configured by using a file transfer, TFTP is listed under the Method heading in the **show ip interface brief** output.

Part 5: (Optional) Use a USB Drive to Back Up and Restore the Running Configuration

A USB flash drive can be used to back up and restore files on a router with an available USB port. One USB port is available on the 4221 routers.

Note: USB ports are not available on all routers, but you should still become familiar with the commands.

Note: Some ISR G1 routers (1841, 2801, or 2811) use File Allocation Table (FAT) file systems, which results in a maximum size limit for the USB flash drives that can be used in this part of the lab. The recommended maximum size for an ISR G1 is 4 GB. If you receive the following message, the file system on the USB flash drive may be incompatible with the router or the capacity of the USB flash drive may have exceeded the maximum size of the FAT file system on the router.

```
*Feb  8 13:51:34.831: %USBFLASH-4-FORMAT: usbflash0 contains unexpected values in
partition table or boot sector.  Device needs formatting before use!
```

Step 1:   Insert a USB flash drive into a USB port on the router.

Notice the message on the terminal when inserting the USB flash drive.

```
*Sep 24 23:00:33.242: %IOSD_INFRA-6-IFS_DEVICE_OIR: Device usb0 added
```

Step 2:   Verify that the USB flash file system is available.

```
R1# show file systems
File Systems:

          Size(b)       Free(b)       Type   Flags   Prefixes
                -             -        opaque    rw    system:
                -             -        opaque    rw    tmpsys:
*      7194652672    6297677824        disk      rw    bootflash: flash:
        256589824     256577536        disk      rw    usb0:
       1804468224    1723789312        disk      ro    webui:
                -             -        opaque    rw    null:
                -             -        opaque    ro    tar:
                -             -        network   rw    tftp:
                -             -        opaque    wo    syslog:
         33554432      33543116        nvram     rw    nvram:
                -             -        network   rw    rcp:
                -             -        network   rw    ftp:
                -             -        network   rw    http:
                -             -        network   rw    scp:
                -             -        network   rw    sftp:
                -             -        network   rw    https:
                -             -        opaque    ro    cns:
```

Step 3:   Copy the running configuration file to the USB flash drive.

Use the **copy** command to copy the running configuration file to the USB flash drive.

```
R1# copy running-config usb0:
Destination filename [running-config]? R1-running-config-backup.txt
2198 bytes copied in 0.708 secs (3105 bytes/sec)
```

Step 4:   List the file on the USB flash drive.

Use the **dir** command (or **show** command) on the router to list the files on the USB flash drive. In this sample, a flash drive was inserted into USB port 0 on the router.

```
R1# dir usb0:
Directory of usb0:/

    6  -rwx    3539   Sep 25 2019 20:41:58 +00:00  R1-running-config-backup.txt
    3  drwx    4096   Sep 24 2019 13:32:26 +00:00  System Volume Information

256589824 bytes total (256573440 bytes free)
```

Step 5: Erase the startup-config and reload the router.

Step 6: Modify the saved file.

    a. Remove the USB drive from the router.

```
Router#
*Sep 24 23:00:27.674: %IOSD_INFRA-6-IFS_DEVICE_OIR: Device usb0 removed
```

    b. Insert the USB drive into the USB port of a PC.

    c. Modify the file using a text editor. The **no shutdown** command is added to the GigabitEthernet0/0/1 interface. Save the file as a plain text file on to the USB flash drive.

```
interface GigabitEthernet0/0/1
 ip address 192.168.1.1 255.255.255.0
 no shutdown
 duplex auto
 speed auto
```

    d. Remove the USB flash drive from the PC safely.

Step 7: Restore the running configuration file to the router.

    a. Insert the USB flash drive into a USB port on the router. Notice the port number where the USB drive has been inserted if there is more than one USB port available on the router.

```
*Sep 24 23:00:33.242: %IOSD_INFRA-6-IFS_DEVICE_OIR: Device usb0 added
```

    b. List the files on the USB flash drive.

```
R1# dir usb0:
Directory of usb0:/

    6 -rwx 3539 Sep 25 2019 20:41:58 +00:00  R1-running-config-backup.txt
    3 drwx 4096 Sep 24 2019 13:32:26 +00:00  System Volume Information

256589824 bytes total (256573440 bytes free)
```

    c. Copy the running configuration file to the router.

```
Router# copy usb0:R1-running-config-backup.txt running-config
Destination filename [running-config]?
2344 bytes copied in 0.184 secs (12739 bytes/sec)
R1#
```

    d. Verify that the GigabitEthernet0/1 interface is enabled.

```
R1# show ip interface brief
Interface            IP-Address   OK? Method Status                Protocol
GigabitEthernet0/0/0 unassigned   YES unset  administratively down down
GigabitEthernet0/0/1 192.168.1.1  YES TFTP   up                    up
Serial0/1/0          unassigned   YES unset  administratively down down
Serial0/1/1          unassigned   YES unset  administratively down down
```

The G0/1 interface is enabled because the modified running configuration included the no shutdown command.

Reflection Questions

1. What command do you use to copy a file from the flash to a USB drive?

_____

2. What command do you use to copy a file from the USB flash drive to a TFTP server?

_____

Router Interface Summary Table

Router Model	Ethernet Interface #1	Ethernet Interface #2	Serial Interface #1	Serial Interface #2
1800	Fast Ethernet 0/0 (F0/0)	Fast Ethernet 0/1 (F0/1)	Serial 0/0/0 (S0/0/0)	Serial 0/0/1 (S0/0/1)
1900	Gigabit Ethernet 0/0 (G0/0)	Gigabit Ethernet 0/1 (G0/1)	Serial 0/0/0 (S0/0/0)	Serial 0/0/1 (S0/0/1)
2801	Fast Ethernet 0/0 (F0/0)	Fast Ethernet 0/1 (F0/1)	Serial 0/1/0 (S0/1/0)	Serial 0/1/1 (S0/1/1)
2811	Fast Ethernet 0/0 (F0/0)	Fast Ethernet 0/1 (F0/1)	Serial 0/0/0 (S0/0/0)	Serial 0/0/1 (S0/0/1)
2900	Gigabit Ethernet 0/0 (G0/0)	Gigabit Ethernet 0/1 (G0/1)	Serial 0/0/0 (S0/0/0)	Serial 0/0/1 (S0/0/1)
4221	Gigabit Ethernet 0/0/0 (G0/0/0)	Gigabit Ethernet 0/0/1 (G0/0/1)	Serial 0/1/0 (S0/1/0)	Serial 0/1/1 (S0/1/1)
4300	Gigabit Ethernet 0/0/0 (G0/0/0)	Gigabit Ethernet 0/0/1 (G0/0/1)	Serial 0/1/0 (S0/1/0)	Serial 0/1/1 (S0/1/1)

Note: To find out how the router is configured, look at the interfaces to identify the type of router and how many interfaces the router has. There is no way to effectively list all the combinations of configurations for each router class. This table includes identifiers for the possible combinations of Ethernet and Serial interfaces in the device. The table does not include any other type of interface, even though a specific router may contain one. An example of this might be an ISDN BRI interface. The string in parentheses is the legal abbreviation that can be used in Cisco IOS commands to represent the interface.

10.6.13 Lab—Research Password Recovery Procedures

Objectives

Part 1: Research the Configuration Register

- Identify the purpose of the configuration register.
- Describe router behavior for different configuration register values.

Part 2: Document the Password Recovery Procedure for a Specific Cisco Router

- Research and record the process for password recovery on a specific Cisco router.
- Answer questions based on the researched procedure.

Background / Scenario

The purpose of this lab is to research the procedure for recovering or resetting the enable password on a specific Cisco router. The enable password protects access to privileged EXEC and configuration mode on Cisco devices. The enable password can be recovered, but the enable secret password is encrypted and would need to be replaced with a new password.

To bypass a password, a user must be familiar with the ROM monitor (ROMMON) mode, as well as the configuration register setting for Cisco routers. ROMMON is basic CLI software stored in ROM that can be used to troubleshoot boot errors and recover a router when an IOS is not found.

In this lab, you will begin by researching the purpose and settings of the configuration register for Cisco devices. You will then research and detail the exact procedure for password recovery for a specific Cisco router.

Required Resources

- Device with Internet access

Instructions

Part 1: Research the Configuration Register

To recover or reset an enable password, a user will utilize the ROMMON interface to instruct the router to ignore the startup configuration when booting. When booted, the user will access privilege EXEC mode, overwrite the running configuration with the saved startup configuration, recover or reset the password, and restore the router's boot process to include the startup configuration.

The router's configuration register plays a vital role in the process of password recovery. In the first part of this lab, you will research the purpose of a router's configuration register and the meaning of certain configuration register values.

Step 1:   Describe the purpose of the configuration register.

Questions:

What is the purpose of the configuration register?

_____

What command changes the configuration register in global configuration mode?

_____

What command changes the configuration register in ROMMON mode?

_____

Step 2:   Determine configuration register values and their meanings.

Questions:

Research and list the router behavior for the following configuration register values.

0x2102

_____

0x2142

_____

What is the difference between these two configuration register values?

_____

Part 2: Document the Password Recovery Procedure for a Specific Cisco Router

For Part 2, you will describe the exact procedure for recovering or resetting a password from a specific Cisco router and answer questions based on your research. Your instructor will provide you with the exact router model to research.

Step 1:   Detail the process to recover a password on a specific Cisco router.

Research and list the steps and commands that you need to recover or reset the enable or enable secret password from your Cisco router. Summarize the steps in your own words.

_____

Step 2:   Answer questions about the password recovery procedure.

Using the process for password recovery, answer the following questions.

_____

Describe how to find the current setting for your configuration register.

_____

Describe the process for entering ROMMON mode.

_____

What commands do you need to enter the ROMMON interface?

_____

What message would you expect to see when the router boots?

_____

Why is it important to load the startup configuration into the running configuration?

_____

Why is it important to change the configuration register back to the original value after recovering password?

_____

Reflection Question

Why is it of critical importance that a router be physically secured to prevent unauthorized access?

_____

Packet Tracer
☐ Activity

10.7.6 Packet Tracer—Use a TFTP Server to Upgrade a Cisco IOS Image

Addressing Table

Device	Interface	IP Address	Subnet Mask	Default Gateway
R1	G0/0/0	192.168.2.1	255.255.255.0	N/A
R2	G0/0	192.168.2.2	255.255.255.0	N/A
S1	VLAN 1	192.168.2.3	255.255.255.0	192.168.2.1
TFTP Server	NIC	192.168.2.254	255.255.255.0	192.168.2.1

Objectives

Part 1: Upgrade an IOS Image on a Cisco Device

Part 2: Back up an IOS Image on a TFTP Server

Scenario

A TFTP server can help manage the storage of IOS images and revisions to IOS images. For any network, it is good practice to keep a backup copy of the Cisco IOS Software image in case the system image in the router becomes corrupted or accidentally erased. A TFTP server can also be used to store new upgrades to the IOS and then deployed throughout the network where it is needed. In this activity, you will upgrade the IOS images on Cisco devices by using a TFTP server. You will also back up an IOS image with the use of a TFTP server.

Instructions

Part 1: Upgrade an IOS Image on a Cisco Device

Step 1:   Upgrade an IOS image on a router.

   a. Access the TFTP server and enable the TFTP service.

   b. Note the IOS image files that are available on the TFTP server.

   Question:

   Which IOS images stored on the server are compatible with a 1941 router?

   _____

   c. From **R2**, issue the **show flash:** command and record the available flash memory.

   _____

   d. Copy the CISCO1941/K9 IOS version 15.5 image for the 1941 router from the TFTP Server to R2.

   Note: In an actual network, if there is more than one interface active on the router, you may need to enter the **ip tftp source interface** command to specify which interface should be used to contact the TFTP server. This command is not supported in PT 7.2 and older versions and is not necessary to complete this activity.

```
R2# copy tftp: flash:
Address or name of remote host []? 192.168.2.254
Source filename []? c1900-universalk9-mz.SPA.155-3.M4a.bin
Destination filename [c1900-universalk9-mz.SPA.155-3.M4a.bin]?

Accessing tftp://192.168.2.254/c1900-universalk9-mz.SPA.155-3.M4a.
bin....
Loading c1900-universalk9-mz.SPA.155-3.M4a.bin from 192.168.2.254: !!!!
!!!!!!!!!!!!!!!!!!!!!!!!!!!!!!!!!!!!!!!!!!!!!!!!!!!!!!!!!!!!!!!!!!!!!!!!!!!!!
!!!!!!!!!!!!!!!!!!!!!!!!!!!!!!!!!!!!!!!!!!!!!!!!!!!!!!!!!!!!!!!!!!!!!!!!!!!!!
!!!!!!!!!!!!!!!!!!!!!!!!!!!!!!!!!!!!!!!!!!!!!!!!!!!!!!!!!!!!!!!!!!!!!!!!!!!!!
!!!!!!!!!!!!!!!!!!!!!!!!!!!!!!!!!!!!!!!!!!!!!!!!!!!!!!!!!!!!!!!!!!!!!!!!!!!!!
!!!!!!!!!!!!!!!!!!!!!!!!!!!!!!!!!!!!!!!!!!!!!!!!!!!!!!!!!!!!!!!!!!!!!!!!!!!!!
!!!!!!!!!!!!!!!!!!!!!!!!!!!!!!!!!!!!!!!!!!!!!!!!!!!!!!!!!!!!!!!!!!!!!!!!!!!!!
!!!!!!!!!!!!!!!!!!!!!!!!!!!!!!!!!!!!!!!!!!!!!!!!!!!!!!!!!!!!!!!!!!!!!!!!!!!!!
!!!!!!!!!!!!!!!!!!!!!!!!!!!!!!!!!!!!!!!!!!!!!!!!!!!!!!!!!!!!!!!!!!!!!!!!!!!!!
!!!!!
[OK - 33591768 bytes]

33591768 bytes copied in 4.099 secs (860453 bytes/sec)
```

e. Verify that the IOS image has been copied to flash.

Question:

How many IOS images are located in flash?

_____

f. Use the **boot system** command to load the version 15.5 IPBase image on the next reload.

```
R2(config)# boot system flash c1900-universalk9-mz.SPA.155-3.M4a.bin
```

g. Save the configuration and reload **R2**.

h. Use the **show version** command to verify the upgraded IOS image is loaded after **R2** reboots.

```
R2# show version
Cisco IOS Software, C1900 Software (C1900-UNIVERSALK9-M), Version
15.5(3)M4a, RELEASE SOFTWARE (fc1)
Technical Support: http://www.cisco.com/techsupport
Copyright (c) 1986-2016 by Cisco Systems, Inc.
Compiled Thu 06-Oct-16 13:56 by mnguyen

ROM: System Bootstrap, Version 15.0(1r)M9, RELEASE SOFTWARE (fc1)

R2 uptime is 21 seconds
System returned to ROM by power-on
System image file is "flash0:c1900-universalk9-mz.SPA.155-3.M4a.bin"
---- output omitted -----
```

Step 2: Upgrade an IOS image on a switch.

a. Access the TFTP server and copy the **c2960-lanbasek9-mz.150-2.SE4.bin** image to S1.

```
S1# copy tftp: flash:
```

b. Use the **boot system** command to configure the switch to load the new IOS image on boot.

   c. Reload S1 and verify the new image has been loaded into memory.

   d. Close the TFTP configuration window if it is still open.

Part 2: Back Up an IOS Image to a TFTP Server

   a. On **R1**, display the contents of flash and record the IOS image.

```
R1# show flash:
```

   b. Use the **copy** command to back up the IOS image in flash memory on **R1** to a TFTP server.

Note: The isr4300 image is considerably larger than the c1900 image. It will take longer to transmit it to the TFTP server.

```
R1# copy flash: tftp:
Source filename []? isr4300-universalk9.03.16.05.S.155-3.S5-ext.SPA.bin
Address or name of remote host []? 192.168.2.254
Destination filename [isr4300-universalk9.03.16.05.S.155-3.S5-ext.SPA.bin]?

Writing isr4300-universalk9.03.16.05.S.155-3.S5-ext.SPA.bin....!!!!!!!!!!!!!!!!!!
!!!!!!!!!!!!!!!!!!!!!!!!!!!!!!!!!!!!!!!!!!!!!!!!!!!!!!!!!!!!!!!!!!!!!!!!!!!!!!!!!!!
!!!!!!!!!!!!!!!!!!!!!!!!!!!!!!!!!!!!!!!!!!!!!!!!!!!!!!!!!!!!!!!!!!!!!!!!!!!!!!!!!!!
!!!!!!!!!!!!!!!!!!!!!!!!!!!!!!!!!!!!!!!!!!!!!!!!!!!!!!!!!!!!!!!!!!!!!!!!!!!!!!!!!!!
!!!!!!!!!!!!!!!!!!!!!!!!!!!!!!!!!!!!!!!!!!!!!! --- output omitted ----

!!!!!!!!!!!!!!!!!!!!!!!!!!!!!!!!!!!!!!!!!!!!!!!!!!!!!!!!!!!!!!!!!!!!!!!!!!!!!!!!!!!
!!!!!!!!!!!!!!!!!!!!!!!
[OK - 486899872 bytes]

486899872 bytes copied in 18.815 secs (83367 bytes/sec)
```

   c. Access the TFTP server and verify that the IOS image has been copied to the TFTP server.

Note: You may have to start and stop the TFTP service on the server so the file appears in the file listing.

10.8.1 Packet Tracer—Configure CDP, LLDP, and NTP

Addressing Table

Device	Interface	IP Address
HQ	G0/0/0	192.168.1.1/24
	G0/0/1	192.168.2.1/24
	S0/1/0	192.168.3.1/30
Branch	G0/0/0	192.168.1.2
	S0/1/0	192.168.3.2/30
HQ-SW-1	VLAN 1	Not configured
HQ-SW-2	VLAN 1	Not configured
BR-SW-1	VLAN 10	
BR-SW-2	VLAN 10	
BR-SW-3	VLAN 10	
NTP Server	NIC	192.168.1.254
PC1	NIC	192.168.2.10
PC2	NIC	192.168.4.10
PC3	NIC	192.168.4.20

Objectives

In this activity, you will configure a router to receive time information over NTP and configure devices with CDP and LLDP.

- Configure CDP to run globally on a device.
- Disable CDP on device interfaces where necessary.
- Configure LLDP to run globally on a device.
- Configure LLDP to send and receive messages according to requirements.
- Configure a router to use an NTP server.

Background / Scenario

A network administrator has been asked to investigate a new client's network. Documentation is incomplete for the network, so some information needs to be discovered. In addition, the NTP server needs to be configured on a router. Discovery protocols must also be adjusted to control traffic discovery protocol traffic and prevent information about the network from being received by potentially unauthorized hosts.

Some of the device IP addresses are unknown to you. You must determine what the IP addresses are so that you can connect to the devices over SSH to configure them. You can enter them into the Addressing Table as you discover them.

Instructions

Use the table below to log on to the Branch switches when you need to do so.

Device	Username	User Password	Enable Secret
BR-SW1	admin	SW1admin#	SW1EnaAccess#
BR-SW2	admin	SW2admin#	SW2EnaAccess#
BR-SW3	admin	SW3admin#	SW3EnaAccess#

Note: Click the **Fast Forward Time** button in the blue bar below the topology to speed up STP convergence. You can also click it several times to speed up the CDP update process.

Configure LLDP as follows:

- Disable CDP on the HQ router.

- Enable LLDP globally on HQ.

- On HQ, configure the links to the switches to only receive LLDP messages.

- Disable CDP on the HQ-SW-1 and HQ-SW-2 switches.

- Enable LLDP on the HQ-SW-1 and HQ-SW-2 switches.

- On the HQ-SW-1 and HQ-SW-2 switches, configure the links to the HQ router to only send, not receive, LLDP messages.

- Disable LLDP completely on the HQ-SW-1 and HQ-SW-2 access ports that are in use.

Configure CDP as follows:

- Activate CDP on the Branch router.

- Connect to switch BR-SW1 over SSH. You will not be able to open a CLI window by clicking the Branch switches.

- Connect to switches BR-SW2 and BR-SW3 over SSH. Configure the access ports that are in use to not send CDP messages out of the ports.

Configure NTP:

- Configure HQ to use the device at 192.168.1.254 as an NTP server.

10.8.2 Lab—Configure CDP, LLDP, and NTP

Topology

Addressing Table

Device	Interface	IP Address	Subnet Mask	Default Gateway
R1	Loopback1	172.16.1.1	255.255.255.0	N/A
	G0/0/1	10.22.0.1	255.255.255.0	
S1	SVI VLAN 1	10.22.0.2	255.255.255.0	10.22.0.1
S2	SVI VLAN 1	10.22.0.3	255.255.255.0	10.22.0.1

Objectives

Part 1: Build the Network and Configure Basic Device Settings

Part 2: Network Discovery with CDP

Part 3: Network Discovery with LLDP

Part 4: Configure and Verify NTP

Background / Scenario

Cisco Discovery Protocol (CDP) is a Cisco proprietary protocol for network discovery on the data link layer. It can share information such as device names and IOS versions with other physically connected Cisco devices. Link Layer Discovery Protocol (LLDP) is a vendor-neutral protocol using the data link layer for network discovery. It is mainly used with network devices in the local area network (LAN). The network devices advertise information, such as their identities and capabilities to their neighbors.

Network Time Protocol (NTP) synchronizes the time of day among a set of distributed time servers and clients. NTP uses the User Datagram Protocol (UDP) as its transport protocol. By default, NTP communications use Coordinated Universal Time (UTC).

An NTP server usually receives its time from an authoritative time source, such as an atomic clock attached to a time server. It then distributes this time across the network. NTP is extremely efficient; no more than one packet per minute is necessary to synchronize two machines to within a millisecond of each other.

In this lab, you must document the ports that are connected to other switches using CDP and LLDP. You will document your findings in a network topology diagram.

Note: The routers used with CCNA hands-on labs are Cisco 4221 with Cisco IOS XE Release 16.9.4 (universalk9 image). The switches used in the labs are Cisco Catalyst 2960s with Cisco IOS Release 15.2(2) (lanbasek9 image). Other routers, switches, and Cisco IOS versions can be used. Depending on the model and Cisco IOS version, the commands available and the output produced might vary from what is shown in the labs. Refer to the Router Interface Summary Table at the end of the lab for the correct interface identifiers.

Note: Ensure that the routers and switches have been erased and have no startup configurations. If you are unsure contact your instructor.

Required Resources

- One router (Cisco 4221 with Cisco IOS XE Release 16.9.4 universal image or comparable)
- Two switches (Cisco 2960 with Cisco IOS Release 15.2(2) lanbasek9 image or comparable)
- One PC (Windows with a terminal emulation program, such as Tera Term)
- Console cables to configure the Cisco IOS devices via the console ports
- Ethernet cables as shown in the topology

Part 1: Build the Network and Configure Basic Device Settings

In Part 1, you will set up the network topology and configure basic settings on the router and switches.

Step 1:   Cable the network as shown in the topology.

Attach the devices as shown in the topology diagram, and cable as necessary.

Step 2:   Configure basic settings for the router.

a. Assign a device name to the router.

b. Disable DNS lookup to prevent the router from attempting to translate incorrectly entered commands as though they were host names.

c. Assign **class** as the privileged EXEC encrypted password.

d. Assign **cisco** as the console password and enable login.

e. Assign **cisco** as the VTY password and enable login.

f. Encrypt the plaintext passwords.

g. Create a banner that warns anyone accessing the device that unauthorized access is prohibited.

h. Configure interfaces as listed in the earlier table.

i. Save the running configuration to the startup configuration file.

Step 3:   Configure basic settings for each switch.

a. Assign a device name to the switch.

b. Disable DNS lookup to prevent the router from attempting to translate incorrectly entered commands as though they were host names.

c. Assign **class** as the privileged EXEC encrypted password.

d. Assign **cisco** as the console password and enable login.

e. Assign **cisco** as the VTY password and enable login.

f. Encrypt the plaintext passwords.

g. Create a banner that warns anyone accessing the device sees the banner message "Authorized Users Only !"

h. Shut down all unused interfaces.

i. Save the running configuration to the startup configuration file.

Part 2: Network Discovery with CDP

On Cisco devices, CDP is enabled by default. You will use CDP to discover the ports that are currently connected.

a. On R1, use the appropriate **show cdp** command to determine how many interfaces are CDP enabled, and how many of those are up and how many are down.

Question:

How many interfaces are participating in the CDP advertisement? Which interfaces are up?

_____

b. On R1, use the appropriate **show cdp** command to determine the IOS version used on S1.

```
R1# show cdp entry S1
-------------------------
Device ID: S1
Entry address(es):
Platform: cisco WS-C2960+24LC-L,   Capabilities: Switch IGMP
Interface: GigabitEthernet0/0/1,   Port ID (outgoing port): FastEthernet0/5
Holdtime : 125 sec


Version :
Cisco IOS Software, C2960 Software (C2960-LANBASEK9-M), Version 15.2(4)E8,
RELEASE SOFTWARE (fc3)
Technical Support: http://www.cisco.com/techsupport
Copyright (c) 1986-2019 by Cisco Systems, Inc.
Compiled Fri 15-Mar-19 17:28 by prod_rel_team


advertisement version: 2
VTP Management Domain: ''
Native VLAN: 1
Duplex: full
```

Question:

What IOS version is S1 using?

_____

c. On S1, use the appropriate **show cdp** command to determine how many CDP packets have been output.

```
S1# show cdp traffic
CDP counters :
        Total packets output: 179, Input: 148
        Hdr syntax: 0, Chksum error: 0, Encaps failed: 0
        No memory: 0, Invalid packet: 0,
        CDP version 1 advertisements output: 0, Input: 0
        CDP version 2 advertisements output: 179, Input: 148
```

Question:

How many packets has CDP output since the last counter reset?

_____

d. Configure the SVI for VLAN 1 on S1 and S2 using the IP addresses specified in the earlier Addressing Table. Configure the default gateway on each switch based on the Address Table.

e. On R1, issue the **show cdp entry S1** command.

Question:

What additional information is now available?

_____

```
R1# show cdp entry S1
-------------------------
Device ID: S1
Entry address(es):
  IP address: 10.22.0.2
Platform: cisco WS-C2960+24LC-L,   Capabilities: Switch IGMP
Interface: GigabitEthernet0/0/1,   Port ID (outgoing port): FastEthernet0/5
Holdtime : 133 sec

Version :
Cisco IOS Software, C2960 Software (C2960-LANBASEK9-M), Version 15.2(4)E8,
RELEASE SOFTWARE (fc3)
Technical Support: http://www.cisco.com/techsupport
Copyright (c) 1986-2019 by Cisco Systems, Inc.
Compiled Fri 15-Mar-19 17:28 by prod_rel_team

advertisement version: 2
VTP Management Domain: ''
Native VLAN: 1
Duplex: full
Management address(es):
  IP address: 10.22.0.2
```

f. Disable CDP globally on all devices.

Part 3: Network Discovery with LLDP

On Cisco devices, LLDP maybe enabled by default. You will use LLDP to discover the ports that are currently connected.

a. Enter the appropriate **lldp** command to enable LLDP on all devices in the topology.

b. On S1, issue the appropriate **lldp** command to give you detailed information on S2.

```
S1# show lldp entry S2


Capability codes:

    (R) Router, (B) Bridge, (T) Telephone, (C) DOCSIS Cable Device

    (W) WLAN Access Point, (P) Repeater, (S) Station, (O) Other

------------------------------------------------
Local Intf: Fa0/1

Chassis id: c025.5cd7.ef00

Port id: Fa0/1

Port Description: FastEthernet0/1

System Name: S2


System Description:

Cisco IOS Software, C2960 Software (C2960-LANBASEK9-M), Version 15.2(4)E8,
RELEASE SOFTWARE (fc3)

Technical Support: http://www.cisco.com/techsupport

Copyright (c) 1986-2019 by Cisco Systems, Inc.

Compiled Fri 15-Mar-19 17:28 by prod_rel_team


Time remaining: 109 seconds

System Capabilities: B

Enabled Capabilities: B

Management Addresses:

    IP: 10.22.0.3

Auto Negotiation - supported, enabled

Physical media capabilities:

    100base-TX(FD)

    100base-TX(HD)

    10base-T(FD)

    10base-T(HD)

Media Attachment Unit type: 16

Vlan ID: 1



Total entries displayed: 1
```

Question:

What is the chassis ID for switch S2?

c. Console into all the devices and use the LLDP commands necessary for you to draw the physical network topology from only the show command output.

Part 4: Configure NTP

In Part 4, you will configure R1 as the NTP server and S1 and S2 as NTP clients of R1. Synchronized time is important for syslog and debug functions. If the time is not synchronized, it is difficult to determine what network event caused the message.

Step 1:   Display the current time.

Issue the **show clock detail** command to display the current time on R1. Record the information regarding the current time displayed in the following table.

Date	Time	Time Zone	Time Source

Step 2:   Set the time.

Use the appropriate command to set the time on R1. The time entered should be in UTC.

Step 3:   Configure the NTP master.

Configure R1 as the NTP master with a stratum level of 4.

Step 4:   Configure the NTP client.

a. Issue the appropriate command on S1 and S2 to see the configured time. Record the current time displayed in the following table.

Date	Time	Time Zone

b. Configure S1 and S2 as NTP clients. Use the appropriate NTP commands to obtain time from R1's G0/0/1 interface, as well as to periodically update the calendar or hardware clock on the switch.

Step 5:   Verify NTP configuration.

a. Use the appropriate **show** command to verify that S1 and S2 are synchronized with R1.

Note: It could take a few minutes before the switches are synchronized with R1.

b. Issue the appropriate command on S1 and S2 to see the configured time and compare the time recorded earlier.

Reflection Question

Within a network, on which interfaces should you not use discovery protocols? Explain.

Router Interface Summary Table

Router Model	Ethernet Interface #1	Ethernet Interface #2	Serial Interface #1	Serial Interface #2
1800	Fast Ethernet 0/0 (F0/0)	Fast Ethernet 0/1 (F0/1)	Serial 0/0/0 (S0/0/0)	Serial 0/0/1 (S0/0/1)
1900	Gigabit Ethernet 0/0 (G0/0)	Gigabit Ethernet 0/1 (G0/1)	Serial 0/0/0 (S0/0/0)	Serial 0/0/1 (S0/0/1)
2801	Fast Ethernet 0/0 (F0/0)	Fast Ethernet 0/1 (F0/1)	Serial 0/1/0 (S0/1/0)	Serial 0/1/1 (S0/1/1)
2811	Fast Ethernet 0/0 (F0/0)	Fast Ethernet 0/1 (F0/1)	Serial 0/0/0 (S0/0/0)	Serial 0/0/1 (S0/0/1)
2900	Gigabit Ethernet 0/0 (G0/0)	Gigabit Ethernet 0/1 (G0/1)	Serial 0/0/0 (S0/0/0)	Serial 0/0/1 (S0/0/1)
4221	Gigabit Ethernet 0/0/0 (G0/0/0)	Gigabit Ethernet 0/0/1 (G0/0/1)	Serial 0/1/0 (S0/1/0)	Serial 0/1/1 (S0/1/1)
4300	Gigabit Ethernet 0/0/0 (G0/0/0)	Gigabit Ethernet 0/0/1 (G0/0/1)	Serial 0/1/0 (S0/1/0)	Serial 0/1/1 (S0/1/1)

Note: To find out how the router is configured, look at the interfaces to identify the type of router and how many interfaces the router has. There is no way to effectively list all the combinations of configurations for each router class. This table includes identifiers for the possible combinations of Ethernet and Serial interfaces in the device. The table does not include any other type of interface, even though a specific router may contain one. An example of this might be an ISDN BRI interface. The string in parentheses is the legal abbreviation that can be used in Cisco IOS commands to represent the interface.

The "Study Guide" portion of this chapter uses a variety of exercises to test your knowledge of the characteristics of scalable network architectures. The "Labs and Activities" portion of this chapter includes the online curriculum Packet Tracer activity instructions.

As you work through this chapter, use Chapter 11 in *Enterprise Networking, Security, and Automation v7 Companion Guide* or use the corresponding Module 11 in the Enterprise Networking, Security, and Automation online curriculum for assistance.

Study Guide

Hierarchical Networks

In this section, you review how data, voice, and video are converged in a switched network.

Video—Three-Layer Network Design

Be sure to review the video in the online course. It uses Packet Tracer to demonstrate a three-layer network design.

Borderless Switched Networks

An example of the Cisco Borderless Networks architecture is shown in Figure 11-1.

Figure 11-1   Cisco Borderless Networks Architecture

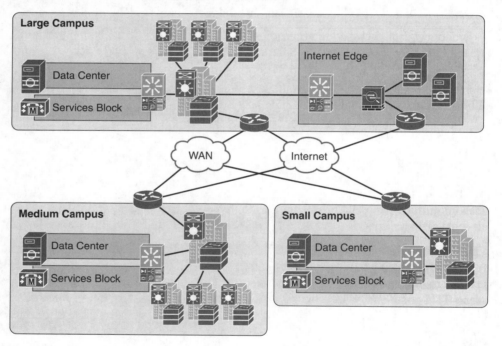

Briefly describe the Cisco Borderless Networks architecture.

_____

_____

_____

_____

Hierarchy in the Borderless Switched Network

Indicate which borderless switched network design principle is best described by each characteristic in Table 11-1.

Table 11-1   Identify the Borderless Switched Network Design Principle

Characteristic	Hierarchical	Modularity	Resiliency	Flexibility
Allows networks to grow and provide on-demand services				
Uses all network resources available to provide data traffic load sharing				
Helps each device on every tier employ a specific role				
Provides a way for the network to always be accessible				

Designing a borderless switched network in a hierarchical fashion creates a foundation that allows network designers to overlay security, mobility, and unified communication features. In Figure 11-2, label the three layers of the hierarchical design model.

Figure 11-2   Three-Tier Model

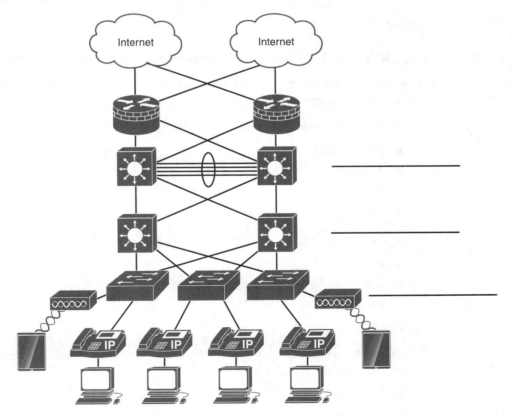

Access, Distribution, and Core Layer Functions

In Table 11-2, identify the layer described for each of the switch functions.

Table 11-2   Identify the Hierarchical Layer

Switch Function	Core	Distribution	Access
Can be combined with the distribution layer to provide for a collapsed design			
Allows data to flow on equal-cost switching paths to the core			
Aggregates Layer 2 broadcast domains and Layer 3 routing boundaries			
The network backbone area for switching			
Includes redundancy as an important feature for switched network access			
Helps applications operate on the network more efficiently and securely			
Provides direct, switched network connectivity to the user			
Interfaces with the backbone and users to provide intelligent switching, routing, and security			
Provides fault isolation and high-speed backbone switch connectivity			

Check Your Understanding—Hierarchical Networks

Check your understanding of hierarchical networks by choosing the BEST answer to each of the following questions.

1. Which term is used to describe a network that is always accessible?

   a. Hierarchical

   b. Modular

   c. Resilient

   d. Flexible

2. Which characteristic of a network allows it to expand and provide on-demand services?

   a. Hierarchical

   b. Modular

   c. Resilient

   d. Flexible

3. Which term describes the ability of a network to use all available network resources and to provide data load sharing?

   a. Hierarchical

   b. Modular

   c. Resilient

   d. Flexible

4. Which network layer provides fault isolation and high-speed backbone switch connectivity?

   a. Core

   b. Distribution

   c. Access

5. Which network layer provides direct, switched network connectivity to the user?

   a. Core

   b. Distribution

   c. Access

6. Which network layer integrates with the backbone and users to provide intelligent switching, routing, and security?

   a. Core

   b. Distribution

   c. Access

Scalable Networks

In this section, you review considerations for designing a scalable network.

Identify Scalability Terminology

Match each definition with the appropriate term. This exercise is a one-to-one matching: Each definition has exactly one matching term.

Definition

a. Supports new features and devices without requiring major equipment upgrades

b. Link-state routing protocol with a two-layer hierarchical design

c. Cisco proprietary distance vector routing protocol

d. Increases flexibility, reduces costs, and provides mobility to users

e. Minimizes the possibility of a single point of failure

f. Allows for redundant paths by eliminating switching loops

g. Isolates routing updates and minimizes the size of routing tables

h. Technique for aggregating multiple links between equipment to increase bandwidth

Terms

_____ EtherChannel

_____ Modular equipment

_____ OSPF

_____ Redundancy

_____ Scalable Routing Protocol

_____ Spanning Tree Protocol

_____ Wireless LANs

Check Your Understanding—Scalable Networks

Check your understanding of scalable networks by choosing the BEST answer to each of the following questions.

1. Which three recommendations may be included in a network design strategy that is focused on scalability? (Choose three.)

    a. Design a hierarchical network.

    b. Use Layer 2 devices to filter and reduce network traffic in the core.

    c. Choose routers or multilayer switches to limit broadcasts and filter other undesirable traffic from the network.

    d. Use expandable, modular equipment or clustered devices that can be easily upgraded to increase capabilities.

    e. Combine the access and distribution layers for easier access and to limit the size of the failure domain.

2. True or false: OSPF is well suited for larger networks because it can be deployed using a hierarchical design.

    a. True

    b. False

3. What three important features should be considered for implementation in a well-designed, scalable network? (Choose three.)

    a. Static routes

    b. Redundant links

    c. Multiple links

    d. Access layer with only wired devices

    e. Expandable, modular equipment

Switch Hardware

In this section, you review how switch hardware features support network requirements.

Switch Hardware Features

Match each business consideration with the appropriate switch feature. This exercise is a one-to-one matching: Each business consideration has exactly one matching switch feature.

Business Consideration

a. Should provide continuous access to the network

b. Switches with insertable switching line/port cards

c. Provides electrical current to other devices and supports redundant power supplies

d. Daisy-chain switches with high-bandwidth throughput

e. Important consideration in a network where there may be congested ports to servers or other areas of the network

f. Depends on the number and speed of the interfaces, supported features, and expansion capability

g. Switches with preset features or options

h. Ability to adjust to growth of network users

i. How fast the interfaces will process network data

j. Refers to a switch's ability to support the appropriate number of devices on the network

Switch Feature

_____ Cost

_____ Fixed configuration

_____ Frame buffers

_____ Modular

_____ Port density

_____ Port speed

_____ Reliability

_____ Scalability

_____ Stackable

_____ Uninterruptible power supply

Check Your Understanding—Switch Hardware

Check your understanding of switch hardware by choosing the BEST answer to each of the following questions.

1. Which category of switches is used to aggregate traffic at the edge of the network?

   a. Campus LAN switches

   b. Cloud-managed switches

   c. Service provider switches

   d. Data center switches

2. Field-replaceable line cards are a feature found on which type of switch?

   a. Modular

   b. Fixed configuration

   c. Virtual

   d. Stackable

3. This is the term used to describe switches that can be interconnected and managed as one larger single switch.

   a. Modular

   b. Stackable

   c. Cloud managed

   d. Multilayer

4. This is the term used to describe the number of ports available on a single switch.

   a. Speed

   b. Scalability

   c. Density

   d. Modularity

5. This is the term used to describe how much data a switch can process per second.

   a. Forwarding rate

   b. Power

   c. Reliability

   d. Wire speed

6. Which type of switch supports routing protocols and can forward IP packets at close to Layer 2 forwarding rates?

   a. Modular

   b. Stackable

   c. Cloud managed

   d. Multilayer

Router Hardware

In this section, you review the types of routers available for small to-medium-sized business networks.

Router Categories

In Table 11-3, select the router category that applies to each description.

Table 11-3   Identify Router Category Features

Router Description	Branch Routers	Network Edge Routers	Service Provider Routers	Industrial Routers
Provide fast performance with high security for data centers and campus and branch networks				
Enable simple network configuration and management for LANs and WANs				

Router Description	Branch Routers	Network Edge Routers	Service Provider Routers	Industrial Routers
Provide enterprise-class features in harsh environments				
Optimize services on a single platform				
Allow end-to-end delivery of subscriber services				
Deliver next-generation Internet experiences across all devices and locations				
Small, compact, and ruggedized for mission-critical applications				
Provide high capacity and scalability with hierarchical quality of service				
Maximize local services and ensure 24/7/365 uptime				
Unite campus, data center, and branch networks				

Check Your Understanding—Router Hardware

Check your understanding of router hardware by choosing the BEST answer to each of the following questions.

1. Which type of router provides fast performance and high security for data centers and campus and branch networks?

    a. Branch router

    b. Network edge router

    c. Service provider router

    d. Industrial router

2. Which type of router provides end-to-end delivery of subscriber services?

    a. Branch router

    b. Network edge router

    c. Service provider router

    d. Industrial router

3. Which type of router provides simple network configuration and management for LANs and WANs?

    a. Branch router

    b. Network edge router

    c. Service provider router

    d. Industrial router

4. Which type of router is designed to provide enterprise-class features in rugged and harsh environments?

   a. Branch router

   b. Network edge router

   c. Service provider router

   d. Industrial router

5. Which type of router delivers next-generation Internet experience across all devices and locations?

   a. Branch router

   b. Network edge router

   c. Service provider router

   d. Industrial router

Labs and Activities

11.5.1 Packet Tracer—Compare Layer 2 and Layer 3 Devices

Objective

Part 1: Compare Layer 2 and Layer 3 Switches

Part 2: Compare a Layer 3 Switch and a Router

Background

In this activity, you will use various commands to examine three different switching topologies and compare the similarities and differences between the 2960 and 3650 switches. You will also compare the routing table of a 4321 router with that of a 3650 switch.

Note: Search the Internet for more details about the *WS-C3650-24PS-L Layer 3 switch* and the *ISR 4321/K9* router.

Instructions

Step 1:   Compare Layer 2 and Layer 3 Switches

    a.   Examine the physical aspects of **D1** and **ASw-1**.

        Questions:

        Each individual switch has how many physical switchports?

        _____

        How many Fast Ethernet and Gigabit Ethernet switchports does each switch have?

        _____

        List the transmission speed of the Fast Ethernet and Gigabit Ethernet switchports on each switch.

        _____

        Are either of the two switches modular in design?

        _____

    b.   The switchports of a 3650 switch can be configured as Layer 3 interfaces by entering the **no switchport** command in interface configuration mode. This allows technicians to assign an IP address and subnet mask to the switchport in the same way that they are configured on a router interface.

        Questions:

        What is the difference between a Layer 2 switch and a Layer 3 switch?

        _____

What is the difference between a switch's physical interface and the VLAN interface?

_____

At which layers do 2960 and 3650 switches operate?

_____

Issue the **show run** command to examine the configurations of the **D1** and **ASw-1** switches. Do you notice any differences between them?

_____

Try to display the routing table on D1 and ASw-1 using the **show ip route** command. Why do you think the command does not work on **ASw-1** but works on **D1**?

_____

Step 2:   Compare a Layer 3 Switch and a Router

In the past, switches and routers have been separate and distinct devices. The term switch was set aside for hardware devices that function at Layer 2. Routers, on the other hand, are devices that make forwarding decisions based on Layer 3 information. They use routing protocols to share routing information and to communicate with other routers. Layer 3 switches, such as the 3650, can be configured to forward Layer 3 packets. Entering the **ip routing** command in global configuration mode allows Layer 3 switches to be configured with routing protocols, which gives them some of the capabilities of a router. Although similar in some ways, Layer 3 switches are different from routers in many other aspects.

a.   Open the Physical tab on D1 and R1.

Questions:

Do you notice any similarities between the two? Do you notice any differences between the two?

_____

Issue the **show run** command and examine the configurations of R1 and D1. What differences do you see between the two?

_____

Which command allows configuration of D1 with an IP address on one of its physical interfaces?

_____

Use the **show ip route** command on both devices. Do you see any similarities or differences between the two tables?

_____

Now, analyze the routing table of R2 and D2. What is present now that was not present in the configuration of R1 and D1?

_____

Which network is in the routing table of D2 that was learned from R2?

_____

b. Verify that each topology has full connectivity by completing the following tests:

- Ping from **PC1** to **PC2**

- Ping from **PC3** to **PC4**

- Ping from **PC5** to **PC6** and **PC7**

In all three examples, each PC is on a different network.

Questions:

Which device is used to provide communication between networks?

_____

Why were we able to ping across networks without there being a router?

_____

Bonus question: We say that routers are Layer 3 devices and conventional (non-Layer 3) switches are Layer 2 devices. However, we can assign an IP address to a management (SVI) interface of a Layer 2 switch. How is this possible if switches are Layer 2 devices?

_____

CHAPTER 12

Network Troubleshooting

The "Study Guide" portion of this chapter uses a variety of exercises to test your knowledge and skills related to troubleshooting enterprise networks. The "Labs and Activities" portion of this chapter includes all the online curriculum Packet Tracer activity instructions.

As you work through this chapter, use Chapter 12 in *Enterprise Networking, Security, and Automation v7 Companion Guide* or use the corresponding Module 12 in the Enterprise Networking, Security, and Automation online curriculum for assistance.

Study Guide

Network Documentation

In this section, you review how network documentation is developed and used to troubleshoot network issues.

Documentation Overview

List three types of documentation a network administrator should have to effectively troubleshoot issues.

_____

_____

_____

Network Topology Diagrams

There are two types of network topology diagrams: physical and logical topology diagrams. Figure 12-1 shows an example of a physical topology.

Figure 12-1   Physical Topology

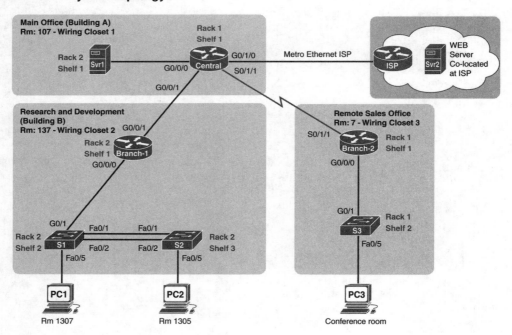

List at least three pieces of information typically included in a physical topology.

_____

_____

_____

_____

Figures 12-2 and 12-3 show examples of logical topologies.

Figure 12-2 Logical IPv4 Topology

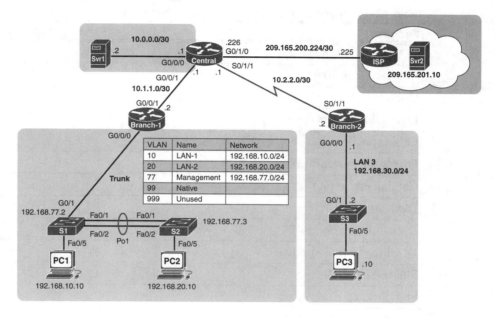

Figure 12-3 Logical IPv6 Topology

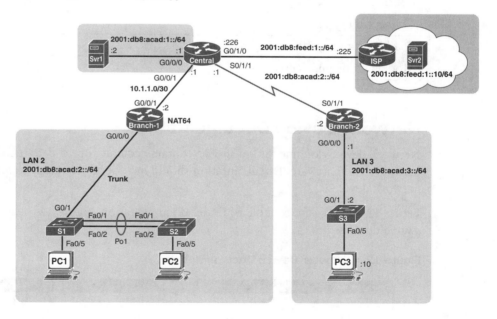

List at least four pieces of information typically included in a logical topology.

_____

_____

_____

_____

_____

In Table 12-1, indicate whether each feature is part of a physical topology document or logical topology document.

Table 12-1 Physical and Logical Topology Features

Feature	Physical Topology	Logical Topology
WAN technologies used		
Interface identifiers		
Connector type		
Device identifiers or names		
Cable specification		
Operating system version		
Cabling endpoints		
Device type		
Data link protocols		
DLCI for virtual circuits		
Site-to-site VPNs		
Static routes		
Cable type and identifier		
Routing protocols		
Connection type		
IP address and prefix lengths		
Model and manufacturer		

Network Device Documentation

Network device documentation should contain accurate, up-to-date records of the network hardware and software. Documentation should include all pertinent information about the network devices.

Figure 12-4 shows an example of router documentation. Figure 12-5 shows an example of switch documentation.

Figure 12-4 Router Device Documentation

Device	Model	Description	Location	IOS		License
Central	ISR 4321	Central Edge Router	Building A Rm: 137	Cisco IOS XE Software, Version 16.09.04 flash:isr4300-universalk9_ias.16.09.04.SPA.bin		ipbasek9 securityk9
Interface	Description		IPv4 Address	IPv6 Address	MAC Address	Routing
G0/0/0	Connects to SVR-1		10.0.0.1/30	2001:db8:acad:1::1/64	a03d.6fe1.e180	OSPF
G0/0/1	Connects to Branch-1		10.1.1.1/30	2001:db8:acad:a001::1/64	a03d.6fe1.e181	OSPFv3
G0/1/0	Connects to ISP		209.165.200.226/30	2001:db8:feed:1::2/64	a03d.6fc3.a132	Default
S0/1/1	Connects to Branch-2		10.1.1.2/24	2001:db8:acad:2::1/64	n/a	OSPFv3
Device	Model	Description	Site	IOS		License
Branch-1	ISR 4221	Branch-2 Edge Router	Building B Rm: 107	Cisco IOS XE Software, Version 16.09.04 flash:isr4200-universalk9.16.09.04.SPA.bin		ipbasek9 securityk9
Interface	Description		IPv4 Address	IPv6 Address	MAC Address	Routing
G0/0/0	Connects to S1		Router-on-a-stick	Router-on-a-stick	a03d.6fe1.9d90	OSPF
G0/0/1	Connects to Central		10.1.1.2/30	2001:db8:acad:a001::2/64	a03d.6fe1.9d91	OSPF

Figure 12-5 LAN Switch Device Documentation

Device	Model	Description	Mgt. IP Address	IOS		VTP
S1	Cisco Catalyst WS-C2960-24TC-L	Branch-1 LAN1 switch	192.168.77.2/24	IOS: 15.0(2)SE7 Image: C2960-LANBASEK9-M		Domain: CCNA Mode: Server
Port	**Description**		**Access**	**VLAN**	**Trunk**	**EtherChannel**	**Native**	**Enabled**
Fa0/1	Port Channel 1 trunk to S2 Fa0/1		-	-	Yes	Port-Channel 1	99	Yes
Fa0/2	Port Channel 1 trunk to S2 Fa0/2		-	-	Yes	Port-Channel 1	99	Yes
Fa0/3	*** Not in use ***		Yes	999	-	-		Shut
Fa0/4	*** Not in use ***		Yes	999	-	-		Shut
Fa0/5	Access port to user		Yes	10	-	-		Yes
...				-	-	-		-
Fa0/24	Access port to user		Yes	20	-	-		Yes
Fa0/24	*** Not in use ***		Yes	999	-	-		Shut
G0/1	Trunk link to Branch-1		-	-	Yes	-	99	Yes
G0/2	*** Not in use ***		Yes	999	-			

List at least four pieces of information that could be included in a network device's configuration documentation.

_____

_____

_____

_____

_____

_____

Figure 12-6 shows an example of end-system documentation.

Figure 12-6 End-System Documentation

Device	OS	Services	MAC Address	IPv4 / IPv6 Addresses	Default Gateway	DNS
SRV1	MS Server 2016	SMTP, POP3, File services, DHCP	5475.d08e.9ad8	10.0.0.2/30 2001:db8:acad:1::2/64	10.0.0.1 2001:db8:acad:1::1	10.0.0.1 2001:db8:acad:1::1
SRV2	MS Server 2016	HTTP, HTTPS	5475.d07a.5312	209.165.201.10 2001:db8:feed:1::10/64	209.165.201.1 2001:db8:feed:1::1	209.165.201.1 2001:db8:feed:1::1
PC1	MS Windows 10	HTTP, HTTPS	5475.d017.3133	192.168.10.10/24 2001:db8:acad:1::251/64	192.168.10.1 2001:db8:acad:1::1	192.168.10.1 2001:db8:acad:1::1
...						

List at least four pieces of information that could be included in an end system's configuration documentation.

_____

_____

_____

_____

_____

_____

Establish a Network Baseline

The purpose of network monitoring is to watch network performance in comparison to a predetermined baseline. In Table 8-2, indicate whether each statement describes a benefit in establishing a network baseline.

Table 12-2   Benefits of Establishing a Network Baseline

Statements	Benefit	Not a Benefit
Enable fast transport services between campuses		
Investigate whether the network can meet the identified policies and use requirements		
Combine two hierarchical design layers		
Locate areas of the network that are most heavily used		
Identify the parts of the network that are least used		
Identify where the most errors occur		
Establish the traffic patterns and loads for a normal or average day		

List the three steps for establishing a baseline.

Step 1. _____

Step 2. _____

Step 3. _____

Data Measurement

When documenting a network, it is often necessary to gather information directly from routers and switches using a variety of show commands. Match each type of information gathered with the appropriate **show** command.

Information Gathered

a. Contents of the address resolution table

b. Uptime and information about device software and hardware

c. Detailed settings and status for device interfaces

d. Detailed information about directly connected Cisco devices

e. Contents of the routing table

f. Summarized table of the up/down status of all device interfaces

g. Summary of VLANs and access ports on a switch

h. Current configuration of the device

i. Useful for collecting a large amount of information for troubleshooting purposes

j. Contents of the IPv6 neighbor table

Command

_____ show ip route

_____ show arp

_____ show vlan

_____ show ip interface brief

_____ show tech-support

_____ show running-config

_____ show version

_____ show ipv6 neighbors

_____ show interface

_____ show cdp neighbors detail

Check Your Understanding—Network Documentation

Check your understanding of network documentation by choosing the BEST answer to each of the following questions.

1. Which topology diagram displays IP addresses?

   a. IP topology

   b. Logical topology

   c. Physical topology

   d. Port topology

2. Which documentation could be referenced to identify the OS on a server?

   a. End-system documentation

   b. LAN switch device documentation

   c. Router device documentation

3. Which three statements does a network baseline answer? (Choose three.)

   a. How does the network perform during a normal or average day?

   b. How much did the network cost?

   c. What are the network policies?

   d. What part of the network is least used?

   e. What part of the network is most heavily used?

   f. Who is responsible for managing the network?

4. True or false: A network baseline never ends and continually gathers information on a yearly basis.

   a. True

   b. False

5. Which command could be used to get detailed information about directly connected Cisco neighbor devices?

   a. show cdp neighbor

   b. show ip interface

   c. show ip route

   d. show version

Troubleshooting Process

In this section, you review troubleshooting methods that use a systematic, layered approach.

General Troubleshooting Procedures

In Figure 12-7, label the four major stages in the troubleshooting process.

Figure 12-7   Major Troubleshooting Stages

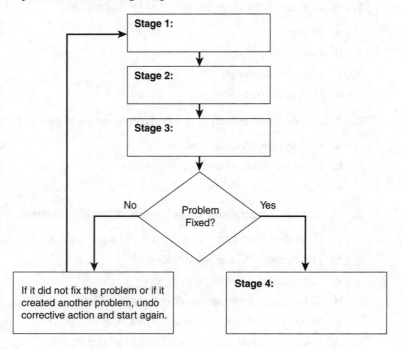

Note: The online course does not label the last stage as Stage 4. However, that is most likely an oversight. Stage 4 is indeed the final and arguably most important stage.

Seven-Step Troubleshooting Process

Figure 12-8 displays a more detailed seven-step troubleshooting process that also represents how some technicians may be able to jump between steps, depending on their level of experience.

Figure 12-8   Seven-Step Troubleshooting Process

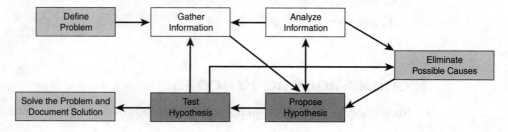

In Table 12-3, briefly describe each of the seven steps.

Table 12-3   Description of the Seven-Step Process

Step	Description
Define the problem	
Gather information	
Analyze information	
Eliminate possible causes	
Propose hypothesis	
Test hypothesis	
Solve the problem	

Gather Information

In step 2, you will most likely use a variety of commands to progress through the process of gathering symptoms. Some of the most commonly used commands are shown in Table 12-4.

Table 12-4   Common Information Gathering Commands

Command	Description
`ping {host | ip-address}`	■ Sends an echo request packet to an address and waits for a reply. ■ The *host* or *ip-address* variable is the IP alias or IP address of the target system.
`traceroute destination`	■ Identifies the path a packet takes through the networks. ■ The *destination* variable is the hostname or IP address of the target system.
`telnet {host | ip-address}`	■ Connects to an IP address using the Telnet application. ■ Use SSH whenever possible instead of Telnet.
`ssh -l user-id ip-address`	■ Connects to an IP address using SSH. ■ SSH is more secure than Telnet.

`show ip interface brief`
 	
`show ipv6 interface brief`
	■ Displays a summary status of all interfaces on a device.
	■ Useful for quickly identifying IP addressing on all interfaces.

`show ip route`
 	
`show ipv6 route`
	■ Displays the current IPv4 and IPv6 routing tables, which contain the routes to all known network destinations

`show protocols`	■ Displays the configured protocols and shows the global and interface-specific status of any configured Layer 3 protocol.
`debug`	■ Displays a list of options for enabling or disabling debugging events.

Structured Troubleshooting Methods

Match each statement with the appropriate troubleshooting method. This activity is not a one-to-one matching: Some troubleshooting methods may be used more than once.

Statement

_____ May not isolate the problem if it exists in multiple devices.

_____ Used for problems that likely involve software settings.

_____ Use when the problem is suspected to be a cabling or device failure.

_____ Reduces the scope of troubleshooting to the links between source and destination.

_____ Disadvantage is it requires you to check every device and interface.

_____ Disadvantage is it requires you to check every network application.

_____ Swap the problematic device with a known-working device.

_____ Start with an informed guess about which OSI layer to begin troubleshooting.

_____ Also called shoot-from-the hip, it may look like random troubleshooting to a less experienced network administrator.

_____ Might lead to a working solution without clearly revealing the root cause of the problem.

_____ Use troubleshooting experience to provide direction for where to investigate a possible cause.

_____ Begins at the OSI application layer.

_____ Also called spot-the-difference between a working solution and a nonworking solution.

_____ Begins at the OSI physical layer.

Troubleshooting Method

a. Bottom up

b. Top down

c. Divide-and-conquer

d. Follow-the-path

e. Substitution

f. Comparison

g. Educated guess

Check Your Understanding—Troubleshooting Process

Check your understanding of troubleshooting processes by choosing the BEST answer to each of the following questions.

1. Which option lists the three troubleshooting stages in the correct order?

    a. Gather symptoms, implement corrective action, and isolate the problem.

    b. Gather symptoms, isolate the problem, and implement corrective action.

    c. Implement corrective action, gather symptoms, and isolate the problem.

    d. Implement corrective action, isolate the problem, and gather symptoms.

    e. Isolate the problem, gather symptoms, and implement corrective action.

    f. Isolate the problem, implement corrective action, and gather symptoms.

2. In which step of the seven-step troubleshooting process would you create a rollback plan that identifies how to quickly reverse a solution?

    a. Analyze information

    b. Define the problem

    c. Eliminate possible causes

    d. Gather information

    e. Propose a hypothesis

    f. Solve the problem and document solution

    g. Test the hypothesis

3. Which are recommendations to be used when communicating with a user? (Choose three.)

    a. Be considerate and empathize with users.

    b. Listen or carefully read what the user is saying.

    c. Speak at a technical level they can understand.

    d. Use acronyms and other technical language that precisely relates to the issue.

4. During the gathering information step, which command would you use to display the configured protocols and the global and interface-specific status of any configured Layer 3 protocol?

    a. show interface

    b. show ip interface brief

    c. show ip protocols

    d. show protocols

    e. show version

5. What is the highest OSI layer that should be considered when troubleshooting routers and Layer 3 switches?

   a. Layer 1

   b. Layer 2

   c. Layer 3

   d. Layer 4

   e. Layer 7

6. Which structured troubleshooting method should be used when a cabling problem is suspected?

   a. Bottom-up troubleshooting

   b. Comparison troubleshooting

   c. Divide-and-conquer troubleshooting

   d. Educated guess troubleshooting

   e. Follow-the-path troubleshooting

   f. Top-down troubleshooting

7. Which structured troubleshooting method should be used when a software-related problem occurs?

   a. Bottom-up troubleshooting

   b. Comparison troubleshooting

   c. Divide-and-conquer troubleshooting

   d. Educated guess troubleshooting

   e. Follow-the-path troubleshooting

   f. Top-down troubleshooting

Troubleshooting Tools

In this section, you review different network troubleshooting tools.

Identify the Troubleshooting Tool

A wide variety of software and hardware tools are available to make troubleshooting easier. You can use these tools to gather and analyze symptoms of network problems. Match each description with the appropriate tool.

Description

a. Online repositories of experience-based information

b. Discovers VLAN configuration and average and peak bandwidth utilization using a portable device

c. Tools that document tasks, draw network diagrams, and establish network performance statistics

d. Measures electrical values of voltage, current, and resistance

e. Tests data communication cabling for broken wires, crossed wiring, and shorted connections

f. Hardware and software performance analysis in switching and routing environments

g. Provides a graphical representation of traffic from local and remote switches and routers

h. Analyzes network traffic—specifically source and destination frames

i. Includes device-level monitoring, configuration, and fault management

j. Tests and certifies copper and fiber cables for different services and standards via a handheld device

Software and Hardware Tools

_____ Protocol analyzer

_____ Cable tester

_____ Portable network analyzer

_____ Baselining tools

_____ Cable analyzer

_____ Network management system tool

_____ Cisco Prime NAM

_____ Knowledge base

_____ Network Analysis Module

_____ Digital multimeter

Syslog Server as a Troubleshooting Tool

Syslog is an important part of network security and troubleshooting. Cisco devices can log information regarding configuration changes, ACL violations, interface status, and many other types of events. Cisco devices can send log messages to several different facilities. List the five destinations to which event messages can be sent.

_____

_____

_____

_____

_____

Cisco IOS log messages fall into eight different levels. In Table 12-5, fill in the keyword for each level.

Table 12-5   Cisco IOS Syslog Messages

	Level	Keyword	Description	Definition
Highest level	0		System is unusable	LOG_EMERG
	1		Immediate action is needed	LOG_ALERT
	2		Critical conditions exist	LOG_CRIT
	3		Error conditions exist	LOG_ERR
	4		Warning conditions exist	LOG_WARNING
Lowest level	5		Normal (but significant) condition	LOG_NOTICE
	6		Informational messages only	LOG_NFO
	7		Debugging messages	LOG_DEBUG

Say that you want a router, RTA, to send syslog messages from level 0 to level 4 to a syslog server located at 192.0.2.1. Enter the commands, including the router prompts, to configure RTA to log and send the messages.

_____

_____

_____

_____

Check Your Understanding—Troubleshooting Tools

Check your understanding of troubleshooting tools by choosing the BEST answer to each of the following questions.

1. Which of these is an online network device vendor resource that can be used as a source of information?

   a. Baselining tool

   b. Knowledge base

   c. Network management system (NMS)

   d. Protocol analyzer

2. Which tool is useful for investigating packet content while packets are flowing through the network?

   a. Baselining tool

   b. Knowledge base

   c. Network management system (NMS)

   d. Protocol analyzer

3. Which hardware troubleshooting tool is a multifunctional handheld device used to test and certify copper and fiber cables for different services and standards?

   a. Cable analyzer

   b. Cable tester

c. Digital multimeter

d. Network Analysis Module

e. Portable network analyzer

4. Cisco IOS log messages fall into eight levels. Which syslog logging level is used to log the highest severity level?

a. 0

b. 1

c. 4

d. 6

e. 7

Symptoms and Causes of Network Problems

In this section, you review how to determine the symptoms and causes of network problems using a layered model.

Isolate the OSI Layer

A network administrator should be able to quickly isolate the OSI layer where an issue is most likely located. In Table 12-6, indicate the layer that is most likely associated with each issue.

Table 12-6   Isolating the OSI Layer Where an Issue Resides

Network Problems and Issues	OSI Layer				
	1	2	3	4	5, 6, and 7
A computer is configured with the wrong default gateway address.					
The DNS server is not configured with the correct A records.					
Traffic is congested on a low-capacity link, and frames are lost.					
STP loops and route flapping are generating a broadcast storm.					
A cable was damaged during a recent equipment installation.					
ACLs are misconfigured and blocking all web traffic.					
SSH error messages display unknown/untrusted certificates.					
The show processes cpu command displays usage far beyond the baseline.					
A VPN connection is not working correctly across a NAT boundary.					
A static route is sending packets to the wrong router.					
The routing table is missing routes and has unknown networks listed.					
SNMP messages are unable to traverse NAT.					

Check Your Understanding—Symptoms and Causes of Network Problems

Check your understanding of symptom and causes of network problems by choosing the BEST answer to each of the following questions.

1. Which OSI layer are you troubleshooting when the cause of network transmission errors is due to late collisions, short frames, and jabber?

   a. Application

   b. Data link

   c. Network

   d. Physical

   e. Transport

2. Which OSI layer are you troubleshooting when investigating a spanning-tree loop?

   a. Application

   b. Data link

   c. Network

   d. Physical

   e. Transport

3. Which OSI layer are you troubleshooting when investigating a routing protocol loop?

   a. Application

   b. Data link

   c. Network

   d. Physical

   e. Transport

4. Which OSI layer are you troubleshooting when investigating an extended ACL-related problem?

   a. Application

   b. Data link

   c. Network

   d. Physical

   e. Transport

5. Which OSI layer are you troubleshooting when investigating a DNS-related problem?

   a. Application

   b. Data link

   c. Network

   d. Physical

   e. Transport

6. Which IOS command can be used to test whether other network protocols are working?

a. ping

b. ssh

c. telnet

d. traceroute

Troubleshooting IP Connectivity

In this section, you review how to troubleshoot a network using the layered model. Be sure you review this section in the online course or *Enterprise Networking, Security, and Automation v7 Companion Guide*. The valuable examples and explanations in those sources are not repeated here.

Knowing which command to use to gather the necessary information for troubleshooting is crucial to effectively and efficiently resolve problems. All the commands you have mastered over the course of your CCNA studies are part of your troubleshooting toolkit. This exercise highlights only a few.

Match the command output with the appropriate command.

Command Output

a. Displays all known destinations on a Windows PC

b. Displays all known IPv6 destinations on a router

c. Can be used to verify the transport layer

d. Clears the MAC-to-IP address table on a PC

e. Displays the MAC-to-IP address table for other IPv6 devices

f. Displays the known MAC addresses on a switch

g. Displays input and output queue drops

h. Displays the IP addressing information on a Windows PC

Command

_____ show ipv6 neighbors

_____ ipconfig

_____ show ipv6 route

_____ telnet

_____ show mac address-table

_____ arp -d

_____ route print

_____ show interfaces

Note: No book or study guide will effectively teach you how to troubleshoot networks. To get proficient at it, you must practice troubleshooting on lab equipment and simulators. This practice works best with a partner or a team because (1) you can collaborate together to resolve issues and (2) you can swap roles and take turns breaking the network and resolving the issue. For readers with access to the Cisco Networking Academy curriculum, the Packet Tracer activities in this chapter are great resources for just such practice sessions with your team. But you also know enough now that you can create your own troubleshooting scenarios to try out on each other. There is no doubt that you will be asked to troubleshoot several issues on the CCNA exam. Practice as much as you can now in preparation for the test. You might be surprised how fun and rewarding it can be.

Labs and Activities

12.5.13 Packet Tracer—Troubleshoot Enterprise Network

Objectives

Part 1: Verify Switching Technologies

Part 2: Verify DHCP

Part 3: Verify Routing

Part 4: Verify WAN Technologies

Part 5: Verify Connectivity

Scenario

This activity uses a variety of technologies that you have encountered during your CCNA studies, including IPv4 routing, IPv6 routing, port security, EtherChannel, DHCP, and NAT. Your task is to review the requirements, isolate and resolve any problems, and then document the steps you took to verify the requirements.

The company replaced routers R1 and R3 to accommodate a fiber connection between the locations. Configurations from the previous routers with serial connections were modified and applied as a starting configuration. IPv6 is being tested on a small portion of the network and needs to be verified.

Note: Passwords have been removed for ease of troubleshooting in this exercise. The typical password protections should be reapplied; however, the activity will not grade those items.

Addressing Table

Device	Interface	IP Address / Prefix	Default Gateway
R1	G0/0/1	192.168.10.1 /24	N/A
	S0/1/0	10.1.1.1 /30	N/A
	G0/0/0	10.3.3.1 /30	N/A
R2	G0/0	209.165.200.225 /27	N/A
		2001:db8:b:209::1/64	
	G0/1	192.168.20.1 /30	N/A
		2001:db8:b:20::1/64	
	S0/0/0	10.1.1.2 /30	N/A
	G0/1/0	10.2.2.1 /30	N/A
		2001:db8:b:10:2::1/64	N/A
R3	G0/1.30	192.168.30.1 /24	N/A
	G0/1.40	192.168.40.1 /24	N/A

Device	Interface	IP Address / Prefix	Default Gateway
	G0/1.50	192.168.50.1 /24	N/A
	G0/1.50	2001:db8:b:50::1/64	
	G0/1.99	N/A	N/A
	G0/1/0	10.3.3.2 /30	N/A
	G0/2/0	10.2.2.2 /30	N/A
	G0/2/0	2001:db8:b:10:2::2/64	
S1	VLAN10	192.168.10.2 /24	192.168.10.1
S2	VLAN11	192.168.99.2 /24	N/A
S3	VLAN30	192.168.99.3 /24	N/A
S4	VLAN30	192.168.99.4 /24	N/A
PC1	NIC	IPv4 DHCP assigned	IPv4 DHCP assigned
PC2	NIC	IPv4 DHCP assigned	IPv4 DHCP assigned
PC3	NIC	IPv4 DHCP assigned	IPv4 DHCP assigned
PC4	NIC	IPv4 DHCP assigned	IPv4 DHCP assigned
	NIC	2001:db8:b:50::10/64	fe80::3
TFTP Server	NIC	192.168.20.254 /24	192.168.20.1
	NIC	2001:db8:b:20::254/64	fe80::2

Instructions

Part 1: Verify Switching Technologies

a. Port security is configured to only allow **PC1** to access **S1's** F0/3 interface. All violations should disable the interface.

Issue the command on S1 to display the current port security status.

```
S1# show port-security
```

b. Enter interface configuration mode for interface F0/3 and set up port security.

```
S1(config-if)# switchport port-security
S1(config-if)# switchport port-security mac-address sticky
```

c. Devices in the LAN on S1 should be in VLAN 10. Display the current state of VLAN configuration.

Question:

What ports are currently assigned to VLAN 10?

_____

d. PC1 should be receiving an IP address from the router R1.

Question:

Does the PC currently have an IP address assigned?

_____

e. Notice the G0/1 interface on R1 is not in the same VLAN as PC1. Change the G0/1 interface to be a member of VLAN 10 and set portfast on the interface.

```
S1(config-if)# int G0/1
```

```
S1(config-if)# switchport access vlan 10
```

```
S1(config-if)# spanning-tree portfast
```

f. Reset the interface address on PC1 from the GUI or by using the command prompt and the **ipconfig /renew** command. Does PC1 have an address? If not, recheck your steps. Test connectivity to the TFTP Server. The ping should be successful.

g. The LAN connected to R3 had an additional switch added to the topology. Link aggregation using EtherChannel is configured on **S2**, **S3**, and **S4**. The EtherChannel links should be set to trunk. The EtherChannel links should be set to form a channel without using a negotiation protocol. Issue the command on each switch to determine if the channel is working correctly.

```
S2# show etherchannel summary
```

```
<output omitted>
```

```
1       Po1(SU)        -        Fa0/1(P) Fa0/2(P)
```

```
2       Po2(SU)        -        Fa0/3(P) Fa0/4(P)
```

Question:

Were there any problems with EtherChannel?

---

h. Modify S3 to include ports F0/1 and F0/2 as port channel 1.

```
S3(config)# interface range f0/1-2
```

```
S3(config-if-range)# channel-group 1 mode on
```

Check the status of the EtherChannel on S3. It should be stable now. If it is not, check the previous steps.

i. Verify the trunk status on all switches.

```
S3# show int trunk
```

Question:

Were there any issues with trunking?

---

j. Correct the trunk issues on S2.

```
S2(config)# int g0/1
```

```
S2(config-if)# switchport trunk native vlan 99
```

k. Spanning Tree should be set to PVST+ on **S2**, **S3**, and **S4**. **S2** should be configured to be the root bridge for all VLANs. Issue the command to display the spanning-tree status on S2.

```
S2# show spanning-tree summary totals
```

```
Switch is in pvst mode
```

```
Root bridge for:
```

l. The command output shows that S2 is not the root bridge for any VLANs. Correct the spanning-tree status on S2.

```
S2(config)# spanning-tree vlan 1-1005 root primary
```

m. Check the spanning-tree status on S2 to verify the changes.

```
S2# show spanning-tree summary totals
Switch is in pvst mode
Root bridge for: default V30 V40 V50 Native
```

Part 2: Verify DHCP

- R1 is the DHCP server for the R1 LAN.

- R3 is the DHCP server for all three LANs attached to R3.

a. Check the addressing of the PCs.

Question:

Do they all have correct addressing?

_____

b. Check the DHCP settings on R3. Filter the output from the **show run** command to start with the DHCP configuration.

```
R3# sh run | begin dhcp
ip dhcp excluded-address 192.168.30.1 192.168.30.9
ip dhcp excluded-address 192.168.40.1 192.168.40.9
ip dhcp excluded-address 192.168.50.1 192.168.50.9
!
ip dhcp pool LAN30
 network 192.168.30.0 255.255.255.0
 default-router 192.168.30.1
ip dhcp pool LAN40
 network 192.168.40.0 255.255.255.0
 default-router 192.168.30.1
ip dhcp pool LAN50
 network 192.168.50.0 255.255.255.0
 default-router 192.168.30.1
```

Question:

Are there any issues with the DHCP configurations?

_____

c. Make any necessary corrections and reset the IP addresses on the PCs. Check connectivity to all devices.

Question:

Were you able to ping all IPv4 addresses?

_____

Part 3: Verify Routing

Verify that the following requirements have been met. If not, complete the configurations.

- All routers are configured with OSPF process ID 1 and no routing updates should be sent across interfaces that do not have routers connected.

- R2 is configured with an IPv4 default route pointing to the ISP and redistributes the default route in the OSPFv2 domain.

- R2 is configured with a default IPv6 fully qualified default route point to the ISP and redistributes the default route in the OSPFv3 domain.

- NAT is configured on R2 and no untranslated addresses are permitted to cross the Internet.

a. Check the routing tables on all routers.

```
R3# show ip route ospf
<output omitted>
      10.0.0.0/8 is variably subnetted, 5 subnets, 2 masks
O        10.1.1.0 [110/649] via 10.2.2.1, 01:15:53, GigabitEthernet0/2/0
O     192.168.10.0 [110/649] via 10.3.3.1, 01:15:53, GigabitEthernet0/1/0
      192.168.20.0 [110/2] via 10.2.2.1, 01:15:53, GigabitEthernet0/2/0
<output omitted>
```

Question:

Do all of the networks appear on all routers?

_____

b. Ping the Outside Host from R2.

Question:

Was the ping successful?

_____

c. Correct the default route propagation.

```
R2(config)# router ospf 1
R2(config-router)# default-information originate
```

d. Check the routing tables on R1 and R3 to make certain the default route is present.

e. Test IPv6 connectivity from R2 to Outside Host and TFTP Server. The pings should be successful. Troubleshoot if they are not.

f. Test IPv6 connectivity from R2 to PC4. If the ping fails, be sure to check that the IPv6 addressing matches the Addressing Table.

g. Test IPv6 connectivity from R3 to Outside Host. If the ping fails, check the IPv6 routes on R3. Be sure to validate the default route originating from R2. If the route does not appear, modify the IPv6 OSPF configuration on R2.

```
R2(config)# ipv6 router ospf 1
R2(config-rtr)# default-information originate
```

h. Check connectivity from R2 to Outside Host. The ping should be successful.

Part 4: Verify WAN Technologies

- The serial link between R1 and R2 is used as a backup link in case of failure and should only carry traffic if the fiber link is unavailable.

- The Ethernet link between R2 and R3 is a fiber connection.

- The Ethernet link between R1 and R3 is a fiber connection and should be used to forward traffic from R1.

a. Take a close look at the routing table on R1.

Question:

Are there any routes using the serial link?

_____

Use the traceroute command to verify any suspicious paths.

```
R1# traceroute 192.168.20.254
Type escape sequence to abort.
Tracing the route to 192.168.20.254

 1    10.1.1.2        1 msec    1 msec    1 msec
 2    192.168.20.254  1 msec    9 msec    0 msec
```

Notice the traffic is being sent via the S0/1/0 interface as opposed to the G0/0/0 interface.

b. The original configurations that came from the previous serial WAN connections were transferred to the new devices. Compare the G0/0/0 interface and Serial0/1/0 interface settings. Notice they both have an OSPF cost value set. Remove the OSPF cost setting from the G0/0/0 interface. It will also be necessary to remove the setting on the link on R3 that connects to R1.

```
R1(config)# int g0/0/0
R1(config-if)# no ip ospf cost 648
R3(config)# int g0/1/0
R3(config-if)# no ip ospf cost 648
```

c. Reissue the traceroute command from R1 to verify that the path has changed.

d. The change has been made to direct traffic over the faster link, however the backup route needs to be tested. Shut down the G0/2/0 interface on R3 and test connectivity to the TFTP Server and Outside Host.

Question:

Were the pings successful?

_____

e. R2 is required to perform NAT for all internal networks. Check the NAT translations on R2.

```
R2# show ip nat translations
```

f. Notice that the list is empty if you have only attempted to ping from R1. Attempt a ping from R3 to Outside Host and recheck the NAT translations on R2. Issue the command to display the current NAT statistics, which will also provide the interfaces involved in NAT.

```
R2# show ip nat statistics
<output will vary>
Total translations: 0 (0 static, 0 dynamic, 0 extended)
Outside Interfaces: GigabitEthernet0/0
Inside Interfaces: GigabitEthernet0/1 , GigabitEthernet0/1/0
Hits: 17   Misses: 27
Expired translations: 17
Dynamic mappings:
```

g. Set the Serial 0/0/0 interface as an inside interface to translate addresses.

```
R2(config)# int s0/0/0
R2(config-if)# ip nat inside
```

h. Test connectivity to Outside Host from R1. The ping should now be successful. Re-enable the G0/2/0 interface on R3.

Part 5: Verify Connectivity

- Devices should be configured according to the Addressing Table.

- Every device should be able to ping every other device internally. The internal PCs should be able to ping the Outside Host.

- PC4 should be able to ping the TFTP Server and the Outside Host using IPv6.

12.6.1 Packet Tracer—Troubleshooting Challenge—Document the Network

Addressing Table

Device	Interface	Device Type (router, switch, host)	IP Address	Subnet Mask	Default Gateway
PC1	NIC	Host			
PC2					
PC3					
PC4					
PC5					
PC6					
PC7					

Objectives

In this lab, you will document a network that is unknown to you.

- Test network connectivity.
- Compile host addressing information.
- Remotely access default gateway devices.
- Document default gateway device configurations.
- Discover devices on the network.
- Draw the network topology.

Background / Scenario

Your employer has been hired to take over the administration of a corporate network because the previous network administrator has left the company. The network documentation is missing and needs to be re-created. You job is to document the hosts and network devices including all the device addressing and logical interconnections. You will remotely access network devices and use network discovery to complete a device table and draw the network topology.

This is Part I of a two-part series of activities. You will use the documentation that you create in this activity to guide you as you troubleshoot the network in Part II, **Packet Tracer—Troubleshooting Challenge—Using Documentation to Solve Issues.**

As you investigate and document the network topology, make note of issues that you discover that do not adhere to the practices taught in the CCNA curriculum.

Instructions

Part 1: Test Connectivity

Ping between the PCs and the Internet server to test the network. All PCs should be able to ping one another and the Internet server.

Part 2: Discover PC Configuration Information

Go to the command prompt of each PC and display the IP settings. Record this information in the documentation table.

Part 3: Discover Information About the Default Gateway Devices

Connect to each default gateway device using the Telnet protocol and record information about the interfaces that are in use in the table. The VTY password is **cisco** and privileged EXEC password is **class**.

```
C:\> telnet IP_address
```

Part 4: Reconstruct the Network Topology

In this part of the activity, you will continue recording information about the devices in the network in the Addressing Table. In addition, you will start to diagram the network topology based on what you can discover about the device interconnections.

Step 1:   Access Routing Tables on Each Gateway Device.

Use the routing tables in each router to learn more about the network. Make notes of your findings.

Step 2:   Discover Non-Gateway Devices.

Use a network discovery protocol to document neighboring devices. Record your findings in the addressing table. At this point you should also be able to begin documenting device interconnections.

Part 5: Further Explore Device Configurations and Interconnections

Step 1:   Access Device Configurations.

Connect to the other devices in the network. Gather information about the device configurations.

Step 2:   View Neighbor Information.

Use discovery protocols to increase your knowledge of the network devices and topologies.

Step 3:   Connect to Other Devices.

Display configuration information for the other devices on the network. Record your findings in the device table.

By now you should know about all the devices and interface configurations in the network. All rows of the table should contain device information. Use your information to reconstruct as much of the network topology as you can.

Reflection

You may have noticed that some of the practices used to configure the network devices are out-of-date, inefficient, or not secure. Make a list of as many recommendations that you have regarding how the devices should be reconfigured to follow the practices that you have learned in the CCNA curriculum.

12.6.2 Packet Tracer—Troubleshooting Challenge—Use Documentation to Solve Issues

Addressing Table

Device	Interface	Device Type (router, switch, host)	IP Address	Subnet Mask	Default Gateway
PC1					
PC2					
PC3					
PC4					
PC5					
PC6					
PC7					

Objectives

In this lab, you use network documentation to identify and fix network communications problems.

- Use various techniques and tools to identify connectivity issues.
- Use documentation to guide troubleshooting efforts.
- Identify specific network problems.
- Implement solutions to network communication problems.
- Verify network operation.

Background / Scenario

In this activity, you will use the documentation that you created in the **Packet Tracer— Troubleshooting Challenge—Document the Network** activity to guide network troubleshooting efforts.

It has been discovered that the network that you worked with in the previous PT activity has developed communication problems. Some hosts are unable to ping other hosts and the Internet server. It is your job to determine what the issues are and to locate and repair them.

Network issues could exist in any device. Be sure to check for comprehensive errors:

- Addressing configuration
- Interface activation
- Routing
- NAT

Instructions

Passwords for all devices are VTY: **cisco**, Enable secret: **class**

Part 1: Assess Connectivity

All hosts should be able to ping each other and the Internet server. Determine if this requirement is met. If not, identify which hosts and networks should be further investigated.

Part 2: Access Network Devices

From the hosts that have communication problems, use ICMP tools to determine where in the network these problems may be located. From the host PCs, access devices in the network and display configurations and operational status.

Part 3: Repair the Network

After locating the issues, reconfigure the devices to repair the connectivity problem. Use your documentation from the previous activity to help you.

Part 4: Document the Issues

Record your issues in the table below.

Device	Issue	Action

Network Virtualization

The "Study Guide" portion of this chapter uses a variety of exercises to test your knowledge of the purpose and characteristics of network virtualization. The "Labs and Activities" portion of this chapter includes the lab instructions.

As you work through this chapter, use Chapter 13 in *Enterprise Networking, Security, and Automation v7 Companion Guide* or use the corresponding Module 13 in the Enterprise Networking, Security, and Automation online curriculum for assistance.

Study Guide

Cloud Computing

In this section, you review the importance of cloud computing.

Video—Cloud and Virtualization

Be sure to review the video in the online course. It covers the following:

- Data centers
- Cloud computer
- Virtualization

Cloud Computing Terminology

Match each definition with the appropriate term. This exercise is a one-to-one matching: Each definition has exactly one matching term.

Definition

   a. Two or more clouds where each part remains a distinctive object but where the clouds are connected using a single architecture

   b. Access to the development tools and services used to deliver applications

   c. Applications and services intended for a specific organization or entity, such as the government

   d. Clouds built to meet the needs of a specific industry, such as healthcare or media

   e. Access to the network equipment, virtualized network services, and supporting network infrastructure

   f. Applications and services made available to the general population

   g. Large numbers of computers connected through a network that can be physically located anywhere

   h. Access to services, such as email, communication, and Office 365, that are delivered over the Internet.

   i. Defines three main cloud computing services

   j. Cloud service extended to provide support for other cloud services

   k. A facility that provides the infrastructure for offering cloud services

Term

_____ Public cloud

_____ Private cloud

_____ Custom cloud

_____ SaaS

_____ Data center

_____ PaaS

_____ IaaS

_____ Cloud

_____ ITaaS

_____ Hybrid cloud

_____ NIST SP 800-145

Check Your Understanding—Cloud Computing

Check your understanding of cloud computing by choosing the BEST answer to each of the following questions.

1. Which cloud service provides programmers access to the development tool and services used to deliver applications?

   a. SaaS

   b. PaaS

   c. IaaS

2. Which cloud service provides users with access to services such as email, communications, and Office 365 delivered over the Internet?

   a. SaaS

   b. PaaS

   c. IaaS

3. Which cloud service provides IT managers with access to network equipment, virtualized services, and a supporting network infrastructure?

   a. SaaS

   b. PaaS

   c. IaaS

4. Which cloud model represents two or more clouds, where each part remains a distinctive object but the clouds are connected using a single architecture?

   a. Public cloud

   b. Private cloud

   c. Hybrid cloud

   d. Community cloud

5. Which cloud model is used to meet the needs of a specific industry, such as healthcare or media?

   a. Public cloud

   b. Private cloud

   c. Hybrid cloud

   d. Community cloud

Virtualization and Virtual Network Infrastructure

In this section, you review the importance of virtualization and the virtualization of network devices and services.

Virtualization Terminology

Match each definition with the appropriate term. This exercise is a one-to-one matching: Each definition has exactly one matching term.

Definition

a. Takes advantage of idle resources and consolidates the number of required servers

b. All of a server's RAM, processing power, and hard drive space devoted to the service provided

c. Separates the application from the hardware

d. Known as a bare metal hypervisor, with examples like KVM, VMware ESXi, Xen, and others

e. Known as a hosted hypervisor, with examples like VirtualBox, VMware Workstation, Parallels, and others

f. The computer on which a hypervisor is supporting one or more VMs

g. Services, OS, firmware, and hardware

h. Protection from a single point of failure

i. Separates the OS from the hardware

j. A program, firmware, or hardware that adds an abstraction layer on top of the real physical hardware

Term

_____ Layers of abstraction

_____ Type 1

_____ Server virtualization

_____ Dedicated server

_____ Virtualization

_____ Type 2

_____ Redundancy

_____ Host machine

_____ Cloud computing

_____ Hypervisor

Check Your Understanding—Virtualization and Virtual Network Infrastructure

Check your understanding of virtualization and virtual network infrastructure by choosing the BEST answer to each of the following questions.

1. What technology separates the OS from the hardware?

a. Web application

b. Virtualization

c. Dedicated servers

d. Firmware

2. What device uses all the RAM, processing power, and hard drive space devoted to one service?

a. Virtual machine

b. Type 1 hypervisor

c. Dedicated server

d. Virtualized server

3. Which technology is a program, firmware, or hardware that adds an abstraction layer on top of the physical hardware?

    a. Web application

    b. Virtualization

    c. Dedicated server

    d. Hypervisor

4. What are the major advantages of virtualization? (Choose three.)

    a. Requires less equipment

    b. Less abstraction

    c. Fewer operating systems

    d. Faster provisioning

    e. Increased server uptime

5. Which technology is installed on top of the existing OS to create and run VM instances?

    a. Type 2 hypervisor

    b. Web applications

    c. Virtualization

    d. Dedicated servers

6. True or false: A Type 1 hypervisor is installed on top of the existing OS; this is called the hosted approach.

    a. True

    b. False

7. True or false: A Type 1 hypervisor requires a management console to manage the hypervisor.

    a. True

    b. False

8. True or false: Management consoles prevent server overallocation.

    a. True

    b. False

9. True or false: East–west traffic is exchanged between virtual servers in the same data center.

    a. True

    b. False

Software-Defined Networking

In this section, you review software-defined networking (SDN).

Video—Software-Defined Networking

Be sure to review the video in the online course. It covers the following:

- Network programming
- SDN
- Controllers

Control Plane and Data Plane

In Table 13-1, select the plane that is described by each characteristic.

Table 13-1   Identify the Control Plane and Data Plane Characteristic

Characteristic	Control Plane	Data Plane
Information sent here is processed by the CPU.		
Typically, the switch fabric connecting the various network ports on a device.		
Uses a digital signal processor (DSP).		
In virtualized networks, the plane that is removed from the device and centralized in another location.		
CEF uses an FIB in this plane.		
The brains of a device.		
Contains Layer 2 forwarding tables.		
Also called the forwarding plane.		
Makes forwarding decisions.		
Contains routing protocol neighbor tables and topology tables.		
Information in this plane is typically processed by a special processor.		
Contains IPv4 and IPv6 routing tables.		
Used to forward traffic flows.		

Check Your Understanding—Software-Defined Networking

Check your understanding of SDN by choosing the BEST answer to each of the following questions.

1. Which characteristic best describes the control plane of a networking device? (Choose three.)

    a. Information sent to this plane is processed by the CPU.

    b. This plane is also called the forwarding plane.

    c. This plane makes forwarding decisions.

    d. This plane contains router protocol neighbor and topology tables.

    e. This plane is responsible for switching frames out the interfaces.

2. Which characteristics best describe the data plane of a networking device? (Choose three.)

   a. This plane is the brains of the device.

   b. This plane is used to forward traffic flows.

   c. Information in this plane is typically processed by a special processor.

   d. This plane contains IPv4 and IPv6 routing tables.

   e. This plane is typically made up of a switch fabric connecting the various ports on a device.

3. True or false: A network administrator accesses the control plane to configure a device.

   a. True

   b. False

4. Which of the following is a network architecture that offers a new approach to network administration and management that seeks to simplify and streamline the administration process?

   a. Network virtualization

   b. SDN

   c. Cisco ACI

   d. Centralized controller

5. Which of the following is a logical entity that enables network administrators to manage and dictate how the data plane of switches and routers should handle network traffic?

   a. Control plane

   b. Data plane

   c. VM

   d. SDN controller

6. Which of the following is a standardized request from the SDN controller to define the behavior of the data plane?

   a. North–south traffic

   b. Northbound API

   c. East–west traffic

   d. Southbound API

Controllers

In this section, you review controllers used in network programming.

Video—Cisco ACI

Be sure to review the video in the online course. It covers the evolution of SDN and Application Centric Infrastructure (ACI).

Types of SDN Controllers

In Table 13-2, select the SDN controller best described by each characteristic.

Table 13-2   Identify the SDN Controller Characteristic

Characteristic	Device Based	Controller Based	Policy Based
OnePK is an example of this type.			
It uses built-in applications that automate advanced configuration tasks via a guided workflow and user-friendly GUI with no programming skills required.			
Cisco APIC-EM is an example of this type.			
Similar to policy-based SDN but without the additional policy layer.			
Devices are programmable by applications running on the device itself or on a server in the network.			
OpenDaylight is an example of this type.			
Does not contain an SDN controller.			
Enables programmers to build applications using C and Java with Python to integrate and interact with Cisco devices.			

Check Your Understanding—Controllers

Check your understanding of controllers by choosing the BEST answer to each of the following questions.

1. Which of the following is a table that matches incoming packets to a particular flow and specifies the functions that are to be performed on the packet?

   a. Neighbor table

   b. Routing table

   c. Flow table

   d. ARP table

   e. Meter table

2. Which of the following is a table that triggers a variety of performance-related actions on a flow, including the ability to rate-limit the traffic?

   a. Neighbor table

   b. Routing table

   c. Flow table

   d. ARP table

   e. Meter table

3. Which type of SDN is a centralized location responsible for managing devices throughout the network?

   a. Device-based SDN

   b. Controller-based SDN

   c. Policy-based SDN

4. In which type of SDN are the devices programmable by applications running on the device itself or on a server in the network?

   a. Device-based SDN

   b. Controller-based SDN

   c. Policy-based SDN

5. Which type of SDN uses built-in applications that automate advanced configuration tasks via a guided workflow and user-friendly GUI, with no programming skills required?

   a. Device-based SDN

   b. Controller-based SDN

   c. Policy-based SDN

Labs and Activities

 ## 13.6.1 Lab—Install Linux in a Virtual Machine and Explore the GUI

Objectives

Part 1: Prepare a Computer for Virtualization

Part 2: Install a Linux OS on the Virtual Machine

Part 3: Explore the GUI

Background / Scenario

Computing power and resources have increased tremendously over the last 10 years. A benefit of multi-core processors and large amounts of RAM is the ability to install multiple operating systems through the use of virtualization on a computer.

With virtualization, one or more virtual computers can operate inside one physical computer. Virtual computers that run within physical computers are called virtual machines. Virtual machines are often called guests, and physical computers are often called hosts. Anyone with a modern computer and operating system can run virtual machines.

In this lab, you will install a Linux OS in a virtual machine using a desktop virtualization application, such as VirtualBox. After completing the installation, you will explore the GUI interface. You will also explore the command-line interface using this virtual machine in a lab later in this course.

Required Resources

- Computer with a minimum of 2 GB of RAM and 10 GB of free disk space

- High-speed Internet access to download Oracle VirtualBox and Linux OS image, such as Ubuntu Desktop

Instructions

Part 1: Prepare a Computer for Virtualization

In Part 1, you will download and install desktop virtualization software and a Linux OS image. Your instructor may provide you with a Linux OS image.

Step 1:   Download and install VirtualBox.

VMware Player and Oracle VirtualBox are two virtualization programs that you can download and install to support the OS image file. In this lab, you will use the VirtualBox application.

    a. Navigate to https://www.virtualbox.org/. Click the download link on this page.

    b. Choose and download the appropriate installation file based on your operating system.

    c. After the VirtualBox installation file is downloaded, run the installer and accept the default installation settings.

Step 2:   Download a Linux Image.

    a. Navigate to the Ubuntu website at http://www.ubuntu.com. Click the Download link on this page to download and save an Ubuntu Desktop image.

Step 3:   Create a New Virtual Machine.

    a. Click **Start** and search for **Virtualbox**. Click **Oracle VM VirtualBox** to open the manager. When the manager opens, click **New** to start the Ubuntu installation.

    b. In the **Name and operating system** screen, type **Ubuntu** in the **Name** field. For the **Type** field, select **Linux**. In the **Version** field, select the corresponding downloaded version. Click **Next** to continue.

    c. In the **Memory size** screen, increase the amount of RAM as long as the amount of RAM for the virtual machine is in the green area. Going beyond the green area would adversely affect the performance of the host. Click **Next** to continue.

    d. In the **Hard disk** screen, click **Create** to create a virtual hard disk now.

    e. In the **Hard disk file type** screen, use the default file type settings of **VDI (VirtualBox Disk Image)**. Click **Next** to continue.

    f. In the **Storage on physical hard disk** screen, use the default storage settings of **dynamically allocated**. Click **Next** to continue.

    g. In the **File location and size** screen, you can adjust the hard drive and change the name and location of the virtual hard drive. Click **Create** to use the default settings.

    h. When the hard drive creation is done, the new virtual machine is listed in the **Oracle VM VirtualBox Manager** window. Select **Ubuntu** and click **Start** in the top menu.

Part 2: Install Ubuntu on the Virtual Machine

Step 1:   Mount the Image.

    a. In the **Oracle VM Virtualbox Manager** window. Right-click **Ubuntu** and select **Settings**. In the **Ubuntu – Settings** window, click **Storage** in the left pane. Click **Empty** in the middle pane. In the right pane, click the CD symbol and select the file location of the Ubuntu image. Click **OK** to continue.

b. In the **Oracle VM VirtualBox Manager** window, click **Start** in the top menu.

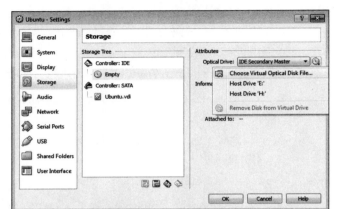

Step 2:   Install the OS.

a. In the **Welcome** screen, you are prompted to try or install Ubuntu. The try option does not install the OS, it runs the OS straight from the image. In this lab, you will install the Ubuntu OS in this virtual machine. Click **Install Ubuntu**.

b. Follow the on-screen instructions and provide the necessary information when prompted.

Note: If you are not connected to the Internet, you can continue to install and enable the network later.

c. Because this Ubuntu installation is in a virtual machine, it is safe to erase the disk and install Ubuntu without affecting the host computer. Select **Erase disk and install Ubuntu**. Otherwise installing Ubuntu on a physical computer would erase all data on the disk and replace the existing operating system with Ubuntu. Click **Install Now** to start the installation.

d. Click **Continue** to erase the disk and install Ubuntu.

e. In the **Who are you?** screen, provide your name and choose a password. Use **iteuser** for **Your Name** and **ITEpass!** for the password. You can use the username generated or enter a different username. If desired, you can change the other settings. Click **Continue**.

f. The Ubuntu OS is now installing in the virtual machine. This will take several minutes. When the **Installation is complete** message displays, return to the **Oracle VM Virtualbox Manager** window. Right-click **Ubuntu** and select **Settings**. In the **Ubuntu – Settings** window, click **Storage** in the left pane. Click the mounted Ubuntu image in the middle pane. In the right pane, click the CD symbol and click **Remove Disk from Virtual Drive**. Click **OK** to continue.

g. In the Ubuntu VM, click **Restart Now**.

Part 3: Explore the GUI

In this part, you will install the VirtualBox guest additions and explore the Ubuntu GUI.

Step 1:   Install Guest Additions.

    a.   Log on to your Ubuntu virtual machine using the user credentials created in the previous part.

    b.   Your Ubuntu Desktop window may be smaller than expected. This is especially true on high-resolution displays. Click **Device > Insert Guest Additions CD image…** to install the Guest Additions. This allows more functions, such as changing the screen resolution in the virtual machine.

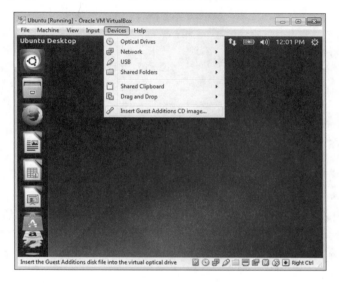

    c.   Click **Run** to install the additions. When prompted for a password, use the same password that you used to log on. Click **Authenticate** to continue.

    d.   If the computer was not connected to the Internet during the installation, click **Devices > Network Settings** in the Oracle VirtualBox menu. Enable network adapters and configure the proper setting for network connections as necessary. Click **OK**.

    e.   When the installation of the additions is done, restart the virtual machine again. Click the menu in the upper-right corner and click **Shut down**. Click **Restart** to restart Ubuntu.

Step 2:   Open a web browser.

    a.   Log on to Ubuntu again. After you are logged on again, you can resize the virtual machine window.

    b.   Open a web browser. Depending on the Linux distribution, you may need to search for a web browser or there is a link to a web browser already on the Desktop.

    c.   Locate a terminal emulator to access the command-line interface. You will be using a terminal emulator in later labs.

    d.   Explore the installed Linux distribution and locate a few applications that you may use.

Reflection Question

What are the advantages and disadvantages of using a virtual machine?

_____

CHAPTER 14

Network Automation

The "Study Guide" portion of this chapter uses a variety of exercises to test your knowledge of how network automation is enabled through RESTful APIs (application programming interfaces that use Representational State Transfer) and configuration management tools. There are no labs or Packet Tracer activities in this chapter.

As you work through this chapter, use Chapter 14 in *Enterprise Networking, Security, and Automation v7 Companion Guide* or use the corresponding Module 14 in the Enterprise Networking, Security, and Automation online curriculum for assistance.

Study Guide

Automation Overview

In this section, you review the concept of automation.

Video—Automation Everywhere

Be sure to review the video in the online course. It provides examples of automation.

Check Your Understanding—Benefits of Automation

Choose whether each of the following scenarios describes automation or does not describe automation.

1. You use online banking to pay a bill.

   a. Automation

   b. Not automation

2. Production levels are automatically tied to demand, eliminating unneeded product and reducing the impact on the environment.

   a. Automation

   b. Not automation

3. Your GPS recalculates the best route to a destination, based on current traffic congestion.

   a. Automation

   b. Not automation

4. The temperature and lighting in your home are adjusted based on your daily routine.

   a. Automation

   b. Not automation

5. A refrigerator senses that you are out of milk and places an order for more.

   a. Automation

   b. Not automation

6. You adjust the volume on the television set with a remote control.

   a. Automation

   b. Not automation

7. Robots are used in dangerous conditions to reduce safety risks to humans.

   a. Automation

   b. Not automation

8. You open your car door with a remote control.

    a. Automation

    b. Not automation

Data Formats

In this section, you review the Hypertext Markup Language (HTML), JavaScript Object Notation (JSON), YAML Ain't Markup Language (YAML), and Extensible Markup Language (XML) data formats.

Video—Data Formats

Be sure to review the video in the online course. It covers the following:

- HTML
- XML
- JSON
- YAML

Identify the Data Formats

In the titles for Examples 14-1 through 14-3, fill in the missing name of the data format.

Example 14-1 _____

```
message: success
timestamp: 1560789260
iss_position:
    latitude: '25.9990'
    longitude: '-132.6992'
```

Example 14-2 _____

```
<root>
  <message>success</message>
  <timestamp>1560789260</timestamp>
  <iss_position>
    <latitude>25.9990</latitude>
    <longitude>-132.6992</longitude>
  </iss_position>
</root>
```

Example 14-3

```
{
    "message": "success",
    "timestamp": 1560789260,
    "iss_position": {
        "latitude": "25.9990",
        "longitude": "-132.6992"
    }
}
```

Check Your Understanding—Data Formats

Check your understanding of data formats by choosing the BEST answer to each of the following questions.

1. Which of the following data formats is typically used to display web pages?

   a. HTML

   b. XML

   c. JSON

   d. YAML

2. Which of the following describes a key/value pair?

   a. A key is a string, and a value is a list

   b. A key/value pair is another name for an array.

   c. A key describes the data, and the value is the data itself.

   d. A key/value pair is used only in JSON.

3. True or false: Whitespace in JSON format is significant and must be correctly formatted.

   a. True

   b. False

4. Which data format is a minimalist format that is very easy to read and is considered a superset of another data format?

   a. HTML

   b. XML

   c. JSON

   d. YAML

5. Which data format is self-descriptive through the use of the <tag>data</tag> structure?

   a. HTML

   b. XML

   c. JSON

   d. YAML

APIs

In this section, you review how APIs enable computer-to-computer communications.

Video—APIs

Be sure to review the video in the online course. It covers the following:

- The definition of API
- Examples of popular APIs
- How to execute an API call in a browser and in Postman

An API Example

A travel service website provides a good example of how you can use APIs to collect information from multiple companies that provide travel services. In Figure 14-1, the travel website presents the data you need by calling multiple APIs from a variety of airline databases.

Figure 14-1 Travel Service Website Calling Multiple Airline APIs

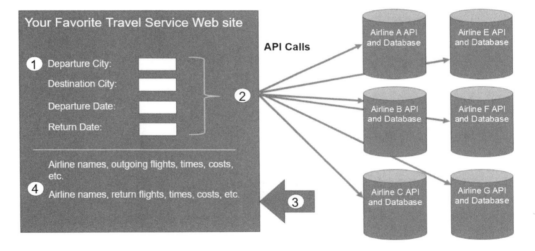

In Figure 14-1, the steps are as follows:

Step 1. The customer enters the minimum information needed to request offers from multiple airlines.

Step 2. The travel service website sends multiple API GET requests to airlines.

Step 3. The airlines respond with the available offers.

Step 4. The travel server website displays the offers to the customer.

Types of Web Service APIs

A web service is a service that is available over the Internet, using the World Wide Web. There are four types of web service APIs:

- Simple Object Access Protocol (SOAP)
- REST

- XML–Remote Procedure Call (XML-RPC)
- JSON–Remote Procedure Call (JSON-RPC)

Table 14-1 compares these web service APIs.

Table 14-1   Web Service APIs

Characteristic	SOAP	REST	XML-RPC	JSON-RPC
Data format	XML	JSON, XML, YAML, and others	XML	JSON
First released	1998	2000	1998	2005
Strengths	Well-established	Flexible formatting and most widely used	Well-established, simplicity	Simplicity

Check Your Understanding—APIs

Check your understanding of APIs by choosing the BEST answer to each of the following questions.

1. True or false: An API is a set of rules describing how one application can interact with another and the instructions to allow the interaction to occur.

   a. True

   b. False

2. Which of the following APIs would be used exclusively between Google and Cisco?

   a. Open or public API

   b. Internal or private API

   c. Partner API

3. Which of the following APIs does Cisco use to provide access to students to complete labs?

   a. Open or public API

   b. Internal or private API

   c. Partner API

4. Which of the following APIs would be used exclusively between computing devices within Cisco?

   a. Open or public API

   b. Internal or private API

   c. Partner API

5. Which of the following APIs provides flexible formatting and is the most widely used API?

   a. SOAP

   b. REST

   c. XML-RPC

   d. JSON-RPC

REST

In this section, you review how REST enables computer-to-computer communications.

Video—REST

Be sure to review the video in the online course. It covers how to execute a REST API request with a web browser, on the command line, using Postman, and using a Python script.

RESTful Implementation

RESTful APIs use common HTTP methods that correspond to these operations: create, read, update, and delete (or CRUD). In Table 14-2, fill in the RESTful operation for each HTTP method.

Table 14-2   HTTP Methods Used by RESTful APIs

HTTP Method	RESTful Operation
POST	
GET	
PUT/PATCH	
DELETE	

URI, URN, and URL

In Figure 14-2, label the uniform resource identifier (URI), uniform resource name (URN), and uniform resource locator (URL).

Figure 14-2   Compare URI, URN, and URL

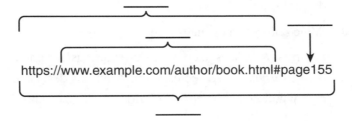

List the parts of the URI shown in Figure 14-2.

- Protocol/scheme: _____
- Hostname: _____
- Path and filename: _____
- Fragment: _____

Anatomy of a RESTful Request

In Figure 14-3, label the parts of a RESTful API request.

Figure 14-3   Parts of a RESTful API Request

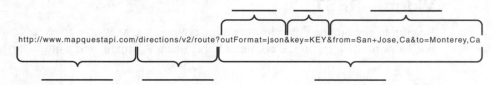

Check Your Understanding—REST

Check your understanding of REST by choosing the BEST answer to each of the following questions.

1. An API is considered RESTful if it has which of the following features? (Choose three.)

    a. Stateful

    b. Stateless

    c. Cacheable

    d. Cacheless

    e. Client/server

    f. Server/server

2. Which of the following is a URL?

    a. https://www.cisco.com/c/en/us/solutions/design-zone.html#~all-guides

    b. https://www.cisco.com/c/en/us/solutions/design-zone.html

    c. www.cisco.com/c/en/us/solutions/design-zone.html

    d. #~all-guides

3. Which of the following is a URN?

    a. https://www.cisco.com/c/en/us/solutions/design-zone.html#~all-guides

    b. https://www.cisco.com/c/en/us/solutions/design-zone.html

    c. www.cisco.com/c/en/us/solutions/design-zone.html

    d. #~all-guides

4. Which of the following is a URI?

    a. https://www.cisco.com/c/en/us/solutions/design-zone.html#~all-guides

    b. https://www.cisco.com/c/en/us/solutions/design-zone.html

    c. www.cisco.com/c/en/us/solutions/design-zone.html

    d. #~all-guides

5. Which of the following make up the query portion of a RESTful request? (Choose three.)

   a. Key

   b. Format

   c. Parameters

   d. Resources

   e. API server

Configuration Management

In this section, you review the configuration management tools Puppet, Chef, Ansible, and SaltStack.

Video—Configuration Management

Be sure to review the video in the online course. It covers the following:

- Configuration management tools, including Ansible, Puppet, Chef, and SaltStack

- Plays, tasks, modules, parameters, and variables in a sample playbook

Compare Ansible, Chef, Puppet, and SaltStack

Ansible, Chef, Puppet, and SaltStack all come with API documentation for configuring RESTful API requests. All of them support JSON and YAML as well as other data formats. Table 14-3 shows a summary of these configuration management tools.

Table 14-3   Configuration Management Tool Comparison

Characteristic	Ansible	Chef	Puppet	SaltStack
Programming language?	Python and YAML	Ruby	Ruby	Python
Agent-based or agentless?	Agentless	Agent-based	Supports both	Supports both
How devices are managed	Any device can be "controller"	Chef Master	Puppet Master	Salt Master
What is created by the tool?	Playbook	Cookbook	Manifest	Pillar

Check Your Understanding—Configuration Management

Check your understanding of configuration management by choosing the BEST answer to each of the following questions.

1. Which of the following are not typically used as configuration tools? (Choose two.)

   a. API

   b. Ansible

   c. Chef

   d. Puppet

   e. SaltStack

   f. SNMP

2. In configuration management, which of the following is the term for programmatically performing a task on a system, such as configuring an interface or deploying a VLAN?

   a. Version control

   b. Automation

   c. Orchestration

   d. Network management

3. In configuration management, which of the following is the term for the process by which all automated activities need to happen (such as the order in which they must be done and what must be completed before another task is begun)?

   a. Version control

   b. Automation

   c. Orchestration

   d. Network management

4. True or false: Agentless means that the controller or master pushes the configuration to the agent.

   a. True

   b. False

5. Which of the following configuration management tools use Python? (Choose two.)

   a. Ansible

   b. Chef

   c. Puppet

   d. SaltStack

IBN and Cisco DNA Center

In this section, you review how Cisco DNA Center enables intent-based networking.

Video—Intent-Based Networking

Be sure to review the video in the online course for an explanation of how artificial intelligence and intent-based networking (IBN) can improve networks.

Intent-Based Networking Overview

Cisco views IBN as having three essential functions: translation, activation, and assurance. These functions interact with the underlying physical and virtual infrastructures. In Figure 14-4, label each box with the correct function.

Figure 14-4   Cisco IBN

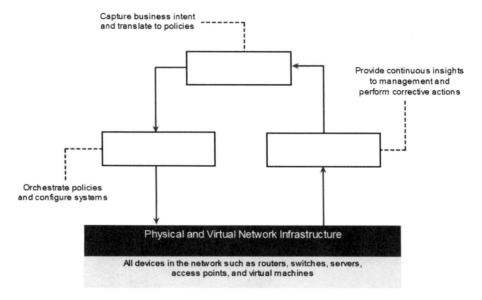

Briefly describe each of the IBN functions.

- **Translation:** _____
_____

- **Activation:** _____
_____
_____

- **Assurance:** _____
_____
_____

Network Infrastructure as Fabric

Fabric is a term used to describe an overlay that represents the logical topology used to virtually connect to devices. The overlay limits the number of devices a network administrator must program, as shown in Figure 14-5.

Figure 14-5 Overlay Network Example

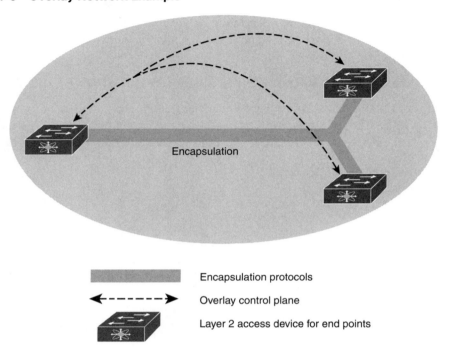

The underlay network is the physical topology that includes all hardware required to meet business objectives. The underlay reveals additional devices and specifies how these devices are connected, as shown in Figure 14-6.

Figure 14-6 Underlay Network Example

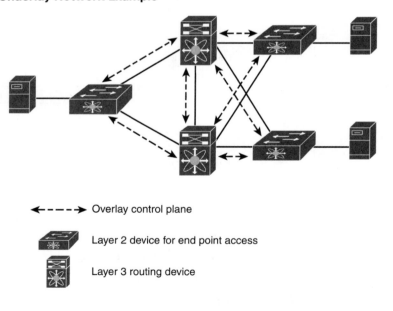

Cisco Digital Network Architecture (DNA)

Table 14-4 lists some Cisco DNA products and solutions.

Table14-4   Cisco DNA Products and Solutions

Cisco DNA Solution	Description	Benefits
SD-Access	■ First intent-based enterprise networking solution built using Cisco DNA. ■ Uses a single network fabric across the LAN and WLAN to create a consistent, highly secure user experience. ■ Segments user, device, and application traffic and automates user-access policies to establish the right policy for any user or device, with any application, across a network.	Enables network access in minutes for any user or device to any application without compromising security.
SD-WAN	■ Uses a secure cloud-delivered architecture to centrally manage WAN connections. ■ Simplifies and accelerates delivery of secure, flexible, and rich WAN services to connect data centers, branches, campuses, and colocation facilities.	■ Delivers better user experiences for applications residing on-premises or in the cloud. ■ Achieves greater agility and cost savings through easier deployments and transport independence.
Cisco DNA Assurance	■ Used to troubleshoot and increase IT productivity. ■ Applies advanced analytics and machine learning to improve performance and issue resolution and predictions to assure network performance. ■ Provides real-time notification for network conditions that require attention.	■ Allows you to identify root causes and provides suggested remediation for faster troubleshooting. ■ Provides an easy-to-use single dashboard with insights and drill-down capabilities. ■ Machine learning continually improves network intelligence to help predict problems before they occur.
Cisco DNA Security	■ Provides visibility by using the network as a sensor for real-time analysis and intelligence. ■ Provides increased granular control to enforce policy and contain threats across the network.	■ Reduces risk and protects the organization against threats—even in encrypted traffic. ■ Provides 360-degree visibility through real-time analytics for deep intelligence across the network. ■ Reduces complexity with end-to-end security.

Cisco DNA Center

Figure 14-7 shows the DNA Center interface launch page that provides an overall health summary and network snapshot.

Figure 14-7   Cisco DNA Center Launch Page

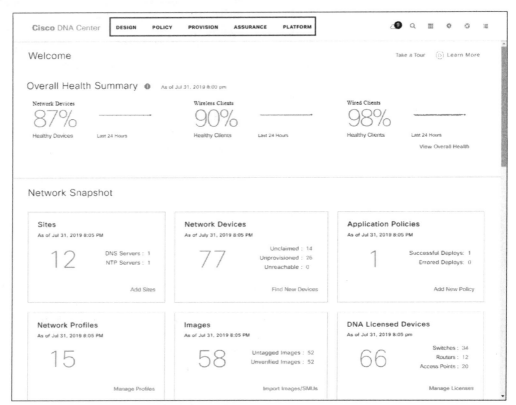

Briefly describe each of DNA Center's five main areas.

- **Design:** _____
  _____

- **Policy:** _____
  _____

- **Provision:** _____
  _____

- **Assurance:** _____
  _____
  _____

- **Platform:** _____
  _____

Videos—Cisco DNA Center

Be sure to review the four Cisco Digital Network Architecture (DNA) Center videos in the online course. They review the following:

- Part One provides an overview of the Cisco DNA Center GUI. It includes the Design, Policy, Provision, and Assurance tools used to control multiple sites and multiple devices.

- Part Two provides an overview of the Cisco DNA Center Design and Provision areas.

- Part Three explains the Cisco DNA Center Policy and Assurance areas.

- Part Four explains how to use Cisco DNA Center to troubleshoot devices.

Check Your Understanding—IBN and Cisco DNA Center

Check your understanding of IBN and Cisco DNA Center by choosing the BEST answer to each of the following questions.

1. Which IBN feature is responsible for continuous validation and verification that the network is meeting the expressed intent?

   a. Translation

   b. Activation

   c. Assurance

   d. Network infrastructure

2. Which IBN feature enables a network administrator to express the expected networking behavior that will best support the business intent?

   a. Translation

   b. Activation

   c. Assurance

   d. Network infrastructure

3. Which IBN feature installs policies that capture intent into the physical and virtual network infrastructure using networkwide automation?

   a. Translation

   b. Activation

   c. Assurance

   d. Network infrastructure

4. True or false: The underlay limits the number of devices a network administrator must program. It also provides services and alternative forwarding methods that are not controlled by the underlying physical devices.

   a. True

   b. False

Labs and Activities

There are no labs or Packet Tracer activities in this chapter.